AL QAEDA NOW

At the invitation of the New America Foundation and the Center on Law and Security at New York University School of Law, a group of authorities on international terrorism and al Qaeda were brought together at a meeting held in the Russell Senate Office Building in Washington, D.C. This volume contains the presentations that were made at this meeting. They constitute a valuable synopsis of current knowledge on al Qaeda and the policies in place to counter threats of future terrorist attacks. The papers in this book will contribute to understanding how al Qaeda has evolved from a movement to an ideology, what influence it has on Middle East stability, and what continued threat it is to the United States, Europe, and other areas of the world. The contributors are from academia, research centers, government agencies, and the media. They represent a cross section of recognized experts on al Qaeda and international terrorism.

Karen J. Greenberg is the Executive Director of the Center on Law and Security at New York University School of Law. She is coeditor of *The Torture Papers: The Road to Abu Ghraib*, editor of the forthcoming *The Torture Debate in America*, and editor of *The NYU Review of Law and Security.*

Al Qaeda Now

UNDERSTANDING TODAY'S TERRORISTS

Edited by
KAREN J. GREENBERG

Center on Law and Security
at New York University School of Law

The New America Foundation

CAMBRIDGE UNIVERSITY PRESS
Cambridge, New York, Melbourne, Madrid, Cape Town, Singapore, São Paulo

Cambridge University Press
40 West 20th Street, New York, NY 10011-4211, USA

www.cambridge.org
Information on this title: www.cambridge.org/9780521859110

First published 2005

Printed in the United States of America

A catalog record for this publication is available from the British Library.

Library of Congress Cataloging in Publication Data

Al Qaeda now : understanding today's terrorists / edited by
Karen J. Greenberg. – 1st ed.
p. cm.
Includes index.
ISBN 0-521-85911-5 (hardback : alk. paper) – ISBN 0-521-67627-4 (pbk. : alk. paper)
1. Qaida (Organization) 2. Terrorism. I. Greenberg, Karen J.
HV6432.5.Q2Q34 2005
303.6′25–dc22 2005019855

ISBN-13 978-0-521-85911-0 hardback
ISBN-10 0-521-85911-5 hardback

ISBN-13 978-0-521-67627-4 paperback
ISBN-10 0-521-67627-4 paperback

Contents

Acknowledgements

This book owes much to the wisdom and foresight of Steven Clemons, Peter Bergen, and the New America Foundation, who, with the able help of Jennifer Buntman, convened the group of participants represented in this book. Peter Bergen also provided much advice and guidance throughout the editing of the manuscript. Thanks go also to Kristin Henderson and Jonathan Voegele for their painstaking editing and research skills. Justin Kitchens worked on listening to bin Laden's speeches and checking the translations. And John Berger, as always, displayed great patience and kind attention. Thanks for this book would not be complete without mention of my children, Adam and Katie Sticklor, and my daughter-in-law Jessica, who provided support, dinners, and patience, enabling me to work long hours without remorse. And as always, thanks go to Stephen Holmes for his unerring sense of judgment and his unsurpassable generosity. Finally, thanks go to the Center on Law and Security for support and guidance.

Preface

In the wealth of responses to 9/11, one has gone overlooked, and that is the vitalization of a once relatively overlooked discipline, the study of terrorism and its companion, counterterrorism. Prior to 9/11, there were a handful of students of terrorism; they included journalists, policy analysts, and scholars. After 9/11, the contours of the discipline expanded vastly; like Xerox copy that has zoomed out, the field was now larger and more complex. As experts and journalists, practitioners and scholars have scurried around after 9/11 to follow the ever-changing nature of Islamic fundamentalism and its attack on the West, a powerful field of study has taken root, with voices from psychology and philosophy, political theory and law enforcement, history and journalism, humanities and the arts all pitching in. This medley of perspectives has created a living, thriving discipline that insists upon a respect for the past and an awareness of each day's events. It has, in essence, provided the world with a new community of thinkers, in a way, the most comprehensive interdisciplinary conversation yet to take place. As such, it is harvest for the global age.

In December 2004, the New America Foundation, in conjunction with the Center on Law and Security at NYU School of Law, hosted a conference that brought into view this development. Titled "Al Qaeda: 2.0," the day of talks began promptly at 8 a.m. and continued, marathon-style, until 6 p.m. There were no breaks, lunch was served to you in your seat, and if you got up, you lost your seat. More than eight hundred participants crowded into the room at the Russell Senate Office Building, where a quick glance around the room told you just how needed this event was. The country's major print journalists, members of policy groups and think tanks, legal experts, and others listened carefully, nodding or shaking their heads with each speaker. The speakers included those students of terrorism who had been documenting the shifts in al Qaeda since well before 9/11 and those who had come more recently to the field. Taking place in the immediate aftermath of the 2004 presidential election, this assemblage of speakers was one of the first to explore the hard policy questions confronting the new administration and its strategy against Islamic fundamentalist terrorism.

Not surprisingly, perhaps, the effect was stunning as a number of points of agreement and disagreement became crystal clear. First, there were conclusions, upon which most panelists agreed, and they included the following: Al Qaeda has become more of a movement, an ideology, than an organization; the profile of a terrorist is skewed more towards that of educated young men exposed to the West than towards that of impoverished, uneducated youth living in the Middle East; strengthening U.S. intelligence services is of the utmost importance; and anti-Americanism is at an all-time high in the Middle East, even in countries we consider our allies. Points of contention were equally astonishing. Panelists discussed the virtues and potential damage of the media in the war on terror, particularly in regard to the favored outlet for al Qaeda, al Jazeera; the current threat assessment of al Qaeda per se; and the long-term and short-term effects of the war in Iraq.

What emerges from this volume is a portrait of al Qaeda as an entity, altered significantly by post-9/11 efforts to stymie its growth and vitality, yet still influential in ever-changing ways; an al Qaeda that, alongside its embrace of Islam, has achieved a sophisticated mastery over the most far-reaching technology of communications, namely, the Internet and the television media. It is a movement that, in fact, needs very little in the way of financing to accomplish its individual missions. It has provided an ideological point of reference that has harnessed the minds of countless youth and continues to do so in a way that is seductive, compelling, and, in today's context, irresistible. But the portrait also emerges of an al Qaeda that is damaged, increasingly uncoordinated, and dispersed.*

* There were a number of editorial decisions that went into this volume, among them the decision to include the Q and A sessions that followed each panel. Often, the questioners were just as knowledgeable and professionally engaged as were the panelists themselves, and just as often, the discussions raised new questions, previously unexplored controversies, and even new answers.

Many of the contributors to this volume refer in their comments to Osama bin Laden's speeches, eighteen of which have been released since 9/11. This volume includes six transcribed audio messages from bin Laden, the first from August 1996 and the last addressed to the American people on October 29, 2004. The trajectory of bin Laden's thinking over time has remained consistent, particularly in regard to the foreign policies of Western countries. What emerges also is his increasing knowledge about the specifics of American culture and American policy. Bin Laden's messages have attracted huge audiences, first through al Jazeera, then through broadcasts by CNN and other worldwide media networks. It is worthwhile to read him in order to gain a better sense of his mission, his attitude toward the West, and his increasing reliance on a media strategy to gain adherents and to spread his ideas.

Much of the thinking in the volume has proven prescient, particularly in light of the July 2005 bombings in London. The events in London followed closely the analyses presented here as to the post-9/11 shape of al Qaeda, Islamic jihad, and our expectations for the future. We can expect more small-scale attacks perpetrated by splinter groups, often a handful of individuals, carrying out bombings, sometimes suicide bombings. We can also expect Europe to be a focal point for such attacks.

From the participants' voices heard here, a clear challenge rings out to Western policy makers, experts, and even citizens; that is, it is imperative to find a way not just to react to the changing forms of al Qaeda as a movement, but to find means of response that are proactive as well; it is important to take seriously the work of those who track al Qaeda and its offshoots each and every day; and it is essential to consider ways in which the image of the U.S. in the world may harm as well as help those efforts. Above all, these collected commentaries are meant to enable constructive discussions on the part of the public as well as in the corridors of decision making, by bringing readers up to date on the current thinking about al Qaeda. From knowledgeable leadership, wise public policy can emerge. And maybe, from informed public debate, wise leadership can learn.

Karen J. Greenberg

Foreword

Writing a book about al Qaeda is a tremendous challenge. Despite the fact that so much has been said and written about international Islamic terrorism, to the point where it sometimes seems as if everybody is an expert on the matter, our understanding of this highly perturbing phenomenon is at best superficial. Hence the importance of a book like this. From a plural perspective, the authors' incisive analyses help us to obtain a clearer picture of this scourge of humanity.

This is not to criticize the public debate that is taking place about al Qaeda, however, since this undoubtedly helps confirm civil society's commitment in the battle against terrorism. The real risk arises when governments and other responsible institutions are on different wavelengths, or when they act unilaterally or without proper coordination. This leaves citizens unprotected and indirectly allows terror to flourish.

An effective response to any form of criminal action, including terrorism, depends on striking a balance between a proactive legal approach and operational actions, and respecting the legal guarantees relating to how the former are implemented. To talk solely about the war on terror while making no reference to these legal checks and balances is to ignore the fact that we live in an international legal community, whose rules exist not just to provide moral or ethical guidance but also to be complied with.

Ensuring that a society is defended from external aggressions also means protecting it from internal attacks, since giving up on the basic advances that have made possible peaceful coexistence effectively amounts to surrendering to the terrorists.

Today the world is facing a variety of threats, some of which have joined forces to wage war on democracy. Only a universal, solid and effective alliance will enable us to take the strongest possible action against this enemy. We must work together.

If a country like the United States decides to go it alone and wages outright war against the international networks of Islamic terrorists without taking into account the experiences of other countries, it will effectively be claiming for itself the title of "universal victim." This approach is bound to fail and, more seriously, it will end up placing its own citizens at greater risk.

If a series of measures are taken that exacerbate security, and the law is used as a means of exacting revenge, we will lose our way in the fight against this form of terrorism, one that has shown itself to be lightning quick in discovering and exploiting the weak points in societies that allow it to unleash its destructive forces. There are many examples, the most recent being in London on July 7, 2005, another terrorist attack which leaves us all feeling defenseless and confused.

Designing common strategies and reaching agreement about what we mean by concepts like security, legal guarantees, intelligence, cooperation and so on; all of this is essential if we are to deal with the explosion of groups and factions united by the same lifeblood, the fanatical ideology of "Alqaedaism."

For too long – in fact, ever since Islamic terrorism emerged – there has been a sterile debate in which religions and nations have been wrongly identified with one another. Furthermore, fundamentalism should not be identified with religion. The word "fundamentalism" may be of religious origin (although it does not come from Islam) but it must not be confused with religion, since lay or political fundamentalism also exists. When it affects religion, in particular Islam, fundamentalism involves indoctrination and proselytism, and the construction of an ideology which lays the foundations for the development of terrorist violence. The use of violence (which is not actually advocated in Islamic sacred texts) becomes a direct means of imposing this ideology and placing it apart from – and even above – the mainstream religion, since those who do not submit to it are seen as having strayed from the true path. This makes them a legitimate target for Islamic terrorists, the theorists and practitioners of this new "religion," which is applied by force both inside and outside a given state, whether on a regional or international basis.

Those in power who do not embrace and apply fundamentalist doctrines in Islamic countries are "the enemy." Those who aid and abet the West, as well as the West itself for its "violent" action against Islamic countries and their people, are also in the terrorists' sights.

This ideology obtains constant succor from one simple source – the unreal and fanatical vision of its followers – and since its objectives are unattainable their reactions become ever more extreme. The jihadist terrorist knows no bounds – methods of attack, means of obtaining resources, committing crimes – everything is valid, since purification is at hand.

The jihadist movement, initially based locally, has become international in nature, in terms of both its members and the diversified objectives that it pursues. This development has not resulted in one main organization on which satellite organizations depend. Instead, with the leadership of Osama bin Laden established and with local cells having sufficient capacity to carry out the jihad themselves, any action does not have to be designed, ordered, or even backed or claimed by him. The ideology has already had its effect, and it is neither necessary nor convenient for any direct central control to exist; they are safer without it.

In this way, the concept of al Qaeda as an ideology for the movement and its network has already achieved its greatest triumph: justifying, claiming as its own, and profiting from any attack that takes place, making it difficult for those attacked to react, as they are unlikely to know who to go after. While they may be able to prevent attacks by the original al Qaeda from taking place, this does not stop the al Qaeda ideology from providing support, in its own very effective way, to the numerous groups or individuals of which it is composed. A good example of this can be found in Iraq. It is therefore necessary to uproot this ideology by convincing those that preach it of the complete error of their ways or, at the very least, by preventing it from attracting more followers, who will be younger and more fanatical.

Despite the extremely serious aggressions that the world has suffered through – the suicidal actions of these groups – now is the best possible time to combat them. We must be *proactive*, keep one step ahead of them, and construct more complex support networks than theirs. In addition, we must take full advantage of all of the legal measures available to us in a democratic system, and I can assure you that there are many.

All we have to do is think together, act together, revitalize different bodies, and put aside the absurd lack of trust that has always divided us. But we must do this now, while we still have an advantage over these new architects of destruction. Believe me, it no longer matters much whether one is American, Spanish, British, French, Arab, or Thai. Because for these new *horsemen of the Apocalypse*, anyone who does not think as they do is to be destroyed. Sometimes they act selectively, other times indiscriminately, striking soft targets like New York, Madrid, London, Bali, or Casablanca. They undoubtedly learn quickly from their mistakes and, without the need for multilateral agreements or meetings, general assemblies, or international conventions, they move on to their next target.

To some extent, these groups and individuals have joined forces, interacting amidst the worrying atomization of the international community, which is aided by the isolationist or selective approach of some countries, the indifference of others, and the slow response of most. Failure to accept that the situation is now so serious that *joint action* is essential would be a mistake of historic proportions.

The combination of terrorist strategies and techniques – the use of chemical, nuclear, or biological weapons cannot be ruled out – and the removal of the boundaries between ordinary crime and terrorism, which now go hand in glove, means that we urgently need a dynamic response, one that has already been too long in coming. How can we protect ourselves? Right now, focusing the response on al Qaeda as a unipolar group may be good for gaining support for the war on terror, but it is not an effective strategy. I do not wish to add an overly long list of suggestions to the points made in the book, but I have no doubt that *legal systems must move closer together* (at present, for example, the U.S. and European models are light years apart) before genuine progress is possible.

It is therefore necessary to find the *common ground* which enables us to build an *integrated system of information analysis and intelligence*. We also need a *proactive approach from the police and judges*, aimed at preventing terrorist acts from taking place; a meeting point where *political action* counteracts the level of fanaticism of these groups or factions; *a more effective and realistic approach from international bodies*, particularly the UN; and *effective financial control* of these networks. On this last point, it is frustrating that we have been unable to find a way of preventing the flows of the huge amounts of money needed to fund the very high levels of operational terrorist activity that have been taking place. Think, for example, of the financing of the insurgency and terrorist organizations in Iraq. Where do the terrorists obtain the enormous sums of money needed to pay for the arms and explosives that day after day take the lives of dozens of people? This is something that we should be thinking long and hard about and investigating in depth, together.

I could also refer to *adequate mechanisms of coordination, joint investigation teams, harmonization of national laws, the disappearance of legal and ideological boundaries, the legal definition of terrorism and the resources needed to combat it.* The task facing us is undoubtedly difficult but we must act. We have managed to equip ourselves with the basic rules that make coexistence possible, supported by a series of rights and responsibilities that protects this system; the future of this system is now at stake.

I, for one, refuse to accept that the civilized world, the democratic world, is incapable of rising to the challenge and tackling successfully this most troubling phenomenon.

Judge BALTASAR GARZÓN REAL

List of Participants

Daniel Benjamin is a Senior Analyst at the Center for Strategic and International Studies and coauthor of *The Age of Sacred Terror.*

Peter Bergen is a Fellow at the New America Foundation, a terrorism analyst for CNN, an Adjunct Professor at the School of Advanced International Studies, Johns Hopkins University, and author of *Holy War Inc.*

Steven Clemons is a Senior Fellow at the New America Foundation and the Publisher of the political blog, TheWashingtonNote.com.

Steve Coll is the former Managing Editor of *The Washington Post* and author of *Ghost Wars: The Secret History of the CIA, Afghanistan, and Bin Laden, From the Soviet Invasion to September 10, 2001.*

Paul Eedle is the founder of *Out There News*, a former Middle East Correspondent for Reuters, and an expert on al Qaeda's use of the Internet.

James Fallows is a National Correspondent for *Atlantic Monthly* and a frequent contributor to *Slate* and the *New York Review of Books.*

Yosri Fouda is the Lead Investigative Reporter for al Jazeera Television Network and author of *Masterminds of Terror*. In 2002 he interviewed Khalid Sheik Mohammed, the operational planner of 9/11.

Reuel Gerecht is a Resident Fellow at the American Enterprise Institute, a Contributing Editor for *The Weekly Standard*, a Correspondent for *Atlantic Monthly*, and a former Middle East Case Officer for the CIA.

Karen J. Greenberg is the Executive Director of the Center on Law and Security at New York University School of Law, coeditor of *The Torture Papers: The Road to Abu Ghraib*, and editor of *The Torture Debate in America*.

Rohan Gunaratna is the Director of the Institute of Defense and Strategic Studies in Singapore and author of *Inside Al Qaeda: A Global Network of Terror*.

Bruce Hoffman is the Director of the Washington Office and a Senior Analyst for RAND Corporation and author of *Inside Terrorism*.

Arif Lalani is the Director of the South Asia Division of the Department of Foreign Affairs, Government of Canada.

Colonel Pat Lang is a former Chief of Middle East Intelligence at the Defense Intelligence Agency, Department of Defense.

Anatol Lieven is a Senior Associate at the Carnegie Endowment for International Peace and author of *America Right or Wrong: An Anatomy of American Nationalism*.

Georg Mascolo is the Washington Bureau Chief of *Der Spiegel* and co-author of *Inside 9-11: What Really Happened*.

Hamid Mir is an Anchor for GEO television in Pakistan and the author of a forthcoming biography of Osama bin Laden. He was the last journalist to interview bin Laden in October 2001.

Ursula Mueller is a Counterterrorism Expert and Minister, Embassy of the Federal Republic of Germany to the United States.

Octavia Nasr is the Senior Editor for CNN Arab Affairs.

Salameh Nematt is the Washington Bureau Chief of *Al-Hayat*.

Marc Sageman is a forensic psychiatrist and a former CIA case officer. He worked with the mujahideen in Islamabad from 1987 to 1989 and is author of *Understanding Terror Networks*.

Michael Scheuer is the former Chief of the CIA Counterterrorist Center's bin Laden unit and author, as Anonymous, of *Imperial Hubris:*

Why the West is Losing the War on Terror and *Through Our Enemies' Eyes: Osama Bin Laden, Radical Islam and the Future of America.*

Henry Schuster is a Senior Producer for CNN and author of the forthcoming book *Hunting Eric Rudolph.*

Steven Simon is a Senior Analyst for RAND Corporation. He is the former Senior Director for Transnational Threats, National Security Council, and coauthor of *The Age of Sacred Terror.*

Jessica Stern is a Lecturer in Public Policy and Fellow in the International Security Program at the Harvard University John F. Kennedy School of Government and faculty affiliate at the Belfer Center for Science and International Affairs. She is also author of *Terror in the Name of God.*

Lawrence Wright is a *New Yorker* staff writer and author of "The Man Behind bin Laden," which won the 2002 Overseas Press Club Award for best magazine reporting.

PART ONE

Al Qaeda after 9/11

The New Face of Terrorism

1 Al Qaeda Then and Now

MODERATOR: **James Fallows,** National Correspondent, *Atlantic Monthly*. PANELISTS: **Peter Bergen,** Fellow, the New America Foundation and terrorism analyst, CNN; **Bruce Hoffman,** Director, RAND Corporation; **Steven Simon,** Senior Analyst, RAND Corporation.

PETER BERGEN

The conventional wisdom is that capturing or killing Osama bin Laden does not really make any difference. But the question of what happens if he is captured or killed should be considered.

Al Qaeda, as general wisdom has it, is now an ideological movement. But it is also more than that. We know now that Osama bin Laden and Ayman al-Zawahiri do not have to be in command and control of al Qaeda anymore. Still, we have twenty-eight video and/or audiotapes from al-Zawahiri or bin Laden since 9/11. Although these tapes – especially the twenty-eighth tape from al-Zawahiri – make it clear that, obviously, they do not retain such power, nevertheless, these audiotapes and videotapes demonstrate that both men continue to influence what happens. These tapes energize the base with the overt message: "Kill Westerners. Kill Americans. Kill Jews." But they also include specific instructions. For example, in December of 2003 Ayman al-Zawahiri called for attacks on President Musharraf. Very shortly thereafter, there were two serious assassination attempts against President Musharraf. And when, following that, bin Laden called for attacks on members of the coalition in Iraq, there were the attacks on the British bank and consulate in Istanbul. These were followed by the attack on the Italian police barracks in Nasiriya in southern Iraq and then finally by the bombing in Madrid on March 11, 2003.

So, the conventional wisdom that it does not really matter whether or not we apprehend bin Laden or al-Zawahiri is wrong, especially if you believe in the "great man" theory of history. It is certainly hard to imagine the Holocaust without Hitler, just as it is difficult to imagine the French army at Moscow in 1812 without Napoleon. Likewise, it is impossible to imagine al Qaeda without Ayman al-Zawahiri and Osama bin Laden. Capturing Khalid Sheikh Mohammed was no doubt important in terms of averting terrorist attacks. But it was bin Laden and al-Zawahiri who created this ideological movement via their ideas and who molded this amorphous group of people who did not have a lot to do with each other, into one organization: al Qaeda, "the base."

We have severely disrupted that base and the organization, yet still the movement continues as the two people who led the movement are at large and continue to influence the debate. It is unlikely that we will capture Osama at this point, but the best thing that we could do is to capture Osama and subject him to the same treatment to which Saddam Hussein was subjected. Checking him for head lice would do more than anything else to deflate his mythic person. Similarly, an international trial would be useful, as is now happening with Slobodan Milošević at The Hague. Though this is an unlikely outcome, it is a desirable one. However, it is much more likely that bin Laden will be martyred in his struggle. What will that actually result in? In the short term, the death of bin Laden might cause a lot of anti-American and anti-Western attacks around the world. In the medium term, it would be a devastating blow to what remains of al Qaeda the organization. And in the long term, unfortunately, it would give tremendous power to bin Laden's ideas. Sayyid Qutb, who is the Lenin of the al Qaeda movement, was a relatively obscure Egyptian writer before he was executed in 1966 by Anwar Sadat. In death, Qutb's ideas took on enormous life. And I think the same thing will happen with bin Laden's ideas after his "martyrdom," but to a much larger degree.

Moving on to another subject, the war in Iraq, the 800-pound gorilla in the room, brings us to three objective benchmarks that demonstrate how this war has been a disaster for our national security interests and the war on terror. The first is polling data. Bin Laden is scoring a sixty-five percent favorability rating in Pakistan, which is higher than President Bush scores in this country. The numbers are similar in Morocco and Jordan, with a favorability rating of fifty-five percent and forty-five percent, respectively. These are our closest allies in the war on terror. In Saudi Arabia we have a favorability rating of three percent, which is essentially zero. When polling is conducted in Saudi Arabia on bin Laden's political ideas, there is a fifty percent favorability rating. Interestingly, though, when we ask, "Would you like bin Laden to be your leader?" the positive response is only five percent.

In sum, either in the run-up to the Iraq war or during the Iraq war, our numbers have gone south and bin Laden's numbers have gone up. Hating the United States does not make you a terrorist but we have obviously increased the pool of people who would like to do damage to us. If you look at election results around the Muslim world in countries like Jordan, Kuwait, Morocco, Bahrain, Pakistan, and the recent Indonesian parliamentary elections, Islamist parties, when participatory, did surprisingly well. Voting for an Islamist party does not make you a terrorist but it does mean that the pool of people who do not like the United States has demonstrably increased.

Second, we need to look at terrorism figures. When the State Department's terrorism figures were revised to their real number, 2003 was the worst year for significant terrorist attacks since 1982. I suspect the trend will hold for 2004.

And finally, while this is not an objective benchmark as our other examples were, I think we can make a prediction that some of the things that happened in the war in Afghanistan against the Soviets are now happening at warp speed in Iraq. Bin Laden fought at the Battle of Jaji near Khost in Afghanistan in 1987. That was seven years after the Soviets invaded Afghanistan.

Foreign fighters arrived in Iraq before the war even began. There are at most fifteen hundred to two thousand foreign fighters estimated to be there. These people are force multipliers. They are, for example, the people carrying out the suicide attacks. If the war ends tomorrow or ten years from now, these people are not going to go back home and open falafel stands or coffee shops. Instead, they will be the shock troops of the international jihadist movement. Unlike bin Laden, who is now forty-eight years old, the people fighting in Iraq are in their early twenties just like bin Laden was when he fought in Afghanistan.

Outside of the war in Iraq, how is al Qaeda evolving? Physicists, who describe light as both a wave and a particle, give us some insights into the debates over al Qaeda. Essentially, we can consider it shorthand for many different phenomena. Al Qaeda is as much an organization as it is a movement. This is not an either/or kind of thing, just as light is both a wave and a particle.

What can we predict about al Qaeda in terms of future attacks? Bin Laden talked about a world Islamic front against the Crusaders and the Jews. But they never attacked Israeli or Jewish targets, something which I have always thought was very puzzling. If you delve inside their cosmology, al Qaeda thought of the Pentagon as a Jewish target. These people are rabidly anti-Semitic and in my book I underestimated that aspect of the story. They saw the Pentagon and the World Trade Center as Jewish targets as much as American targets. Nonetheless, they had never really attacked Israeli or Jewish targets until Danny Pearl's kidnapping and murder. And since then, there has been a very rapid acceleration of attacks on Jewish targets. In Casablanca there was an attack on the Jewish community center. In Istanbul there was an attack on two synagogues. Taba saw attacks on Israeli tourists. In Mombassa there was an attack on the Israeli-owned hotel, and later an attempt to bring down an Israeli passenger jet. And this trend is going to accelerate.

Another trend going forward is the prevalence of attacks on financial targets. You know bin Laden gloated in the last videotape that 9/11 represented the best leveraged investment in history. He said that for every dollar al Qaeda spent it cost the United States $1 million in damages. Al Qaeda spent $500,000. It cost the U.S. $500 billion. Al Qaeda never really thought about economic targets before 9/11. They attacked American embassies. They attacked American warships. They tried to attack American military bases. But they did not really care about economic targets. It was not part of the cosmology. They care about economic targets now because they understand that this is the best way, in a sense, to attack the West.

Bin Laden and al-Zawahiri made this official policy a year after 9/11. They released audiotapes calling for attacks on Western economic targets.

Shortly thereafter the attack in Yemen on the French oil tanker, the *Limburg*, occurred, and also the attack on the disco in Bali. Tourism and oil are obviously central to the global economy. And if you think about it from the perspective of bin Laden, al Qaeda is now beginning to have strategic successes. It may give you psychological satisfaction to blow up a synagogue if you are a member of al Qaeda. But it is not really a strategic success. Jacking up the price of oil is a strategic success. There is some debate about how much we are paying in regard to a "fear premium" on the price of oil. But we are paying something. The recent attacks on Saudi oil installations, on people working in the oil business, and in Iraq are all affecting the price of oil. The Madrid election following the March 2004 bombing was yet another strategic success.

A third group of targets that we can expect to see hit in the future is that of Western brand names. We've seen the beginning of this trend already: attacks on the JW Marriott in Jakarta, on the Sheraton in Karachi, and on the Hilton in Egypt. It used to be that leftist terrorists attacked McDonald's. Now Islamist terrorists have started to attack McDonald's. Recently, there was a string of sixteen coordinated attacks on Shell gas stations in Pakistan. These did not get a lot of coverage; no one was killed. I would predict, going forward, that this will also be a trend that accelerates.

Another worrisome trend is the fact that al Qaeda and the Kashmiri militant groups have essentially morphed together. This connection existed before 9/11 but is rapidly accelerating now. Harkat-ul-Mujahideen and al Qaeda shared training camps in Afghanistan before 9/11. Jaish e-Mohammed, the group that murdered Danny Pearl, is a subsidiary of al Qaeda. Out of a working relationship, these groups seem to have morphed into one.

The reason this combination is particularly problematic is that the war on terror is being conducted largely in Pakistan. Moreover, we have seen that, without exception, the senior leadership of al Qaeda has been arrested in Pakistani cities. And, if indeed al Qaeda is morphing with the Kashmiri militant groups, it is of particular importance to note that these groups are very popular. When Lashkar-e-Toiba has its annual gathering, hundreds of thousands of people show up. It has twenty-two hundred offices around the country. We can conclude, therefore, that the group is popular and that it is hard for law enforcement to be effective against it.

The conventional wisdom that bin Laden is in the tribal territory seems to be very wrong. But there are cities like Gujarat, Rawalpindi, Quetta, and Karachi that are also likely. Think about the bin Laden videotape from October 2004. Here he is a man talking about the supplemental funding for the Afghan and Iraq war. In this video, he is paying very close attention to what is happening in the United States and he has very recent information. He mentioned, for instance, a talk that was delivered at the World Institute of International Affairs in London, which is the equivalent of the Council on Foreign Relations here in the United States. Now most Americans would have no idea what the Council on Foreign Relations is. Bin Laden was paying some very granular attention to the news. This is important because it implies that bin Laden is somewhere where there are newspapers and/or the Internet. He is not in the tribal territories where there is no electricity, and where you can forget about making videotapes. Bin Laden is likely to be in a smaller town, just as every apprehended member of the senior leadership of al Qaeda has been found in cities.

One final thing to point out in terms of the present and future of al Qaeda is the critical importance of Europe. Consider the attacks that have occurred or have been averted which involve both Europe and the United States. Richard Reid, the so-called shoe bomber, was a British Jamaican. The events of 9/11 could not have happened without the Hamburg cell. Ahmed Rassam, an Algerian who went to Corsica, then to Afghanistan, and then to Canada, tried to blow up LAX Airport. A British citizen, Abu Esa al-Britani, who was arrested in August 2004, was casing American financial institutions.

There have been no serious terrorism cases in the United States at all except for Richard Reid, the alleged shoe bomber, and Iyman Faris who had the bright idea of trying to cut through the cables of the Brooklyn Bridge – not a very serious kind of terrorist plot. Nor does it appear to me that there are sleeper cells in this country. There has been no evidence from the legal cases we have seen that there were such sleeper cells. The threat is from people outside and from what is happening in Europe.

Europe is of central importance for two reasons. First, Europe has a huge demographic problem. They have to import labor from outside and they have to extend the social welfare benefits to people bringing income into the country. Now there are twenty million Muslims in Europe and that number is obviously going to increase. Secondly, I would argue that there is a problem with alienation. It is not a class issue in Europe. Look at Omar Sheikh, a graduate of the London School of Economics (LSE), who came from a very privileged background but who felt some alienation because of the inherent racism that exists against Pakistanis in Britain as against Algerians in France. Going forward, it is this group of people that we should be concerned about.

BRUCE HOFFMAN

Let me make three broad observations on al Qaeda and terrorism. First, the good news is that the threat that al Qaeda poses is changing. We have forced it to change. This is a reflection of the successes and the progress that we have achieved in the war on terror in the past three plus years. As President Bush has pointed out, we have killed or captured three-quarters of the al Qaeda leadership. In addition, our allies have arrested upwards of four thousand members of al Qaeda worldwide. We have tracked down more than $140 million in their funding, and we have deprived al Qaeda of its operational bases in Afghanistan.

That is all to the good. But the bad news is that al Qaeda and the threat it poses are changing precisely because they are capable of changing. And what we see is that their ability to change is a reflection of their determination, their adaptiveness, their resiliency, and indeed the fact that they are a particularly implacable and formidable foe. What this means is that terrorism is emerging as a highly dynamic phenomenon, something akin to the archetypal shark in the water. Just as the shark must constantly move to survive, terrorist groups by definition must constantly attack. This is the means by which they catapult themselves back into the headlines. They reinsert themselves into the limelight and they garner the attention and publicity, which they then attempt to use and to harness as a form of coercion and intimidation.

If the threat we face is constantly changing and evolving, so must our thinking on how most effectively to counter this animal change and evolve as well. We cannot afford to rest on past laurels and previous successes. The way we approach this problem must constantly be evolving and adjusting.

Second, we have obviously declared a war on terrorism. But our adversaries are pursuing a war of attrition. We saw this very clearly in bin Laden's statement of October 29, 2004. This has enormous implications for the way we look at the struggle. All to the good, we have gotten used to war as lasting a matter of months if not weeks, as was certainly the case of the first Gulf War and the military invasion of Afghanistan in March and April 2003. These wars were measured in terms of weeks. But this is a fundamental problem. Our adversaries, in defining the struggle as a war of attrition, have embarked on a campaign that they recognize will take years, if not decades. This is important for our own patience and for our own time horizon.

Third, I have to say that, having studied terrorism now for nearly thirty years, the subject itself has become exponentially more difficult to categorize and to pitch and hold on to than it ever was. Consequently, it is now more difficult to understand. What we see today is a more diffuse phenomenon, with less centralized and more opaque relationships and a far less transparent command and control structure.

Let me move on to al Qaeda today. Al Qaeda has proven itself to be a remarkably nimble, flexible, and adaptive entity. It rebounded from the loss of Afghanistan to an extent I do not think was ever fully appreciated. More recently, however, al Qaeda has been able to reconfigure itself into an organization more reflective of an ideology than it once was. Consequently, al Qaeda has been able to transform itself into an entity that is more difficult for us to defeat today than it was on 9/11.

It is no longer a pseudo- or quasi-army as it was in Afghanistan when it could be defeated on the battlefield. Nor is it a bureaucratic entity as it was in Afghanistan, able to be crushed. Instead, it is a transnational movement that is true to its name. The result is that there are many al Qaedas today and not just one. And the threats that they each pose are more complex, significantly more difficult, and ultimately more challenging.

Despite this remarkable transformation of al Qaeda, the basic pattern and *modus operandi* of the jihadists remains remarkably the same. As demonstrated in the abortive plots against the financial centers in New York City, Newark, New Jersey, and Washington, D.C., this past summer, and even more importantly in the plots that were uncovered in the United Kingdom to attack infrastructure, mass transit, and financial targets, al Qaeda and the radical jihad have lost none of its grandiose ambitions nor its homicidal intentions. What we see, as we saw on 9/11, is a continued focus on economic targets, multi-year planning, and detailed reconnaissance and surveillance, all planned to lead up to what al Qaeda hopes will be a stunning impact. Simultaneity, the ability to perpetrate more than one operation at the same time, remains a singularly important metric, perhaps the most important metric for the jihadists. We have seen this in recent years with the attacks in Mombassa, in Istanbul, and in Madrid. But in this respect we have to recognize that al Qaeda has never had an either/or strategy. They have always planned spectacular events to be planned and executed at the direction of some central command authority, while alongside of this centralized planning and execution, there were attacks by affiliates and associates operating independently, completely apart from al Qaeda but out of sympathy with its aims. What is different today, when compared to the past, is the emphasis and encouragement given diaspora communities, particularly in Europe.

There are numerous examples of the threat from the disapora. The expatriate communities of Algerians in London were implicated in the ricin plot in January 2003. The Moroccans carried out the bombing in Madrid and the van Gogh murder in the Netherlands. But a further, emergent issue is the problem with sleepers, people like Lionel Dumont and Willie Brigitte. Dumont, apprehended in Germany, was completely off law enforcement lists and intelligence screens until his apprehension. Brigitte, a member of Lashkar-e-Toiba, who was apprehended in Australia, was similarly unknown. And then there are two particularly interesting cases in London; namely, those of Asif Mohammed Hanif and Omar Khan Sharif, two British Muslims of Kashmiri extract who were attracted to radical jihadism by al Muhajiroun through the Finsbury Mosque. Both were completely assimilated, both perfectly comfortable, both from middle-class backgrounds. One of them, like Omar Sheikh, had the distinction of being an LSE graduate. They were deliberately recruited, became enmeshed in terrorism, and embarked on a journey that somehow diverted them from what I believe was their plan to attack in Iraq. Instead, they struck on April 30, 2003, at Mike's Place in Tel Aviv.

When you look at these diaspora individuals and leaders, they may be less capable than the professionals who carried out the 9/11 attacks. But, at the same time, they may also be more bloody-minded. Even cells of these radical jihadists who may be relatively low on the terrorist food chain in terms of professionalism and in terms of skill nonetheless have a proclivity to think very big. You just have to look at the group of Algerians who were involved in the ricin plot and who were apprehended in London in January 2003. Here you have almost the archetypal, unsophisticated group of terrorists including a bunch of adolescents. But they were thinking in grandiose terms, as al Qaeda aspires to do, by attempting to use a biological weapon, ricin.

Now, given these changes, given what we see are the trends in terrorism, what should we do in the future? In the December 2004 issue of *Current History* I presented an expansive list. But let me conclude on what I think is the one key point as we move forward in confronting this challenge. And that is this: *that the concept of a war on terror has outlived both its usefulness and its relevance.* As we move ahead, rather than looking at this as a war on terrorism, we have to reconceive of this as something more akin to a global insurgency or a global counterinsurgency. And here we know that, as Field Marshal Sir Gerald Templar – arguably the world's leading example of implementing a successful counterinsurgency which he did in Malaya nearly fifty years ago – famously declared: countering insurgency is only twenty-five percent military. Seventy-five percent consists of political, diplomatic, economic, and information operations. It was very important during the first two phases of terrorism to rely on our military instruments to weaken our enemies in order to break the backs of their power. But if we are to achieve continued success in this struggle we have to move away from a metric that focuses almost exclusively on kill-and-capture to something that focuses more on breaking the cycle of terrorist recruitment and replenishment that we have seen unfold over the past three years.

To do this we have to think and plan strategically, to counter not just the current generation of terrorists out there, but the generation beyond the existing one as well.

STEVEN SIMON

Let me begin with an overview of the main developments or trends in the fight against al Qaeda. First, there has been a transition from group to movement, a development which by now has become the conventional wisdom. The chief point of difference between group and movement is how recruitment takes place. And it looks as though that recruitment has evolved into a process that is largely one of self-selection. It is no longer top-down identification and indoctrination of members.

This is a key difference. One of the phenomena that has fed this is what I like to call Ummah-itis, which is an unhealthy preoccupation with one's membership in a supranational group. In this case, the obsession is with the Ummah, the Muslim community. And there are some interesting statistics on this. Pew administered polls in June 2003, which showed that large majorities in eight of nine Muslim survey groups either completely agreed or somewhat agreed that this obsession with belonging, this Ummah-itis, existed. This was the case for eighty percent or more of the respondents in Indonesia and Pakistan and at least seventy percent of those surveyed in Lebanon, Nigeria, and Jordan. Pluralities in Kuwait, Morocco, and the Palestinian Authority also reported a similar deepening of solidarity.

This is a phenomenon that is being fed and will be further fueled by the nature of mass communications, whether it is the Web or videotapes or cable TV or the like. In combination with this phenomenon of Ummah-itis, you have a grafting process. Groups like Jama'at al-Tawhid wal-Jihad – that is the group of Abu Musab al-Zarqawi in Iraq – graft themselves onto al Qaeda. The GSPC [Salafist Group for Preaching and Combat] in Algeria has done the same thing. This has contributed to a blurring of the lines between the movement we see now and your father's al Qaeda. And it is especially relevant in this context to bear in mind that we are not dealing with a candy mint or breath mint phenomena. Is it a candy mint or is it a breath mint? Is it a movement or something else?

In this general domain of the transition from group to movement, the only other thing I want to point out is the Salafist critique. When you consider the power of that critique in combination with the generalized antipathy towards the U.S., the emergence of the U.S. as an undifferentiated symbol of everything that is wrong, and bin Laden's own folk hero status in many parts of the Muslim world, you can be sure there is more trouble brewing.

Yet another change has been in the model of resistance. Al Qaeda was at one point all about the collective defense of Muslims through military engagement. That's what it was. Al Qaeda was a standing army of a notional sovereign Dar al-Islam, the world of Islam. In Afghanistan, you could see that articulated in a very explicit way by bin Laden himself in his 1996 declaration of war and then further played out in Chechnya, Kashmir, Tajikistan, in the seventh brigade of the Bosnian army, and, of course, in Somalia which was a formative experience for the group. That was then and this is now. There was a transition sometime in the 1998 time frame, probably spurred by the attacks against American interests in Saudi Arabia, in Riyadh, and in Dhahran in 1995 and 1996.

The paradigm of resistance began to encompass an explicitly offensive component. And this was embodied in the 1998 fatwa against Jews and crusaders. So even though jihad was still something that was foisted on the Ummah and was defensive in origin, it had taken on a very different character. This had the additional effect of expanding the group's target set; it was not just the enemy's military or the instruments of the enemy's power that were targeted, but anyone affiliated with the enemy as well. Bin Laden called this striking at the head of the snake.

Another way in which this development has shaped their targeting doctrine and which is worth focusing upon is the way "combatant" has been defined. In World War II, the United States and its allies actually had a very broad view of who the combatants were on the other side. So if you were working in Dresden in a factory making precision optics for the *Luftwaffe*, you were essentially a combatant and were susceptible to legitimate violence. We have been moving away from that concept but al Qaeda has been moving in the opposite direction. To them, everyone is a legitimate target and they have advanced a number of explanations for this, including a number of very formal legalistic justifications for this widening of the target set. It is a trend that we need to be watching very carefully because, among other things, this target set now takes into account children under a doctrine of reciprocity. This is what Beslan was about. So, watch out.

A third trend is a reorientation to some degree of their targeting activity, which is to say they have gone back home. At the same time that they remain focused on the U.S. as a target, they have gone home, particularly to Saudi Arabia where the number of attacks between September 11, 2001, and June 2004 is quite impressive. There have been twenty separate attacks in Saudi Arabia, leading to the deaths of at least fifty security personnel and the wounding of many more.

Now in a way this should not be surprising, since according to Khalid Sheikh Mohammed, about seventy percent of the population of the training camps in Afghanistan were Saudi. And the Saudi security forces have asserted that about fifteen thousand to twenty-five thousand Saudi youths have passed through the camps in Afghanistan. Iraq of course is another front where the movement has gone back home and returned to attacking the near enemy.

I will close with two more trends that I would like to discuss briefly. The first is the splintering of the movement. We are looking at variations of this not only in Iraq but in Morocco, Tunisia, and Indonesia, which were previously thought to be immune to this sort of thing. Now this is in part a by-product of what amounted to an enormous recruiting drive launched initially by the electrifying attack against the World Trade Center. It was a galvanizing event; it was awe-inspiring to many youths who were ripe for recruitment. But although this was an enormous recruiting drive, there existed no capacity to absorb all the recruits. There was no way to channel that enormous surge of energy. So the group necessarily splintered, and newly empowered jihadists struck out on their own.

There are a couple of great examples of developments that have enhanced this splintering of the movement. The lines of command that had existed hitherto are beginning to disintegrate and in some places have disintegrated. So for example if you looked at Pakistan after the capture of Khalid Sheikh Mohammed, you began to see new groups popping up. The poster boy for this was a statistician at the University of Karachi named Atta-ur Rehman who is now in Pakistani custody. He was involved in a conspiracy to kill President Musharraf. He simply got together with his friends; they knocked over a bank, they stole $70,000, and they set themselves up as a terrorist organization.

This is happening in many places. It is therefore not surprising that the nature of the jihad has taken on a somewhat unfocused aspect. This is something to watch out for especially in the context of Europe. New fields of jihad are emerging. Europe has been ripening in this way for a long time. It may now be maturing.

What do we do about that? To begin with, it is not enough to change opinions about the United States; it is not sufficient to propagandize. The RAND Corporation has done some very interesting studies about what are euphemistically called the military information operations. In these studies, precedents have been scrutinized. How, for example, did we try to influence opinion in Vietnam? How did we try to influence opinion in postwar Germany? How did we try to influence opinion in Eastern Europe? The one constant theme that returns again and again is that context is everything. When the message of the United States seems to cohere with the context in which the message is transmitted, there can be success. When we transmitted to Eastern Europe that we were the alternative, the only alternative, the magisterial, the definitive alternative to Soviet rule and Soviet ideology, it worked because we were seen to be acting in a way that was consistent with our message. The context was right.

But today, at this point in time, the context, for complicated reasons, is not right. Our message is not going to stick, and as we think about this long-term conflict and how we are going to deal with its ideological component, we need to think about the mismatch between context and message.

AL QAEDA THEN AND NOW

Question and Answer Session

Q. JAMES FALLOWS: To me one of the most striking themes concerns the conflicting themes of dynamism. We see al Qaeda being presented as dynamic in almost every way, in terms of new forms, new rationales, new spheres of influence. The question is whether or not the United States can be comparably dynamic in adapting to that threat. How do you (the panelists) want to answer that question? What has been the effect of the war in Iraq in terms of creating an environment in which more and more people come to see the United States as an avenue towards terrorism instead of away from it?

A. STEVEN SIMON: The war in Iraq tended to confirm key planks in bin Laden's platform. It depicted the United States or the West or the infidels as interested in controlling or conquering Muslim lands, exploiting Muslim resources, and being committed to the humiliation of Islam. And there is no question that these themes have been accelerated by the war in Iraq and by damaging images such as those from Abu Ghraib. The problem is that the images of what actually happened have lent credence now to any image emerging. The most recent example of this was a fabricated image of an American soldier shooting an unarmed Iraqi civilian. This photo circulated on the Web before there was a real incident of a U.S. Marine who, for whatever reasons, and under presumably very stressful circumstances, shot an unarmed Iraqi. So, we are caught in an inescapable loop of imagined reality on the part of our adversary and actuated reality on our part. It is a difficult cycle to escape in the context of a brutal counterinsurgency.

A. **PETER BERGEN:** You know, in the most recent Ayman al-Zawahiri tape, he actually talks about how happy he is that Saddam is gone. In other words, he was an enemy of jihad. Bin Laden and Ayman al-Zawahiri have been rather happy about Saddam's departure from the scene. After all, Saddam, like Assad, was opposed to the jihadists. And – following what Steve Simon has just said and what Mike Scheuer said – if Osama believed in Christmas, the Iraq war would be under his Christmas tree. He has really stirred up a Sunni and Shi'a fundamentalist insurgency in the country, and we have deposed somebody who was a rabid secularist.

Q. **MICHAEL KENNEY [Pennsylvania State University and Stanford University]:** I would like to ask about the theme of the decentralization of al Qaeda, the shift from an organization to a movement. What implications does that change have for the knowledge structures within the movement? Are we talking about former al Qaeda mid-level people that now are in charge of their own groups and are drawing on their previous knowledge and experience to conduct their attacks? Or are we talking about new leaders of groups that are starting from square one, which has obvious implications for the terrorist learning curve?

A. **BRUCE HOFFMAN:** It is all of the above, and I think that is precisely what al Qaeda's strength is. It doesn't make these choices and, therefore, it is able to operate on a number of different planes, to mix and match approaches, skill sets, recruits, and so on. That is what makes them so formidable a challenge. It is not one set *modus operandi* or one set footprint but it is rather – I think deliberately – a much more diverse and different one.

Q. **MATTHEW LYONS [Archivist and independent historian]:** Obviously, the sentiment in the Ummah towards the West is a key component of the decision to join the global jihad. However it is not immediately obvious that the only recourse against grievances from the West against the Ummah is to join the jihad. To what extent do you think a lack of faith of the social institutions of the Muslim world contributes to the global jihad movement?

A. PETER BERGEN: I think it is not an accident that so many people in al Qaeda are from Egypt or Saudi Arabia, places that are intolerant of any form of dissent. And I think the reason that al Qaeda springs up is that there is no political space to express this view of the world is, and so you are thrown into the arms of the radicals. I think if we created a political space to express such opinions that we may not particularly like, but are not violent, it would go a long way to really sabotaging al Qaeda.

Q. MATTHEW LYONS: And how can we move towards that?

A. PETER BERGEN: That is a $64 million question. We have done a terrible job so far. We have barely begun talking about winning the war of ideas. The Cold War was not only won with battle tanks in Germany but also with a kind of multi-pronged approach. In the Cold War we did this both overtly and covertly with quite a lot of success, whether it was funding Christian democratic parties, funding liberals opposed to communism, or funding certain kinds of magazines. Right now, because of the Iraq situation and the discrepancy between message and context, it is quite hard for us probably to be very effective. But the Iraq war will end one day. This problem is going be much longer than the Iraq war, so we need a strategy, a multi-pronged strategy.

Q. RAY McGOVERN [Veteran Intelligence Professionals for Sanity]: At the end of Bruce Hoffman's presentation, he talked about how to get away from the kill-capture metrics and how we might break the cycle of recruitment. Steve Simon did something similar when he talked about the message not cohering with the context in which the message is transmitted. Have we done anything to address the problem of the context, i.e., the Israeli-Palestinian dispute and our support for repressive regimes in Arab countries?

A. STEVEN SIMON: If you look at the Palestinian-Israeli conflict in the way that plays into broad, popular antipathy towards the United States and the way it has been instrumentalized by bin Laden, then I am not sure that it is possible for the United States to do anything, at least in the near term, that is going to change those perceptions, in part because bin Laden has set us up. He set us up by staking out the line that Muslims are being duped in a massive and comprehensive way, that anything emerging from the adversary is a lie. In fact, Muslims have been trapped by this web of lies. So he will say, as he has said, that when we say we are behind the roadmap and we'd like to see a Palestinian state, this is just another example of one of those lies, because what we really are talking about is perpetuating the enslavement of Palestinians and so forth. So in addition to all the other problems, we have the bin Laden effect in the way he has set us up.

A. **PETER BERGEN:** *The 9/11 Commission Report* is a masterpiece narrative of what happened, but its recommendations were strangely silent on three very important issues: the Israel-Palestine dispute, Kashmir, and Chechnya. Waving a magic wand over all these is not going to put al Qaeda out of business. But if we could, we would be taking away either core grievances or training grounds, both of which would be helpful.

A. **JAMES FALLOWS:** Let me say something about the Israel-Palestine dispute. I don't think we should be under any illusion that if we somehow magically inserted ourselves into the process and resolved this longstanding and nearly intractable conflict, that terrorism, and especially al Qaeda, is going to disappear. One only has to recall that in 1998, at the height of the Oslo Accords and when Palestinian-Israeli relations were arguably at their zenith, that bin Laden and al Qaeda were taking root, the time when bin Laden was blowing up our embassies.

The key is that if the U.S. is seen as more equitable, it will reduce some of the enmity that is generated against the United States repeatedly and regularly on a daily basis, enmity that links U.S. military operations in Iraq reflexively with IDF [Israeli Defense Forces] operations in the West Bank of Gaza. That, in and of itself, would be an improvement, at least in mitigating some of the hostility towards the United States.

But, as it stands, we are behind the curve. The biggest challenge is that the audience share now is calculated not just in reference to al Jazeera or al Arabiya, but increasingly by mouthpieces of the terrorist organizations themselves, whether it's on the Internet where terrorists are completely bypassing our media or by outfits like al Manar. Hezbollah has a TV station that is regularly watched more than its competitors in Jordan, for example, in times of crisis and for breaking news. So I think it is making up for lost time. It astonished me that during the Cold War, we were amazingly adept and sophisticated at what has become almost as pejorative a term as terrorism and propaganda. Now it's called information operations. Somehow we have completely surrendered this capability. We do very little of it now, and when we do, we recognize the importance of it too late. I think one important step forward would be, rather than stiff-arming and ignoring al Jazeera and al Arabiya, at least to have our Arabic-speaking diplomats and Arabic-speaking Americans go on these outlets much more and be much more of a presence.

Q. AUDIENCE PARTICIPANT: Steve Simon mentioned that terrorism has become largely self-recruitment. Can you say something about the ability of some of these smaller groups to obtain financing? How difficult is it for them and what sort of resources may they have to turn to?

A. STEVEN SIMON: Setting aside Europe and maybe the U.S. for a moment, the interesting case is the one I raised of Atta-ur Rehman, where he and his friends turned to crime. In their case, it was a dramatic crime, but one that netted a lot of money right away and gave them operational funding for the kinds of things they were planning. What we saw before September 11th was a lot of self-funding. I mean people go to work, they have jobs. They engage in minor crime, credit card fraud, check forgery, and things like that which get them money. And there have been, and still are, charitable sources of money that can be diverted for criminal purposes. So there is plenty of money out there, and terrorism is inexpensive really.

A. PETER BERGEN: Yes, terrorism is a very cheap form of warfare. The first World Trade Center attack cost something like $10,000. Ahmed Ressam was planning to blow up LAX Airport with $12,000. It is sort of a feel-good exercise when we say we are going to cut down the money supply, and the Treasury Department closes down $150 million or so in terms of terrorist financing. But it is not about money, it is about belief.

You cannot persuade people in their twenties to fly passenger jets into large buildings because of money. I think we have overestimated the importance or the efficacy of going after the money.

A. BRUCE HOFFMAN: The other thing, too, that I think is important to note is that, although we were successful in hunting down the sources of financing for terrorism in the immediate aftermath of 9/11, those sources have changed and evolved as well. This is another example where Iraq has been, as Mike Scheuer describes it, a Christmas tree for al Qaeda. It has been a boon, not just to recruitment, but also to financing, to contributions, and to radical jihadist groups.

Q. MICHAEL SCHEUER: I just have a short comment, first on Mr. Bergen's description of the narrative of *The 9/11 Commission Report* as being superb, and I think it is. But I also think it is a terrible hoax on the American people in that it is always easy to write history if you start at the end and work backwards. It is like looking at the Civil War; if you start from Mr. McClean's porch at Appomattox, the Union victory looks certain. If you start from John Brown's raid, it is not so certain. One of the tremendous flaws in this now-accepted piece of American scripture is that, somehow, any intelligence analyst on earth could have known any of that information.

It is becoming an accepted notion that Osama bin Laden and Ayman al-Zawahiri are no longer in command and control of their organization, that al Qaeda is broken and gone forever. But have you ever heard of any terrorist group that has suffered the loss of three quarters of its leadership and four thousand fighters and is still capable of detonating a weapon of mass destruction in the United States? What I am afraid of here is that the word terrorist for al Qaeda is such a misnomer that we are really working with a body count at the moment. There is no order of battle. What are we deducting three quarters of the leadership and four thousand fighters from? I have had a little experience chasing Mr. bin Laden, and I am reluctant to think that we should toss off the idea that he is no longer in command and no longer capable of attacking us or running an organization. My question is simply, how do we know?

A. STEVEN SIMON: I take your point. First of all, there is no turnstile to begin with that shows who is going in, let alone who is rising, in the organization. There still is evidence of command and control, but we can't go into that. We need to take into account our predisposition to deal with this as we dealt with the counternarcotics problem – basically deploying a kingpin strategy. You have the big board. And on that big board you have the faces of the bad guys, and as each one is arrested or rendered, extradited or killed, a bar is drawn through his face. It is a body count approach to this thing.

A. BRUCE HOFFMAN: The crux of your statement is that we fasten onto these metrics of kill-capture. That may have been important and necessary in the immediate aftermath of 9/11, but that also is outliving its relevance. That is why I suggest that we should be thinking beyond the current generation and not looking at this as a deck of cards. Because actually when we look at Iraq we can see that getting the deck of cards has not ended the insurgency there.

Do we know of any organizational entity anywhere, at any time in history, that could survive the loss of three quarters of its senior and middle management, that could see the arrests of thousands of its followers, and still be in business in one fashion or another? Just the fact that bin Laden can still exert such a commanding presence on TV, the fact that there is still terrorism that occurs throughout the world and that others want to harness al Qaeda's name for themselves, this in and of itself is a towering achievement of survival. It suggests that this is going to be a very long struggle not least because their adversaries have defined it as a long struggle. They have defined it as a war of attrition, which raises challenges. The challenge in a war of attrition is to maintain focus and to maintain momentum even at times of relative quiescence. We cannot be lulled into thinking that the latest arrests or roundups are sounding the death knell of a rather more intractable enemy, that it has become much more of an ideology than an actual terrorist group.

Finally, looking at bin Laden's achievements, what terrorist group in history had thousands of people? Unlike many other terrorist leaders who are philosophers or historians or political scientists, bin Laden's background and acumen is in business, in the sciences of management. And that is what he has applied towards making this very unique terrorist movement.

A. **STEVEN SIMON:** Bin Laden transformed a relatively small group of stone-cold Egyptian killers and Saudi eschatological lunatics into a worldwide movement, and that is incredible.

Q. **AUDIENCE PARTICIPANT:** My question is for Peter Bergen. You explained the prominence of Saudis and Egyptians in this movement by the repressive nature of those regimes. Would you care to speculate on why we have not heard more about people from Syria and the former Soviet Central Asian Republics?

Q. **PETER BERGEN:** On Syria, there is a one-word answer, which is "Hama," the massacre in which all those people were killed in 1982. On the Central Asians, we actually are seeing some terrorism in Uzbekistan. Ahmed Rashid has written very well on this subject, and he says the Uzbeks are making a huge mistake in turning Hizb-ut-Tahir, which is a sort of quietist organization into a terrorist organization. And this may become a self-fulfilling prophesy in that the Hizb-ut-Tahir movement may replace the Islamic movement, making Uzbekistan a serious threat.

Q. **MATTHEW JOSEPH [Terror Free Tomorrow]:** My question is for Mr. Simon. You indicated that if the context is not right, our message does not stick. So what can we actually do to change the context so that our message does stick?

A. **STEVEN SIMON:** We are now perceived to be the enemy par excellence of Islam. There are some ways in which that reputation is unavoidable. This is because there are certain U.S. policies that are immutable and which contribute to this perception; support for Israel, for example. The U.S. connection to regimes that are perceived to be apostate and depressive is another thing that is difficult to escape.

Now how do we really disentangle ourselves from these relationships just when the war on terrorism requires us to bind more closely to some of these governments because we need their tactical cooperation? The socioeconomic traumas that contribute to the recruitment and radicalization of the bourgeois terrorists who are actually doing the killing are so great that it is difficult to see how we can work quickly to diminish them. It costs a lot of money to deal with issues like those, and it cannot be done by us alone. It requires allies, and right now our alliances are not in the best of repair. Nor do we have an alliance strategy for dealing with these underlying problems.

Since so much of the discourse on the other side is cast in religious terms, how should we respond to it? You know, we are now expressing ourselves more openly in religious terms. Formerly, it pretty much stopped at the water's edge, that is, if you do not count missionary activity. This is not the case any more. Perhaps this is a good development. Maybe you can have something like a faith-based dialogue or faith based diplomacy with others and engage in a dialogue on shared terms. On the other hand, the way in which we deploy our religious rhetoric might in fact sharpen perceptions on the other side, rejecting a fundamental clash of cultures and religions which is precisely the perception we do not want to encourage. This just adds to the complexity of what faces the United States in dealing with this issue.

Q. AUDIENCE PARTICIPANT: This question is directed to Mr. Bergen. You said that we have not begun the war of ideas. I just would like to hear what your response will be to the press when they continuously say that the detainees down in Guantánamo Bay, Cuba, have been there two plus years and have not provided anything relevant to the war on terror.

A. PETER BERGEN: I think it is factually correct to say that the press has repeatedly said that the information coming out of Guantánamo is not particularly useful.

Q. MARK SANTILLIS [Terrorism Research Center]: My question is for Peter Bergen. You mentioned that Kashmiri separatist groups in al Qaeda were being fused together. I was wondering if you could elaborate more on specific examples where they have fused together or collaborated?

A. PETER BERGEN: Look at the assasination attempts on Musharraf or what is happening in Karachi, one of the world's most dangerous cities, the scene of three attacks on the American consulate. Look at Danny Pearl's kidnapping or the attack on the Sheraton Hotel that killed twelve French defense contractors. All of these attacks are a form of joint operations between al Qaeda and the Kashmiri militant groups.

2 Who Joins al Qaeda?

MODERATOR: **Steve Coll,** author of *Ghost Wars: The Secret History of the CIA, Afghanistan and Bin Laden, From the Soviet Invasion to September 10, 2001.* PANELISTS: **Yosri Fouda,** Lead Investigative Reporter for al Jazeera Television Network; **Jessica Stern,** Lecturer in Public Policy and Fellow in the International Security Program at Harvard University; **Marc Sageman,** forensic psychiatrist and former CIA case officer.

STEVE COLL

Perhaps we can define the difference between the discussion we just concluded and the one we are about to begin by mentioning the elusiveness of any quantitative census of al Qaeda or the movement that al Qaeda represents. What we are interested in is the qualitative census of that movement. We are interested in the problem of counterinsurgency.

If this is really a campaign of counterinsurgency or at least a campaign analogous to counterinsurgency, then one of the challenges is to separate the most nihilistic, violent elements of that movement from those who could be converted to ordinary politics in the manner of counterinsurgencies throughout history. That requires an understanding of where the most violent adherents began, how they were radicalized, and from what social strata they came. Why, from among the many, many millions of angry young Muslim men with grievances toward the West, has a relative handful chosen to participate in this sort of nihilistic violence?

Our first speaker is Yosri Fouda, an investigative reporter for al Jazeera who has the distinction of having interviewed both Khalid Sheikh Mohammed and Ramzi Binalshibh prior to their arrests in Pakistan. He has lived with this story, and with the characters who have thrust themselves fully into our agenda, throughout his professional life.

YOSRI FOUDA

Thank you to the New America Foundation and the Center on Law and Security for daring to invite somebody from al Jazeera. That tells me a lot about this country. This is a great country and I am proud to stand here today. America has every right to defend itself, its people, its land, its values.

When I first opened my eyes in that safe house in Karachi, I found Khalid Sheik Mohammed in front of me. If I had been asked at the time whether I would like to meet Mr. bin Laden or Mr. Khalid Sheikh Mohammed (KSM) with the bonus of Mr. Ramzi Binalshibh, I would have definitely gone for the latter option. One of the very first things that KSM said to me when I was sitting on the floor with him was, "When they, the Americans, will come to you, they will show you some pictures and this is what you will have to say: 'Take it or leave it.'" And when I thought of it, I thought what I was in for was much more precious than the little promises that I had to make. Ever since then I have been waiting for a phone call.

And it really made me wonder, "Why haven't I heard from somebody in this country who is in a position to do something about the world after 9/11, especially given my profile, the kind of programs that I have been making with al Jazeera and before al Jazeera with the BBC, the fact that I live in London, the fact that I am so accessible?" Only a few of my fellow journalists, like Peter Bergen, took the trouble of calling me. Only one or two of the lawyers representing the victims' families have tried to be as helpful as possible.

I did not, having come back from Karachi, feel that there was much of a moral or ethical nature about the story. It had to do with the past and that was enough for me not to take the trouble of trying to seek somebody out. I set the standard for myself when I was asked aggressively by one American journalist why I had the audacity not to try and call somebody out. And I said I would need three conditions for that.

First, I would call if I had specific information about an imminent attack on a civilian target. Other than this, I am not prepared to do somebody else's job. When KSM was seeing me off after forty-eight hours, he looked me in the eye. He had been scrutinizing me, judging every move that I made when I was with them. But he left me with this thought and I did not know how to reply to it. He said, "Brother Yosri, You know something?" I said, "What?" He said, "You can make the perfect terrorist." I was stunned and I said, "Why would you think so?" He said, "Look at yourself. You are young. You live in London. You are single. You speak good English. You are intelligent. You know what you want." He compared me to Mohammed Atta, the Egyptian guy. I happen to have been born in Egypt. I am Egyptian and I have been living in London for the past twelve or fifteen years or so. I am proud of being both Egyptian and British. But it told me about the kind of mentality that someone like KSM, with all his experience and background, had about someone like me.

That is why I have been going across America for the last month or so revisiting the whole issue all over again. I was in San Diego where the spearhead of al Qaeda descended sometime in 1999 or maybe before; I mean namely Khalid al-Mihdhar and Nawaf al-Hazmi. At that time KSM was not very happy with them until Mohammed Atta showed up in the picture. Then KSM demoted Nawaf al-Hazmi from the ring leader of what he called the airplane operation to Atta's deputy. Those are his qualifications for valuing somebody. He has first of all to be somebody who would be willing to die for Allah. This is the most important thing. KSM told me that they started planning for what came later to be known as the 9/11 atrocities some two and a half years prior to it. I am talking about specific planning for the operation. Nobody knew what it was all about. The knowledge was on a need-to-know basis. Only Mohammed Atta knew some of the details. Nobody from the rest knew anything about the operation except for the fact that it was going to be a martyrdom operation.

I happen to have graduated from the American University in Cairo, where I also taught for a while. This year the president of the university was in London. He invited me to dinner, trying to persuade me to take part in a fund-raising campaign for new campuses. I did so happily but I also advised him to try and come here, to this place, the United States, to the Senate and to sell the new campus on 9/11 grounds. He was a bit surprised, but I tried to explain what I deeply believe from what little experience I have accumulated with al Qaeda, the organization and issues related to them. It is education. If you take the nineteen hijackers and forget all about the supporting themes and the leadership, how many of them knew anything about anything in life? How many of them were educated?

Perhaps other than the Egyptian Mohammed Atta and the Lebanese Ziad Jarrah, the rest provide us with actual ways out of the conditions we are living in now. The war on terror is perceived in the minds of many in our part of the world as more of a war *of* terror rather than a war *on* terror.

Bin Laden became the hero of so many people, not because he attacked the United States, but simply because he spoke the minds of so many people. He dared to ask the right questions. We have to make the distinction between al Qaeda the organization and al Qaeda the idea. We also have to make the distinction between what bin Laden says and how he says it and what bin Laden does and how he does it. I can hardly think of a single Arab or a single Muslim who does not want to become an American citizen. Bin Laden played on this sensitive chord.

Bin Laden also played on some other sensitive chords. He played on the U.S. association with corrupt Arab regimes, the kind of rulers preferred by Washington, because it is always easier for the White House to pick up the phone and tell them what is expected from them. In my opinion this is a serious issue and should be addressed. Like Peter Bergen and some of my fellow speakers noted before, *The 9/11 Commission Report*, as comprehensive as it is, and despite all the work that has been put into it, failed to address vital issues like this. As long as this is the case, we will always be running the risk of another bin Laden coming from the people and pretending or claiming truly to represent them.

What about a war on illiteracy? What about a war on ignorance? What about a war on poverty? You cannot even begin to persuade somebody that something has to be done about terrorism if they are hungry, if they are ignorant, or if they are not represented in any sense. This, in my opinion, is the rule for everything. Now bin Laden has taken advantage of this. But who becomes a member of al Qaeda in a situation like this? I could think of just about everyone.

It took me awhile to understand why someone like KSM should take the trouble of inviting, all the way from London, someone of my profile, with my reputation, and with my constituency as a secular journalist. But on my way to him, I thought that he might be interested in talking to a certain type of people. And this type of people is the type of people that I am most concerned about: the mainstream people, the moderates, the seculars.

When I say seculars I do not mean the non-believers. I just mean those who do not believe in violence as a way out, those who believe in dialogue and in talk. Luckily the vast majority in our part of the world are this sort of people. The terrorists are only the minority, and I do not think that it is really understood or taken into consideration in the context of the war on terror. I think the approach is not really the right one for several reasons that bin Laden is now trying to take advantage of.

And whether bin Laden is there or whether he's not there, I don't think that will be the end of al Qaeda. The polarization is frightening, not only between East and West, but between Islam and Christianity. Even in the United States I have been horrified.

There is one very simple question that I would like to leave you with. Does America feel safer now? If yes, why? If no, why not? This is a most crucial question that we have to always remind ourselves of. Otherwise we will be playing into the hands of the extreme right wing on both sides.

JESSICA STERN

My book, *Terror in the Name of God*, is a book about a study of terror in the name of God across religions. I started out in the United States and went around the world, beginning in Texas actually, talking to Identity Christians. I also talked to people who kill; to abortion providers, doctors, and clinic personnel. I went to Jordan and tried to speak to Hamas but failed. (I have a Jewish name and I never pretend to be someone that I am not, and I had to reveal my name.) From there I took a bus into Gaza; if you know one family with doctors in it, then it is very easy to get to Dr. Abdel Aziz al-Rantissi, who was briefly the leader of Hamas. I also met with Abu Shanab, the head of the Society of Engineers, who was a political leader of Hamas. Both of them have since been killed. I went into Israel and talked to Jewish terrorists, including the man who intoned the Aramaic prayer, the pulsa denura, in which he lays claim to the death of Rabin. That prayer has only been used once before in the 20th century, allegedly leading to the death of Leon Trotsky. I went to Lebanon and spoke with Hezbollah. I went to refugee camps. I went to India. I met with leaders of Bajrang Dal and the other members of the Sangh Parivar, the group of Hindu nationalists and extremists. I went to Indonesia and talked with Lashkar-e-Toiba.

The place I know the most about is actually Pakistan. What Peter Bergen is referring to are the Kashmiri groups, the most interesting of which are actually based in Pakistan. They are interested in releasing Kashmir from Indian control, but most of them are based in Pakistan. There I met with quite a few of them: Lashkar-e-Toiba, Lashkar-e-Jhangvi, Harkat-ul-Mujahideen, Harkat-ul-Ansar, Jaish-e-Mohammed, Jamaat-ul-Mujahideen, and so on. And I am told I am the best-known American among the mujahideen in Pakistan, which used to be amusing and actually no longer is so amusing. (Although there's an offer to have a big book party for me where these leaders would come and celebrate me. I have declined – so far.)

Let me tell you why I think they talk to me, because that is one of the first questions that people ask me. One reason is that some of the people I spoke with were very, very lonely; for example, Paul Hill, who was on death row and has since been executed for murdering two people at an abortion providing clinic. He was really anxious to speak with people, especially with a woman who was going to hang onto his every word and not interrupt him. Mir Aimal Kansi, a Pakistani national who shot and killed a couple of CIA employees, initially was quite reluctant to talk to me. He insisted that I pay him. We had a correspondence. And when I said I could not pay him, he suggested that I donate money to a charity that he would choose and I said I could not do that either. Eventually, he decided that he wanted to talk to me. I think, again, it was really because he was lonely. He wrote me a letter saying that he hoped my book was a great success and that I would eventually be able to buy a Mercedes Benz.

In almost every case, the people I spoke with wanted to convert me. The situation Yosri Fouda is describing is apt. They wanted to convert me, either to get me to donate money to the terrorist cause or just to convert me to the religion. That happened almost every time. Or in the case of the Jewish terrorists and extremists, they wanted to convert me to be a more serious Jew. And they all wanted me to donate money to their cause.

In one case, that of James Dalton Bell, who was an MIT-trained chemist – who is, I would say, the most frightening terrorist I have spoken with and who is now in prison – the subject had an unusual reason for wanting to talk to me. He was about to get out of prison, and he really wanted to go to his MIT reunion. I also went to MIT, and he was really hoping that I would accompany him to this reunion.

In every case, of course, they wanted their grievance to get attention and I understand that they were using me in order to publicize their grievance. But since I thought it was important for us to understand their grievance, I did not mind being used in that way. In the case of the Pakistani jihadists, they initially thought that I might be there on behalf of India's intelligence agency, RAW [Research and Analysis Wing]. But by looking me in the eye, they decided that that was not the case. They decided that I was not actually there to kill them on behalf of RAW, but was there instead for the CIA. They felt neglected by the CIA. It was not a problem. They wanted to be taken seriously in the late nineties. I think they felt that they were not treated as seriously as, for example, Hamas and Hezbollah. And so this was, I think, flattering to them.

These groups are all quite different from one another in terms of their size, and in terms of their religion. By the way, I did not cover Buddhist terrorists, but there are Buddhist terrorists. They are different obviously, in terms of what they say their grievance is, but it is important to realize that in almost every case, you sit down and try to suspend judgment while you are in the conversation. You try to follow the moral logic that leads them to make the profound moral errors that they make. In many cases, if not all the cases, the grievance is compelling. It is not the grievance. It is the action that we condemn. And it is important for us to understand that.

We need to understand the grievance. For example, one common theme arises in almost every group I investigated, and that is the opposition to globalization. They have different ways of describing their opposition. For Hezbollah, globalization is McDonaldization. Abu Shanab has described globalization as bad for the human being. Mohammed Ajmal Qadri, who is the leader of one of the three branches of the Jamaat Ulema-e-Islam, told me he believes in a clash of civilizations. He had read Samuel Huntington and was a big admirer, and he is certain that the Islamic world will win this clash because the West is rotting from within. Our family structures are disintegrating, he feels, sounding very much like certain Americans.

Another commonality is the way these groups mobilize. In a way, they offer a basket of goods for the commander- and cadre-style organization, for the terrorist army. The most important benefits they offer are material benefits that take various forms. This is not true for the so-called leaderless resistance of virtual networks, but for all the organizations that are real organizations, including terrorist bureaucracies such as al Qaeda and many of the jihadi groups in Indonesia and in Pakistan. It could be, as in many cases, the payment of operatives. It was a big surprise for me to realize the extent to which payments, especially at the managerial level, can become very important. Terrorism becomes a job and terrorists become professionals. Over time, the money can become more important than everything else. That is very important for us to understand because sometimes we are able to take advantage of that. And I think we probably could take advantage of it more often than we do.

Of course, there are rewards for the families of the so-called martyrs, so the material rewards can come in that form. One of the Pakistani jihadi charities took me around to show me the things that they were doing for the families of the so-called martyrs. They showed me very proudly one family that they had moved from a mud hut to a cement house. This family had, in their words, donated their oldest son to the jihad. The two middle sons were working for the father, whom I met. The youngest son, whom I also met, was going, in his mother's terms, to be donated to the jihad. I asked him what he wanted to do when he grew up, and he said that he wanted to be a mujahideen and join in this losing holy war, this hopeless holy war, to become cannon fodder.

There are also very important spiritual and moral rewards. You've all heard about the seventy-two virgins. This is now an issue for women as well. Sheikh Ahmed Yassin, the head of Hamas until he was killed recently, said that women could be involved in martyrdom operations provided they wore the hijab, they were accompanied by a male relative, and that there were no men available to do the job. Now of course Sheikh Yusuf al-Qaradawi has removed even that stricture and has said that women can go in any dress, and they do not need to be accompanied. He has also talked about spiritual rewards for them. He has not mentioned virgins *per se*, something which might not be particularly appealing to women, but he has hinted that there are rewards for women as well.

It is the leader's responsibility to make the follower feel that jihad, the thing he is about to do, which violates every religious tradition and everything his mother told him about what is right and wrong, is the morally and spiritually correct thing to do. In Yosri Fouda's interview of Ramzi Binalshibh, Binalshibh said that jihad is a tax that we have to pay to serve. Jihad is a public good, and those who can participate in the jihad are paying a tax. It is a collective action problem and there needs to be a way for leaders to persuade followers that they should pay what Binalshibh called a tax.

The most important reward, and the one I think we need to be most aware of, is the emotional one. I think that people join these extremist organizations, as they join extremist religious organizations that don't promote violence, because they are seeking a clear identity. Globalization creates a tremendous amount of confusion for all of us in terms of our identity. And those who are particularly at sea in regard to this uncertain identity can sometimes be drawn to extremist movements, including those that promote violence. "It's a glamorous life," I heard again and again. "It's an adventure." We know, for example, that a member of al Qaeda said that he wanted to go to Afghanistan to join al Qaeda because he felt it would be an adventure. He was training to be a chef, but he thought it would be more exciting to be a mujahideen.

Perhaps the most important finding of my interviews is the idea of humiliation as something that may be organic to the individual or the society, but that can be strengthened or even created by an astute leader. Let me give you a couple of examples. The leader of one of the Identity Christian organizations, actually the second-in-command, told me that he had been sickly as a child. He had had bronchitis. He was forced to take the girls' gym class. The first time that he felt strong was when he was surrounded by a group of armed men. The leader and founder of another organization, who was retired when I met him, told me that he had heard about the deliberate humiliation of the Islamic world by the West in an extremist mosque in Kashmir. He said that he founded that organization, not for nationalist reasons, but because he felt that the way to overcome this humiliation was by getting involved in a jihad. You can look at the words of al-Zawahiri, who says exactly the same thing. You can actually search on the word humiliation in his autobiography and you will see that he says that the way to overcome this humiliation, both for individuals and for Islamic society, is by picking up a gun. It is a cleansing. Violence and jihad are cleansing. It is purification.

I think there is a lot we are doing right in the war on terrorism. And most of what we are doing right has to do with going after today's stock of terrorists. We have been pretty good, and we are getting better at locating and capturing today's stocks of groups. We are less good at penetrating, but we have made some progress. Yet we are making a very profound error in focusing almost exclusively on today's terrorists rather than on who becomes a terrorist and why. We are paying insufficient attention to the flow of new recruits, to what facilitates recruitment.

What facilitates new recruits? Well, obviously, festering conflicts. The Arab-Israeli conflict, and Chechnya, for example. It is also important to look at the high male-to-female ratio, which seems to be associated with an increased risk of internal terrorism, though the data is uncertain. Failed states are risk factors, and not just failed states, but failed pockets within states. The CIA has identified fifty such pockets, and if you look at a map that is referenced on page 562 in *The 9/11 Commission Report*, you will see that the stateless zones identified there include European cities with expatriate Muslims in them. That's an important area of risk. Also, prisoners in the United States and immigrants, especially illegal aliens in the United States, I would predict, are going to be important sources of recruitment.

It's very important for us to remember that terrorists require support from the broader population, even though it's a very rare human being who would be willing to become a terrorist. We have to understand that there are people who are going to look the other way, or not provide critical intelligence. We need to pay attention to the views of that broader population even if we understand that only a tiny fraction will become terrorists. This is why the horrific divide between the United States and the rest of the world, especially but not exclusively the Islamic world, is so distressing. Where are we going to get the intelligence we need to follow someone like al-Zarqawi, for example? We need it from Jordan, which is why when we see polls that suggest that majorities in Jordan have more confidence in bin Laden than in President Bush, we need to be disturbed by this fact. It is not that it is a popularity contest. It's that we need intelligence from ordinary people because the threat is coming from the people, not from the states.

STEVE COLL

Thank you, Jessica, for the fascinating reminder that evaluating the sort of qualitative census of the al Qaeda movement requires the assembly and mapping and evaluation of personal narrative, often personal narratives of radicalization, so that we can try to identify some of the patterns in those narratives.

MARC SAGEMAN

[Editor's note: text not transcribed.]

Question and Answer Session

Q. STEVEN CLEMONS: If the movement that al Qaeda represents is self-selected how do you think that self-selection has changed since the beginning of 2002? Is there a difference in the character of self-selection since 9/11? If so, what is it?

A. YOSRI FOUDA: I don't think there is a difference in nature as much as a difference in the intensity. The extent of polarization has complicated things in my opinion to the point that it is becoming a bit difficult now to explain to the average, mainstream Arab or Muslim how bin Laden is a mad guy. I don't think that the vast majority would believe that bin Laden is mad. Certainly the vast majority, if not every single person who has something between his ears, wouldn't even begin to agree with the way bin Laden decided to express what he thought, even though many agree that he had fair cause for such thinking.

It all goes into this vicious circle of alienation and of more and more polarization. Now, in my opinion, 9/11 has been hijacked by a few groups. For better or worse, I am one of those who believe that America has every single right to make sure that its borders, its people, its values, and its interests are protected in the way it sees fit. The danger or the risk is that the way America does this may lead to more and more polarization. I think one or two things are not quite right about the way the war on terror is being waged.

Q. TIM ROCKWOOD [Journalist and producer of *Avoiding Armageddon*]: Jessica Stern, have you noticed a change in the willingness of terrorist recruits to use WMDs since 1998 when your book *The Ultimate Terrorists* came out, or since 9/11?

A. JESSICA STERN: First, I need to point out that, in most cases, unless a group has already been known to have acquired these weapons, I don't ask that question. But I think that biological weapons, as the head of the Montana Militia put it to me, are in the air. They are in fashion among American right-wing extremist groups. It is just something that they find quite fascinating. It does not mean that they will ever be able to pull off anything significant. But in regard to al Qaeda, they are clearly extremely interested, and have been seeking weapons of mass destruction for quite a while. Has there been a change? I think there's an interest and there's been an interest for a long time. Whether or not any of these groups can actually pull something off, especially in terms of detonating a nuclear device, remains unclear for the present.

Q: JEROME C. GLEN [American Council for the United Nations University]: It is correct that a military solution is not possible. And if it is correct that this is now a social movement, then isn't the ultimate defense really the maturation and growing up of the American people and how American people from Kansas to New Mexico operate and act in the world?

A. JESSICA STERN: I guess probably all three of us agree with you. A military response is only effective against today's terrorists. It obviously does nothing about tomorrow's terrorists. Indeed, it is likely to result in additional recruits, even if they are not formally recruited. So we are in a bind. On the one hand, a military response is required where there is a known terrorist haven. But at the same time, if we are going to focus on the long term, we need another strategy. And that strategy probably has to do with undoing this misapprehension that the United States is deliberately out to humiliate the Islamic world. That's an enormous challenge. What would it mean to undermine that lie? What would it mean to promote dignity among those who feel humiliated? How can one do it without making things worse? These are big questions. I think none of us, unfortunately, has the answers.

Q. JAMES FALLOWS: This question actually stems from what Jessica Stern was just saying, but I'm going to direct it to Marc Sageman. In a previous panel (see Chapter One) we were discussing the fact that the war of ideas changes the context that makes it easy to recruit people to terrorist organizations. If we took seriously your assessment of the social origins of this movement, what specific changes in American policy would be required to counteract this? Is there anything that the United States can do? What are the practical implications of your assessment?

A. MARC SAGEMAN: American foreign policy is very much what transforms local grievances into global ones. Look at the policy or perceived lack of fairness in the Palestinian-Israeli issue. Look at Iraq and at Kashmir and so on. Iraq is really the big issue. And that's why our approval ratings have dropped precipitously in the Middle East and everywhere in the world except Poland and Russia, I think. I think that we have a great message. I think the American Dream is a great message. And I think that Yosri Fouda is absolutely right. A lot of people want to become American citizens. What they don't like is American foreign policy. I'm not saying that American foreign policy has caused terrorism, but it is one of the catalysts that makes it explode, transforming a few small groups that might have no consequence into this whole social movement. So what we need to do is have our deeds match our words. We have some very nice words that we tell the world, but we're just seen as a hypocritical bully in the Middle East. And we have to stop.

Q. PHILLIP SMUCKER [Journalist, author of *Al Qaeda's Great Escape*]: What attraction does an actual war have for people who would become future jihadists? The inferno of Afghanistan produced Al Qaeda 1.0. What is going to come out of Iraq now? What is the allure of war and what does it mean to future jihadists?

A: YOSRI FOUDA: It would really depend on the type of jihadist or mujahideen to which you refer. Don't forget that many of the mujahideen who were there in Afghanistan, the so-called Afghani Arabs, actually had to stay in Afghanistan after the Soviets were out. Everybody knows that it was America along with Saudi Arabia, in particular, and indeed most of the world that backed bin Laden.

3 Al Qaeda in Europe

Today's Battlefield

MODERATOR: **Steven Clemons,** Senior Fellow, The New America Foundation. PANELISTS: **Rohan Gunaratna,** Director, Institute of Defense and Strategic Studies; **Ursula Mueller,** Minister, Embassy of the Federal Republic of Germany to the United States; **Georg Mascolo,** Washington Bureau Chief, *Der Spiegel.*

ROHAN GUNARATNA

Why did al Qaeda attack America's most iconic landmarks on 9/11? I ask this question of my American friends and they tell me that al Qaeda does not like our values. I want to tell you that al Qaeda has no problem at all with your values. Al Qaeda's problem is with your foreign policy. And if we look at the founding charter of al Qaeda, it was created as the pioneering vanguard of the Islamic movement.

Al Qaeda was created for the very purpose of leading this fight. The predecessor organization of al Qaeda, known as Makhtab al-Khidamat (MAK, the Afghan Services Bureau), played a very critical role in the anti-Soviet, multinational, Afghan Mujahideen campaign, a campaign that finally led to the defeat of the largest land army at that time in Afghanistan.

In many ways the battle that al Qaeda is conducting today is an attack on the remaining superpower. The strategic threat posed by al Qaeda has been underestimated by the Americans and by their allies and friends. Specifically, the Western response to fighting al Qaeda has been an event-driven response. It must be a campaign-driven one. The current response to al Qaeda has been largely a response that I would say is called a Rumsfeld approach.

The Rumsfeld approach is to target terrorist cells that are planning and preparing attacks. By only attacking the terrorist cells that are planning and preparing attacks, you can never destroy a terrorist organization. Terrorists, especially the al Qaeda brand of terrorists, have a very high capacity for replenishing human losses. In order to fight terrorism, it is very important in parallel with the strategy of targeting al Qaeda operation cells, to attack their ideological bases.

If one only targets the operational infrastructure and does not target the ideological motivation, then certainly these organizations will survive. That means we will have to fight terrorism for another one hundred years. So there must be some new thinking on how to fight the organization that poses a strategic threat.

With that introduction I want to very quickly move to the threat – the networks. The terrorist networks currently based in Europe pose a serious threat to the United States. If you look at the last fifteen years, almost all of the major terrorist attacks that were attempted – with the exception of the Oklahoma City bombing, which was by a local group – were successfully staged from European networks.

These attacks have been staged mostly by migrants or terrorist organizations that have infiltrated migrant and diaspora communities. The majority of Muslims, say ninety-five percent of Muslims in the United States, Canada, and Europe, do not support terrorism. Still, we have seen that the small percentage that does sympathize with and support terrorism is sufficient for terrorist organizations to mount sustained operations. And if you look at the 9/11 operation and the operation that was disrupted in Britain, traditionally Europe and Canada have been the two launching pads or staging areas for conducting attacks against the United States.

I will focus on the British operation, which was disrupted in the first week of August in Britain. This operation was planned to attack some of the key targets in the United States, namely the IMF building in Washington, D.C., the Prudential building in New Jersey, and the stock exchange and the Citigroup building in New York. This case illustrates the fact that the Europeans and the Canadians have been very tolerant of terrorist support networks.

Support networks differ from operational networks, which conduct terrorist attacks. Support networks distribute propaganda, raise funds, procure supplies, and manage safe houses. In the post-9/11 environment especially, we have seen many of the support networks that exist in Europe and in North America mutating into operational or attack networks. This is the real threat. The Madrid bombers certainly belonged to a support network, but after 9/11 and following some of the developments that have taken place, they mutated into an operational network.

The operation that was planned in Britain was a cell of British Muslims, but they were all of Asian, mostly Pakistani, origin. So while the 9/11 operational leaders were of Arab origin, the cell that was based in Britain was of Asian origin. This shows a new trend, because traditionally, we have seen that many of the terrorist groups were of Middle Eastern origin. Not only are we seeing a significant number of groups emerging that are of Asian origin, but the nine people who were arrested in Britain in August all had university degrees. Some of them even had advanced degrees, and one of them was about to complete his Ph.D.

The operational leader of the cell in Britain is named Esa al-Britani, the name by which he was known whenever he traveled outside with me. In Britain he was known as Esa al-Hindi because he was born in Gujarat, India. He came to Britain when he was two years old, and when he was twenty years old, he converted to Islam. In 1995 he went to Kashmir, where he fought, gained experience, and wrote a brilliant book called *Islamic Army of the Medina.* After that, he served as an instructor in Afghanistan and subsequently as an instructor in a camp in the southern Philippines before he was asked by Khalid Sheikh Mohammed to come to the United States to mount surveillance on strategic targets in three principal states.

When this cell was disrupted, a number of attack plans were recovered. Not only was the U.S. plan found, but a fully transferable template for conducting terrorist operations elsewhere was found as well. This is the clearest demonstration to us that, even three years after 9/11, al Qaeda still poses a very significant threat. I am not speaking of al Qaeda–associated groups. I am speaking of the small group, al Qaeda.

But let us quickly look at the associated groups of al Qaeda. We have seen about fifteen of the associated groups of al Qaeda active in Europe and in Canada. In many ways the Western intelligence community, especially the U.S. community, has been focusing on al Qaeda, and I believe that this is one of the biggest weaknesses of the Western intelligence community. There is an excessive focus on al Qaeda, yet we have seen a number of associated groups also capable of mounting large-scale operations. In many ways, these groups have been inspired and instigated to operate like al Qaeda.

Let me quickly look at the implications of Iraq on Europe and on North America. In our assessment, the U.S. invasion of Iraq has increased the threat of terrorism severalfold, not only to the United States but to the rest of the world as well. We can consider Europe to be the most endangered geographic zone. This is because we have seen that some of the terrorist networks based in Iraq have built networks into the Levant in the Middle East and also into Europe.

Over the past three years about 150 members of Abu Musab al-Zarqawi's group, Tawhid wal-Jihad, have been arrested. Earlier this year, al Qaeda had difficulty communicating to the outside world and maintaining coordination with their cells. This role has been taken over, at least partially, by the Tawhid wal-Jihad group in Iraq. I can also share with you that his network is not only communicating with the Middle Eastern and the European cells but also with the Asian cells.

The point I want to make is demonstrated by looking at the anti-Soviet, multinational, mujahideen campaign in which those young Muslims who went to fight against the Soviets returned to their home countries. What was it they wanted to do? They wanted to propel those regimes out and to create Islamic states instead. Today, substantial numbers of Muslims, both cradle and convert Muslims, from North America and from Europe, have left for Iraq. We have seen the rich Muslims of Western Europe going to Eastern Europe and the Balkans to recruit poor Muslims and ask them to go to Iraq.

When they return, what will happen? Two months ago, there were seventy-five car bombings in Iraq. Certainly, we all practice what we have been taught. In many ways, Iraq has become the new land of jihad, and as we saw with the previous generation of terrorists that came from Afghanistan, Bosnia, and Chechnya, we will see that the next generation of terrorists will come from Iraq. And in many ways, the Europeans have failed to control the flow of these radicals from Europe to Iraq.

But there is an even greater danger. The greater danger is that Europe has not suffered an attack on the scale of 9/11. As a result, we have seen European governments largely attacking operational cells – cells planning and preparing attacks – but not the support, cells – those cells that are raising funds, recruiting, procuring supplies, and managing safe houses. That is why it is very important for there to be a true partnership, because if Europe and Canada lag behind the United States in law enforcement and in counterterrorism policy and strategy, certainly each region will suffer.

The United States has not suffered a terrorist attack in the past three years for three reasons, and it is important to understand these three reasons. One is heightened public vigilance. As long as that vigilance is maintained, it will be difficult for terrorist groups to mount big attacks. The second is unprecedented law enforcement, security, and intelligence cooperation. Prior to 9/11, your intelligence community shared only a very small percentage of intelligence with the military and the law enforcement agencies. This has changed. You must continue to maintain the cooperation you have established with the Middle East and Asia and, in particular, with the Muslim countries because ninety percent of terrorist groups emanate from Asia and the Middle East. As long as you empower those governments and their law enforcement and intelligence agencies, the battle will be fought there. Third, the mindset of the Americans has changed but not that of other Western nations. That is to say, you were fishermen before 9/11. You waited until an attack occurred, then you did a brilliant investigation, a brilliant post-blast investigation. Today you have become hunters because you have been directly affected by terrorism.

It will be unfortunate if Europe waits to suffer another large-scale attack in order for the European nations and Canada to target terrorist support cells. Their strategy for fighting terrorism rests in targeting not only the cells that are planning and preparing attacks, but the support infrastructure that enables those operational cells to work. Finally, you must negotiate with groups that are willing to negotiate. We are seeing that in this environment, there are still a number of groups that we can talk to and bring into the political mainstream.

URSULA MUELLER

I was asked to speak about al Qaeda in Europe. Well, Europe consists of twenty-five countries with a population of 450 million people, so let me just focus on a few points. Al Qaeda as an organization as such is not present in Europe but it is alive as a movement, as an ideology that inspires local groups. What we see in Europe is that al Qaeda is decentralizing, deregulating, and regionalizing. The current trend is moving away from a central figure or leader who is the brains behind the planning and who needs willing participants to implement his plans towards decentralized groups who initiate their own attacks. In other words, it is now a bottom-up approach. These groups are not only launching their own initiatives but also at some stage the final endorsement might come from someone linked to al Qaeda who gives the, if you will, religious go-ahead.

The trend shows that the terrorist elements are not candidates for suicide bombers. Furthermore, they act on very short notice, while al Qaeda operatives engage in long-term planning. This is a trademark of al Qaeda's: long-term and very precise, detailed planning. The trend can be seen when looking at some of the recent attacks. In Casablanca in May 2003, we see a clear reference to al Qaeda with Kareem Altohami al-Mohati. The Madrid attacks followed on March 11, 2004. There, the name Amer Azizi came up; he certainly has a mujahideen past. Then late in March/April 2004, six hundred kilograms of explosives were used by a nonaligned group. And finally, in October 2004, there was an attack in Madrid on the Spanish prosecutor Baltasar Garzón, which was carried out by local jihadists.

These attacks all share the following characteristics, demonstrating the new trend. The operational groups have had no training in Afghanistan or in Bosnia with a common jihadi experience. In all cases, a mosque was the breeding ground in which jihad was preached, very often by a visiting imam. These groups were formed around a clerical authority and indoctrinated in those mosques. Many of them were indoctrinated in prisons and established their contacts in prisons in Europe. As a consequence of the decentralization of al Qaeda, the indoctrination and recruiting for the jihadi mission in Europe now take place in and around urban centers where the new generation is rising up, for instance, in the suburbs of

Paris. There they find eager recruits in the deprived and marginalized segments of society.

We assume that al Qaeda remains active and continues to plan terrorist attacks in Europe. They might plan fewer attacks, but they continue to focus on catastrophic attacks. They plan over a long period of time, several years for instance, as in the case of Istanbul. But the planning and execution have become more difficult. Al Qaeda is more security conscious and very cautious in its planning and implementation. They are now trying to recruit non-Arab operatives, including Islamic converts in Europe, and that is cause for great concern.

Europe is a target area, and at the forefront is the UK, with its British and Israeli-Jewish interests and targets. What is the threat assessment for Europe? There are some indications that Europe is at a greater risk for terrorist attacks than the U.S. There were numerous threats this summer, many of which could be attributed to al Qaeda copycats. This past summer, Italy tracked down twenty-seven threats of this kind on various Internet Web sites. The threats for the most part are directed against U.S. coalition partners in Iraq. The UK, Italy, and Spain are at the greatest risk, however, Germany also remains a target. Recall that the al Qaeda video of bin Laden was aired with German subtitles on al Jazeera television. In that video, bin Laden offered a ceasefire with Europe if it withdraws from Iraq and Afghanistan. Germany is a coalition partner in the fight against terrorism. We are part of Operation Enduring Freedom in Afghanistan. Germany deployed twenty-two hundred soldiers in the Multinational Security Assistance Force in Afghanistan and is the lead nation for the training of Afghan police. In a joint German-U.S. effort, thirty thousand Afghan policemen have been trained in Afghanistan in an effort to bring stability to Afghanistan, which was a breeding ground for al Qaeda.

The European Union, including Germany, remains fully committed to the fight against terrorism and uses a whole array of tools, including diplomacy, the military, drying out financial sources, intelligence, and aggressive law enforcement. By working together, a string of attacks was averted in Europe. These included the arrest of an Algerian man in Paris who was planning an attack against the Russian Embassy at the end of 2002; the ricin plot in London in January 2003; an attack against a Jewish synagogue in Berlin that was planned by the Tawhid wal-Jihad group, the terrorist cell linked to al-Zarqawi; the March/April 2005 plan in which explosives that were intended to blow up a high-speed train in Madrid were detected and defused; and finally, the plans against Heathrow Airport were disrupted. This last was a classic al Qaeda operation, led by Khalid Sheikh Mohammed. Al Qaeda typically remains focused on the same targets for a long period of time, and we continue to believe that al Qaeda still has targets in Europe.

GEORG MASCOLO

Der Spiegel headquarters are in Hamburg. It is a fifteen-minute drive to Marienstrasse, where some of the 9/11 mass murderers lived, and it is a five-minute walk to the mosque which turned seemingly model students into fervent Islamists. Perhaps the next Mohammed Atta will again come from Europe. Today, liberal societies are still fertile ground for the development of radicals.

The structures evolved back in the eighties when asylum seekers who came to Europe were members of the Algerian GIA or the Muslim Brotherhood. True to the Arab saying that you do not spit into the soup that you eat, there was a general belief that they would not act contrary to the interests of the host countries. That proved to be a wrong assumption. Now we know that these radicals played a very important role in the indoctrination of young Muslims, and we should have stopped them much earlier.

Meanwhile, this first generation has become dispensable, for the mechanism of radicalization functions perfectly without their help. It begins with disapproval and separation, with young Muslims covering their eyes when they see half-naked women on TV. Radical imams still preach in the mosques, although much less frequently now. Only three weeks ago, in Berlin, one of them made quite an inflammatory speech about "the stinking Germans." It is harmless compared to the videos and cassettes that are sold under the table or downloaded from the Internet. A satellite dish brings al Jazeera and other Arabic stations straight into the living room. At the end of this process, you have Muslims who hate the society that has given them a home. "Oh Europe, I know for certain that you are doomed," wrote the murderer of the Dutch film maker Theo van Gogh.

However, not all these radicals will turn into terrorists. The question is who will cross this last barrier. That is where our dilemma in Europe starts. Thousands of Muslims known to be followers of radical Islam are listed in the computers of the European secret services. Those belonging to the scene are generally known. In Germany, a list of those deemed most dangerous has been compiled and contains about three hundred names. The French judge, Jean-Louis Bruguière, one of the best al Qaeda experts in Europe, has compared the organization to the AIDS virus. It mutates, changes and when one believes to have found effective means to combat it, it reappears in a new, even more dangerous form.

After 9/11, the search focused on a type of perpetrator similar to that of the pilots. The biographies of these jihadists were atypical. More commonly, they are minor criminals known to the police only as drug dealers or pushers of stolen cars. They never become integrated into Western society and they are searching for new meaning in their lives. One described it clearly during a police interrogation: "I could not get a job so I started to pray." Their anchor is a religion. The release for their criminal energy is the jihad. In Germany, it has been mentioned that targeted radicalization is now even taking place in prisons.

In Europe, the fight against al Qaeda has become a battle fought with observations and telephone taps, a dangerous walk on the edge. By means of such controls, the authorities hope to find out who might make the final step into terrorism. The nightmare of European politicians is an attack perpetrated by terrorists who are known to the authorities. The probability of this, as the Netherlands and Madrid attacks showed, is very high. I would like to quote from a telephone conversation to give you an idea of this fear. Two Arab sympathizers suspected to be al Qaeda members talk. The conversation is taped, and is as follows:

"What we say now is being listened to by them. They listen to everything."

"As far as I'm concerned, they can listen. What are we talking about anyway?"

"I just wanted to inform you and to show you how mean these dogs are."

"Yeah, I'll let them listen then. They are welcome."

"Did you notice just now how this sound fluctuated? One moment the sound is low and then suddenly it is louder."

"Well why don't you change your telephone?"

"Are you kidding? They will discover the new number in a flash."

It is interesting to study the papers of American terrorism trials. It seems to me that here, arrests are made at a very early point when there are still no discernable plans for attacks. In Europe, there are now great differences in the practice of arresting someone, but in my observation no country goes as far as the United States. The European concept of a state founded on the rule of law will not allow that anyway, but that is not the only consideration. Past experience fighting terrorist groups has taught a very valuable lesson. If the state suspends its own principles of law, it runs the risk of losing the ideological confrontation, which in turn can create the next generation of terrorists.

Therefore, there will never be a European Guantánamo, even though, quite a few politicians secretly wish for it if only to sleep better. But the societies of Europe are beginning to fight back by other means. The limits of liberalism are being newly defined. The demand for a clear separation of the peaceful Muslims from their radical brothers is getting increasingly louder. Laws are called for to speed up extradition of those who so disgracefully abused the laws of their host countries. This is very tricky because many could likely expect the death penalty or torture if they are returned to their home countries. On the other hand, one cannot be expected to accept the fact that those who lived with, prayed with, and shared Mohammed Atta's radical convictions should today still be allowed to study in my home town, Hamburg.

Let me share a thought with you. America today is more threatened from the outside, from perpetrators entering the country to launch attacks. Europe's threat is growing from inside. A critical mass, a group of Muslims determined to employ any means, can develop anytime and anywhere; it no longer needs an order from the al Qaeda leadership. These radicals consider themselves to be under direct orders from Allah. I am afraid that the situation will become much more precarious. As in the past, when Muslims rushed to fight in Afghanistan, today they are drawn from Europe to Iraq. From Germany alone, about fifty are thought to be on their way. How many actually arrived is not known, but whoever manages to get there and survive will return one day battle-hardened and honored by his brothers. He who has been in battle is held in highest esteem by radical Muslims. We know that such a veteran, Mohammed Zammar, who fought in Bosnia, recruited the Hamburg 9/11 pilots for al Qaeda. Perhaps those who will return from Iraq will one day play a similar role.

Question and Answer Session

Q. STEVEN CLEMONS: One of the dilemmas that we are debating in the United States is the question, "How sustainable is our vigilance?" For instance, because I am one who thinks that we are not paying enough attention to real threats and are paying attention instead to cosmetic things, I think it is important to note that it is hard to get on an airplane nowadays. Funding for the training of TSA [Transportation Security Administration] employees, for instance, has just been slashed by forty percent. Air marshalls flying in and out of the airlines at Reagan National Airport have been cut back drastically. When you add to that the parts of the U.S. infrastructure that have not even received the kind of funding and support to take care of some of these insecurities, it demonstrates to me that the great, heightened alert that we had at some point, wanting to throw money at problems, is waning. Even the money is beginning to disappear.

So my first question to Rohan is, do you worry that the vigilance that you said that we have might in fact be eroding? And secondly, I heard all of you imply that al Qaeda or its inspired groups have somehow focused on Europe or the West as its target. This is very different from some of the comments that I have heard from Peter Bergen, who said that the West has essentially been caught in a civil war with Islam. So I think it's really important to ask this question, "Is it destabilizing the home they now have in Germany or elsewhere? Or are we really dealing with inspired groups who are still trying to lead a civil war within Islam, a scenario which has a very, very different set of political objectives?"

A. **ROHAN GUNARATNA:** In the post-9/11 period, about sixty or seventy terrorist operations have been detected and disrupted, and most of that detection has been a result of the flow of public information. So it is very important to keep the public alert, especially the Muslim, migrant communities that are living in the United States and in Europe, because as long as governments reach out to the Muslim communities, there will be a greater flow of information. Contrary to public perceptions, most Muslims do not support terrorist organizations. They may have a disagreement with the United States, but in terms of supporting terrorism, support for terrorism is very limited.

I will give you one example of how public vigilance prevented an attack – Richard Reid, the shoe bomber. What prevented him from detonating that shoe on that transatlantic flight? It was the alert passengers. I think that it is difficult to maintain that level of vigilance over a long period of time, but you can certainly maintain it at different scales over a period of time. That is why it is so important for governments periodically to release threat information to the public domain, because it has a very important effect in keeping people alert, not alarmed.

A. **URSULA MUELLER:** I agree with Rohan that you have to keep the public alert but not paranoid. And no, al Qaeda is not destabilized in Europe. They still pursue their interests, such as U.S. targets and Israeli-Jewish targets. You might be interested to learn that exactly two weeks ago, there was a huge demonstration in Cologne. Twenty-five thousand people, mostly Muslims, were protesting against extremism and showing their willingness to integrate. The German authorities, for instance, are engaging Muslim communities. We have 4.2 million Muslims in Germany.

A. **GEORG MASCOLO:** Going back to Germany and looking at all the cases we have had, I learned one thing. You have to check every single biography. It doesn't make any sense to talk about al Qaeda and what the general view might be. You have to go to every single radical and you have to check out how he reaches this point and what he is able to do, and then you can figure out what the next attack might be.

Q. JAROD KRISSMAN [The Nixon Center]: My question is for Rohan. You made the distinction between support structures for terrorism and those that are more operational. Getting back to the cell of Pakistanis that were in Britain, the nine that were arrested, have we been able to identify what support structures fueled the militancy?

A. ROHAN GUNARATNA: The cell that was disrupted in Britain in August 2004 was clearly an operational cell. I will give you four characteristics of that cell that will make you understand the distinction between an operational and a support cell. Look at Esa al-Britani. He never used a mobile phone. He always used public phones. He never had his own vehicle, he always used public transport. He had no financial history. He never had a credit card or a bank account, he always paid with cash. And finally, he never stayed in one home, he always moved every three to four days from home to home. It was clearly a clandestine secret cell. But if you look at the vast majority of cells operating in Europe and also in the United States, even after 9/11, we see that these cells are support cells. These are cells that recruit. These are cells that procure supplies. And these are cells that send members to conflict zones.

Q. JAROD KRISSMAN: I think the question really is, who is doing the recruiting? For example, who is recruiting the Pakistani people living in Britain? Who is providing them with the propaganda? Who counts as the foundation?

A. ROHAN GUNARATNA: Traditionally, a number of virulent imams or ideological leaders have been tolerated by Europe and by Canada, even by the United States before 9/11. There were so many extremists who were preaching, and the recruitment was primarily through those institutions of worship.

Q. AARON MANNES [Author, *Profiles in Terror: A Guide to Middle East Terrorist Organizations*]: Professor Gunaratna, in your book one thing you've mentioned that has not come up so far is the alliance between Hezbollah and al Qaeda, and I was wondering if you could say a few words about that? As we are seeing al Qaeda factionalize, regionalize, *et cetera*, how might Hezbollah, which maintains a discrete and worldwide and effective network, play into that?

A. **ROHAN GUNARATNA:** As you know, al Qaeda's headquarters was in Sudan from 1991 to May 1996. During this period, one of the organizations that supported al Qaeda was the Iranian security service, MOIS [Ministry of Intelligence and Security]. And we have seen that Iran sponsored a number of training camps. But we have seen that, during that time, a few al Qaeda members went to Lebanon to train. The assistance was provided both by the Iranians and by Hezbollah. Since Osama bin Laden moved to Afghanistan in May 1996, we have not seen an Iran–Hezbollah–al Qaeda link. But we are now seeing some links between the Sunni groups and the Shi'a groups and Iran, especially after the U.S. invasion of Iraq.

Q. **AUDIENCE PARTICIPANT:** My question is about prison recruitment. Do you think that the pending release of Fateh Kamel and the Roubaix gang has had, or will have, any impact on al Qaeda or terrorist activity within Europe? And do you think that they influenced future jihadists during their time in prison?

A. **URSULA MUELLER:** Well it is just a fact that recruitment is taking place in prison, not only in Europe, but also in the U.S. That's when they are lonely and are searching for an identity. They make contacts and they find a mission.

Q. **AUDIENCE PARTICIPANT:** If somebody were to obtain a European Union passport, they would be able to travel, relatively, without restrictions. They could live, work, and travel within the fifteen countries of the EU, essentially connecting to the Eastern bloc countries, down towards Turkey and Bosnia, where there is a large Muslim presence. What countermeasures are the independent European states, as well as the EU itself, taking to meet this challenge of essentially unrestricted movement within Europe?

A. URSULA MUELLER: You are right. As long as you hold a European passport, you can move relatively without restriction within the EU. That's why counterterrorism cooperation are so important. The cooperation did not start after the attacks in Madrid, but long before. Intelligence cooperation and law enforcement cooperation are very close. Not only is there the new position of EU coordinator for counterterrorism, but the Ministries of the Interior and Justice and the law enforcement agencies all work together much more closely now.

A. GEORG MASCOLO: How do you restrain people inside of European from traveling when they are holding European passports? The decision in Europe, and I guess this is pretty similar to what the 9/11 Commission discovered, is simply to share the information. Let the information flow because what you always find out at the end of any terrorist attack is that you had part of the government or the police or the secret service who simply did not know what other guys already knew. So, letting information flow is the main lesson.

Q. TIM ROCKWOOD [Journalist and producer of *Avoiding Armageddon*]: What can we, as journalists, do to put forward more dialogue about terrorism and al Qaeda? How can we do our job better so that this key issue will be more interesting to people in the United States and in Europe?

A. ROHAN GUNARATNA: Prior to 9/11, terrorism was regarded as a law-and-order problem and a public nuisance. But after 9/11 it became a national security threat. Now, many play an important role – the enforcement and the intelligence community, the health sector, the education sector, the banks and the financial institutions, and also the media.

The media can certainly highlight certain events, certain organizations, certain individuals. For instance, there are a number of groups that are engaged in political violence, and who are willing to negotiate with governments. The madrassas also deserve media attention. Madrassas are considered by the West to be jihadist factories, but our research has found that, of the 14,500 madrassas in Indonesia, only forty madrassas have produced jihadists. So I think the media can play a very important role, especially in not demonizing the Muslim-community, because the West requires the support of the Muslim community in order to win this campaign. I think the media can show what is really happening in those countries. As long as the media touches on those important issues, U.S. policy and decision makers will be better informed.

Q. **STEVEN CLEMONS:** Rohan, in regard to your statement about the transition in the West from being fishermen to being hunters, do you find it is possible within Muslim-dominated states for Muslim interests to be the hunters of these elements?

A. **ROHAN GUNARATNA:** The Muslims have become hunters only when they have suffered attacks. For example, since the May 2003 attacks in Saudi Arabia, we have seen significant movement on the part of the Saudi government to go after al Qaeda cells. But until those attacks occurred in Saudi Arabia, they were tolerant of those networks. So I think that it is a great tragedy that many countries will really hunt terrorists only once they suffer from terrorism. And as we have seen, the Indonesians similarly tolerated Jemaah Islamia until the attack in Bali. After that, they moved against these networks. But the attack eventually has to occur in order to galvanize a response, in order for there to be public support for politicians who advocate aggressive law enforcement and intelligence action against terrorist organizations.

A. **GEORG MASCOLO:** I want to add one thing about Saudi Arabia. There is no doubt that they are hunting at home, but I am not sure if they are doing the same abroad. When you go to Europe, you have a lot of mosques where these cells started. Where does the money come from for these mosques? Who supports them? You still find a lot of Saudi money in these radical mosques.

Q. **CHUCK PEÑA [Cato Institute]:** Rohan started his comments with a statement I agree with, namely that al Qaeda's grievances are based largely on U.S. foreign policy. How much does the threat in Europe emanate from al Qaeda or radical Islam and how much is a result of U.S. foreign policy? And what would you recommend to the United States, beyond the standard solve-the-Israeli-Palestinian-issue, in terms of changing foreign policy in order to lessen the threat in Europe?

A. ROHAN GUNARATNA: The United States can do a number of things and I would just mention three. One relates to the fact that as we have seen, most of the terrorists have been produced in regional conflict zones – Kashmir, Chechnya, Iraq now, Afghanistan in the past. For example, for ten years Afghanistan was a terrorist Disneyland. Many thousands of terrorists were trained while the international community did nothing. So one needs to develop the capabilities to end conflicts in those regional conflict zones not only by peace enforcement, but by bringing warring parties and factions together and ending conflicts. That is one thing that the U.S. can do.

Secondly, the United States should invest significantly, as should European countries, to end the Palestinian-Israeli dispute. And I think if the U.S. had put into Israel ten percent of the effort it put into Iraq, you would have resolved the Israeli-Palestinian dispute.

The third point that I want to make is that the U.S. has been very generous in the past to the Middle East and has given much assistance to Middle Eastern governments. But many of the Middle Eastern leaders who have taken U.S. assistance have taken that assistance while teaching their own subjects that America is bad. It is important for the U.S. to invest more in public diplomacy and to give more assistance to nongovernmental organizations in the Middle East. I know the Americans don't like so much to hear about NGOs. But I think it is important to invest more in the nongovernmental organizations and to give more assistance from the U.S. government to the NGO sector. In this way, the U.S. may be able more effectively to change the public perception of the United States that people in the Middle East have. Eventually, you have to build bridges with the Muslim public. That is one way of reducing the long-term strategic threat to the United States.

Certainly, you must still keep the operational effectiveness on the ground. You must maintain the effectiveness that comes with targeting cells, and with planning and preparing attacks. But to reduce the strategic threat you must win over the Muslim public support.

A. URSULA MUELLER: It is crucial that the United States uses its leverage to solve the Israeli-Palestinian conflict because the suffering of the Palestinians is all over the Arab television networks. Secondly, public diplomacy has to be effective and the message has to be consistent with the action. And thirdly, international cooperation has to be increased because it is crucial to fighting international terrorism effectively.

4 Militant Islam

On the Wane or on the Rise?

MODERATOR: **Peter Bergen,** Fellow, New America Foundation and terrorism analyst, CNN. PANELISTS: **Salameh Nematt,** Washington Bureau Chief, *Al-Hayat*; **Michael Scheuer,** author, as Anonymous, *Imperial Hubris: Why the West is Losing the War on Terror.*

SALAMEH NEMATT

One of the things that was not mentioned about what exists in common among the terrorists who are perpetrating these acts is the fact that almost every single one of them, if not every one of them, is a Sunni Muslim. None of them, none of the groups, none of the individuals have been Shiite, for example. I think this is significant. The fact that the Taliban regime that was ruling Afghanistan was a Sunni Muslim regime is also significant. The fact that Pakistan is a Sunni Muslim state is important; the fact that after 9/11 the U.S. administration decided to target the Taliban regime first is also significant. In my view, the overthrow of the Taliban regime was very important because Pakistan has a nuclear weapon. After the defeat of the Soviet Union in Afghanistan, the U.S. government thought that Pakistan would contain the new order in Afghanistan. What happened was that instead of Pakistan containing the Taliban, the Taliban was containing the Pakistani military security establishment. This extremist Sunni regime was getting close basically to putting its hand on the first Muslim nuclear weapon.

Now there is another question that nobody has addressed and that is why 9/11 happened in 2001 and why we have been witnessing this rapid increase in the frequency of terrorist attacks all over the world. What has happened in the last five years? What has happened in the last ten years?

Islam has been around for fourteen hundred years. Injustice has been around for that long too. Grievances have been around for that long. And if we want to think about airplanes, airplanes have been around for about one hundred years.

Why didn't anybody do this before? How do you explain the timing? I think it is very important to understand this. One of the most important developments in the Arab context is that ninety percent, if not more, of the terrorists come from the Middle East. This is where I come from, too, but I am not a terrorist.

I basically believe that the biggest development over the past ten years has been the proliferation of state-controlled and state-run Middle Eastern satellite channels. And al Jazeera, of course, is the most prominent one. Make no mistake. These are completely government-run and state-controlled media. And these governments are not democracies that believe in freedom of expression. These are governments that believe in directing the media towards serving their strategic interest, which means staying in power. Is there a link between the rise of Islamic terrorism and the rise of pan-Arab media and technology and satellite channels? I think there exists an important link.

My thesis is that suicide bombers will not do it unless they know that they will get their fifteen minutes of fame. We know that all suicide bombers, if they don't leave letters, make videotapes of themselves giving statements. These are statements that otherwise would never, ever get any air time or be published. The only reason for the fact that, today, the voices of Osama bin Laden and Abu Musab al-Zarqawi are much higher than the voices of heads of state throughout the world is because they associate their message with spectacular acts of murder, of mass murder. This is how they get their message heard. Now, their message is not new in the sense that people all over the world have been talking about the injustices of American policies in the Middle East. They have been complaining about Western and U.S. support for dictatorships that are ruling them in the Middle East. Why is there so much interest now in the bin Laden message and there was no interest for decades? The same message has been expressed by the people of the Middle East but there was no attention given to them in the rest of the world because there was no spectacular mass murder event associated with their message.

Another thing in common between the terrorists is they all came from countries that have dictatorships, countries where there is no democracy. This is a fact. Unfortunately, most of the Arab states are not democracies. Most of them came from dictatorships that were backed by the United States or financed and armed by the United States, meaning Egypt, Saudi Arabia, and Jordan.

Basically, another fact at which we have to look is the anti-Americanism of the people in states in the Middle East which are "allied" with the United States. Anti-Americanism is higher in Middle Eastern countries that are economically backed by the United States, countries such as Egypt and Jordan. Consider anti-Americanism in Jordan and Egypt, where they receive annual foreign aid from the United States and are considered friends of the United States. Anti-Americanism there is higher than in Iran and in Syria, where the regimes are hostile to the United States. What is the explanation? This is never discussed. The explanation is that the people in the countries that are friendly to the United States hate America twice. First, it is because of U.S. policies in the Middle East, and secondly, because the Americans support the regimes that are oppressing them. So they are victims twice; that is why anti-Americanism in these countries is high. It is very interesting that the Bush administration has picked up on the connection between lack of freedom and the militant extremism that leads to terrorism. That is why the U.S. government has adopted, together with the group of aid countries, a strategy for freedom in the Middle East. And President Bush is convinced that one of the main problems that produced terrorism is the lack of freedom.

There is a further factor that has not been explored in terms of these acts of terrorism that we have witnessed in the last few years. If you think of al Qaeda as an umbrella organization for Islamist terrorist groups – a generic name, a brand name just like McDonald's and Burger King where every Burger King produces hamburgers but not every hamburger is produced by Burger King – their main agenda is not to change America or the rest of the world. Their agenda is to change the countries where they came from, the countries of the Middle East, the Muslim countries which have been dominated in the past eighty or ninety years by secular regimes.

To understand the rise of Islamic extremism, we have to understand what happened to produce this kind of extremism. Over the past one hundred years, the secular regimes, some of which emerged at the end of British and French colonialism, maintained their links with the former colonialists. Often their closest relations were with the former colonialists – the Algerians with the French, Jordan and Egypt with Britain, Iraq with Britain, *et cetera*. They established this pattern of relationships between Western countries and secular dictators, secular corrupt dictators. Some of these regimes survive today by inheritance, i.e., the president dies, his son takes over, and so forth.

While America talks about a forward strategy for democracy in the Middle East, it says it wants to cooperate with the countries of the region towards implementing that strategy. This means cooperating with these autocratic dictatorships to overthrow them by establishing democracy. And the U.S. thinks that they are going to cooperate? The U.S. does not understand that democracy in the Arab world is regime change, period. So, of course, we will have to wait and see. Until now we have not seen any action by this administration, or anybody else for that matter, towards democratization, at least not since 9/11. I think terrorism is on the rise but for many, many factors, only one of which is U.S. foreign policy, particularly U.S. foreign policy that backs dictatorships against their own people. This is a bigger factor, in my view, than the Arab-Israeli conflict or any other regional policy problem that the people have with the United States.

As for the media, many people would not commit such acts of terrorism if they knew they were not going to be exposed, if they knew they were not going to have an audience. Terrorists always need audiences. Even petty criminals, for example those who take hostages in a bank or in a building, first ask for television coverage. It is ridiculous for them to do it if nobody is going to pay attention, if nobody is going to know about it. That is why the terrorists target the most spectacular targets possible – like the World Trade Center.

They need the pictures because this is how they recruit. Now, in the process of the fight against terrorism, what is the pan-Arab satellite media doing in terms of helping? They are doing exactly the opposite of what they should be doing. Because the media is not free throughout the

Arab world, these satellite channels focus on two stories every day, every night. They focus on Americans killing Iraqi Muslims in Iraq and on Israelis killing Muslim Palestinians in Palestine.

This media pours blood and civilian deaths into people's living rooms every night. This is what is recruiting terrorists. Now you are saying, "But it is happening." Yes, it is happening but what is the spin? The pan-Arab satellite media is not balanced. It is media with an agenda, media with an agenda set by authoritarian regimes and dictatorships. We should not forget that. People think, "Oh well, al Jazeera is very popular because, you know, they are free." They are not free. They are fully controlled in their editorial policy and everything else. Everyone who works in al Jazeera is a government employee. Some of them are brilliant journalists. Some are not just mouthpieces. Some of them are really good journalists. But then, they do not set the editorial agenda. The owner of the station sets the agenda. What does this mean? This means that countries, even countries that say that they are cooperating with the United States in fighting terrorism, are basically doing everything possible internally at home to produce more terrorists.

Let's look at Jordan. I come from Jordan. The Jordanian government is probably number one on the list of countries cooperating on security matters with the United States. The Jordanian media continues to speak as if it is run by Saddam Hussein, and it is not like you have to look deeply for this. Just look. Read the leading government-run newspaper. Watch the programs on TV. The Egyptians do the same thing. Why are they doing it? Why are they cooperating on one front and basically being very destructive on the other front? I think it's a deal. Just like al Jazeera is owned by a country that has the biggest military base in the Middle East. So the deal is this: these families rule these countries in exchange for giving the Islamist opposition a voice, because over the years they successfully crushed all kinds of opposition, except of course for the mosques. They could not close down the mosques.

This is why Islam emerged as the only challenge to the secular, corrupt dictatorships. It did not emerge just like that. Fifty years ago there was no such thing as the Muslim Brotherhood. It did not exist. There was no need for it as a political movement based on religion. To sum it up, I would like to say that the media is now the oxygen which the terrorist organizations breathe. They can be stifled. They would suffer their biggest blow if the media stops broadcasting their message and carrying their images and showing their success.

I am willing to bet that if you offered Osama bin Laden the regime of Saudi Arabia, if you said "Here it is. Take over Saudi Arabia with its oil, the biggest oil reserves in the world, with one condition, that you give up on al Jazeera," he will say "No, I will take al Jazeera and I will give up on Saudi Arabia." It is much more important for him than taking over the richest oil-producing country in the world.

MICHAEL SCHEUER

I personally think that it is a bad idea to censor any media, anywhere in the world, especially al Jazeera. Al Jazeera is a tremendous asset to the American intelligence community simply because it brings to us the words of Osama bin Laden and Ayman al-Zawahiri as well as Abu Musab al-Zarqawi. It puts together roundtables consisting of experts who, whether or not you agree with them, are usually eloquent gentlemen who explain what's going on in much more realistic terms than we generally hear. Salameh Nematt talked about the hypocritical nature of our support for tyrannies across the Muslim world. Well, there is nothing that makes an American look more hypocritical than calling for the censorship of media and the end of free speech. The vision of Secretary Powell, or of Secretary Albright before him, fuming against al Jazeera television is, I think, an embarrassment to us as a country and little more than ineffective whining.

I don't believe that al Jazeera caused Osama bin Laden. I think what happened was that, in a Muslim world devoid of leadership, Osama bin Laden happened on the scene when Arabic language television came to maturity. When we put it the other way around, we vastly underestimate the power of bin Laden and of the Internet. If al Jazeera were not there, if al Arabiya were not there, the Internet would still be there, and the Internet is a very difficult thing to shut down. I would also add that in the Muslim world rhetoric is very important. What bin Laden says, he means, and it is perceived in the Muslim world that he means what he says. We should listen to it and we don't. We were joking over dinner last night that when a tape comes into al Jazeera and is then shown on television, the serious part of the intelligence community listens to what bin Laden says and studies his words. But the vast majority of flapping around that occurs is another matter, such as when they call in the geologists to see if the rock in the background is part of Afghanistan. The Germans at one time thought they heard a bird and they called in an ornithologist to identify the chirp to see if they could locate that bird, that species in Afghanistan. And when Osama bin Laden made his speech with the rocks in the background, the CIA thought it was important to get a geologist to see if that particular brand of limestone or sandstone was only available in part of Afghanistan. It's all nonsense. Pardon the expression. What is important about the bin Laden videos is not anything except what he says. To this end, I think al Jazeera serves a tremendously important purpose. Does it aggravate me as an American? You bet it does. But I would much rather know what my enemy is thinking and saying than have to try and guess at it.

The Western media has done a spectacularly poor job in covering Osama bin Laden in the sense of what he says. I think the first whole speech we saw of his was during the election campaign when *washingtonpost.com* mounted the transcript on its Web site. If it was not for that jewel of the American government, the Foreign Broadcast Information Service, we would probably not know one-tenth of what bin Laden has said since 1996.

Let me point out, or at least suggest, that we have not begun to fight this war yet. And I think it is indeed a war as Bruce Hoffman described it, a war of attrition. One of the most astounding things that came out of *The 9/11 Commission Report* and out of Mr. Richard Clarke's book was a criticism of the intelligence community for not having the imagination to expect someone to fly an airplane into a building.

But I don't think we suffer from a lack of imagination. I think we have plenty of it, and it has led us down a disastrous road. Let me suggest what kinds of things have come not only from imagination, but from a failure to see the world as it is and not as we want it to be, for example: WMDs in Iraq; a close tie between Saddam Hussein and Osama bin Laden; the idea that wars can be fought without casualties; the notion that 9/11 was the result of an intelligence failure; and the 9/11 Commission's recommendations that somehow a massive public diplomacy campaign will fix things, as if the unwashed Muslim masses cannot understand that our foreign policy is really designed to help them. The other one I thought was very good was the educational fund for Muslim training and travel in the United States that sounded like we were going to resurrect "Abu Harry Hopkins" and "Abu Harold Ickes" to have a New Deal for the Muslim World. These are examples of other things that come from the imagination of people: that we are being attacked because of who we are and what we do, or who we are and what we believe, rather than what we do, or the idea that Osama bin Laden is just a thug, a criminal, and a gangster. There are literally dozens of these things that are just patently absurd and really block the ability of Americans to assess the threat to them.

I come at this problem from a very nationalistic viewpoint. I am perfectly satisfied to be an American citizen and not a citizen of the world. I really am most interested in protecting this country. We have very little contact with reality, that is, with the world as it is. That is our own fault. Even today we don't have a panel that discusses the role of Islam. We talk a lot about Islam and about Muslims that are participating in this war against us, but there is no discussion of how important religion is as a motivating factor. And I know I disagree on this part with Mr. Sageman and he disagrees with me. But I do not think the conflict we are engaged in is understandable unless you factor in how religion motivates the issue.

Peter Bergen mentioned that during the Cold War we had a panoply of ways to fight off the Soviet Union, and one of them was to challenge the validity of the doctrine of communism. No one was, of course, politically correct in the sense of not wanting to offend the spirit of Lenin or of Karl Marx. We are indeed reluctant to say that religion has everything to do with this war and it escapes me how our leaders, our political leaders, our elites, Democrats and Republicans, have just not grasped that. If we want to say that we are at war with Islam, I think we ought to acknowledge the data. The hard data is that a large and increasing percentage of Islam is at war with us.

We need to understand that our policies are indeed an offense to the Muslim religion. During the recent election campaign, the Christian right delivered the election to President Bush. I think they turned out in that number because they saw their God and their religion threatened by policy. Whether it is gay rights, abortion, or gay marriage, a religion under attack by policy will defend itself. In North America we respond by voting. I don't think it is very different in parts of the Muslim world. Their religion is more pervasive in the sense of their daily lives than Christianity is in most of America. And they perceive their religion as being under attack by our policies. That analogy has not been made. It is not a perfect analogy, but I still think it is not surprising that religious people who view their God or their religion as being attacked will respond vigorously.

I am really very pessimistic about where we stand against this war. I think it is increasingly a war that cannot speak its own name. This is a shame because Americans are going to die, unnecessarily probably, and certainly it will bankrupt us at some point. Salameh Nematt said that these Muslims were changing their own world more than ours. And I think they *are* changing their own world. But I think you will recall that just after the war in Afghanistan started, Osama bin Laden appeared and said, "I am not going to appear as much as I have been appearing. First of all, by dint of circumstance, I am going to have to be less available to foreigners." He also said, "I am not going to become engaged in a tit-for-tat response in a dialogue with the Americans or anyone else." More importantly he said, "I don't need to be on the television to terrorize the Americans. All I need to do is to make the statement and carry out an attack once again because the Americans will terrorize themselves. They will eventually constrict their own civil liberties. They will eventually bring their society to a state that is not recognizable with what it was before 9/11."

I think we are certainly doing that. Anyone who has tried to take their grade-school daughter's class to the Presidential Visitors' Center and has seen fourth-graders frisked and run over with the electronic detection kit can say that somehow America has changed. Try to get on an airplane. Look at the concentric rings around the White House, giving the current President much more defense than Franklin Roosevelt had when he was fighting two fascist empires.

I had the great good fortune of not going to one of America's great universities for my education. I went to a small Jesuit school in Buffalo,

New York. The Jesuits are very interesting people. They taught me that you may need to manipulate others as you go through life, but never fool yourself. And for better or worse, Americans are fooling themselves if they think we are making progress in this war. I think it is primarily the case that the fault lays primarily with the leadership of both parties, neither of which have squared with the American people.

Question and Answer Session

Q. PETER BERGEN: I would like to ask Salameh to do a thought experiment over the fact that there was no coverage of al Qaeda before 9/11. There was simply no media coverage at all. And then 9/11 happened. The 9/11 planning started in 1996, the very year that al Jazeera came into existence. Moreover, CNN did an interview with bin Laden in 1997. The embassy bombing plot had begun back in 1993. That plot was going to happen whether we did an interview with bin Laden or not.

At least we have an understanding of why we are being attacked. I would like Salameh to respond to the idea that there was absolutely no coverage at all, and also to respond to the notion that perhaps what he is saying is somewhat tautological in a sense. We live in a world that is entirely dominated by the media, and whether you are Madonna or President Bush or Osama bin Laden, you are going to take advantage of that.

A. SALAMEH NEMATT: I cannot disagree with what you said, except that you are taking it for granted that the Arab media and the pan-Arab media like al Jazeera are basically reporting it the way the American media does. But this is not the case. The way it is reported in the Arab world gives it legitimacy. They do not portray terrorism as a bad thing. Al Jazeera blurs the line between legitimate and illegitimate jihad. It legitimately targets the military in the context of occupation, let's say in Iraq, where you cannot argue with resistance when it is targeting military personnel. But when you go and behead people, innocent people, and you blow up Iraqi children, and you go and give that legitimacy in your media as if it is legitimate resistance, this is where I have a problem.

The problem now is that we have a generation in the Arab world of young people, teenagers, who look at Osama bin Laden and Abu Musab al-Zarqawi as heroes because this is how al Jazeera and other TV channels portray them. This is a very, very dangerous phenomenon. And I think that I wouldn't mind if it was being reported the way the American media reports it, but it is not.

I don't know if anybody you know who knows Arabic listens to it. There is a legitimization and there is a glorification of acts of mass murder in al Jazeera and other Arab media. Of course, I am not excluding al Jazeera here or exclusively attacking al Jazeera or targeting it, but it is the most prominent one. The other channels and newspapers are doing similar things. So we have got to do something about this. Because where do we stop if you give legitimacy to incitement, to murder, despite the fact that there is nothing in Islam that allows suicide? Actually, Islam bans suicide. And it is supposed to be Islamists, pious Islamists, who believe in God. How come they are breaking God's word by committing suicide and killing innocent people? Where is it in Islam that allows killing innocent people? I want to understand.

We speak about bin Laden as if he is a legitimate spokesman of Islam. He is not. He broke ranks with mainstream Islam, and he broke ranks with his own country, with his own regime. He is an outsider who hijacked Islam simply because he gets more media coverage. Why does he get more media coverage? He commits spectacular acts of mass murder. Not because he is more convincing than, let's say, King Abdullah of Jordan or Hosni Mubarak of Egypt when they talk about Islam.

A. MICHAEL SCHEUER: In many ways I agree with my knowledgeable colleague here that the one thing we need to understand is that Qatar, Saudi Arabia, Kuwait, and the United Arab Emirates are not American allies. Certainly, the content of al Arabiya and al Jazeera is meant to redirect the Islamic militants in their countries towards the United States. It is a matter of self-preservation for them. They send slick-speaking diplomats to America to convince us otherwise. But they, for example during the Afghan War, let many, many, many of their young men who are militants go to Afghanistan in the hope that they would kill Soviets and be killed in return. That sort of backfired. Not all of them got killed. But it is not a coincidence at the moment that so many Saudis, Kuwaitis, Algerians, Tunisians, and Jordanians are being killed in Iraq.

I cannot prove it but my guess is that the system that worked for Afghanistan is being used in Iraq and that these countries are unloading people who were imprisoned for militant Islamic activities who, by nature are against the ruling party, and who have been released from prison as long as they go to Iraq and try to kill Americans and hopefully, from the perspective of their governments, be killed by the Americans. It is a kind of a realistic geopolitical fact and it is not so much the content of what is on al Jazeera as it is the political goal of the countries that we continue to believe are our allies when they are indeed much more Islamic imperialists than are any of bin Laden's words.

Q. PETER BERGEN: I want to ask Yosri Fouda to respond to some of the things that have been said about al Jazeera, since he is their lead investigative reporter.

A. YOSRI FOUDA: I really did not want to intrude into a session that is not mine. I think I have really had more than my share. I thank Mike Scheuer a lot for his ideas, for sticking up for al Jazeera and for what al Jazeera means not only for the Arabs, but perhaps more importantly for this country and for Western civilization. I am a little bit surprised that Salameh Nematt should think this way. Salameh is a very good friend of mine and our relationship goes back for many years. We used to work for the BBC. I can tell you, Salameh, that now with al Jazeera I am enjoying much more freedom than I ever did with the BBC. I know that this is a big statement, but I can tell you that the Saudis offered me and a few others from al Jazeera a lot of money to join al Arabiya. Some joined, but some didn't because we believed in something.

I think it is very theoretical to assume that there is a perfect media outlet. Of course, somebody has to pay for the service. Of course, whoever pays for the service sometimes expects something in return, including every single media outlet in this country whether it is market-oriented or interest-oriented or whatever. In the end, what matters is what you get on the screen. I can tell you from my own experience that my boss did not know what I was doing in Karachi until I came back with it. So it is not about an agenda. My boss never told me, "Yosri, you either do this or you are fired." My boss was upset with me that I did not put him in the picture, but he did not fire me. I don't know if you have worked a little bit too long for the Saudis, but I think that the Saudis have been all about buying people off. From the 1970s until now, I have had so many Saudi friends. Some of them are very, very good journalists. I can tell you that if al Jazeera closes down today, al Arabiya would close down tomorrow because the very reason that al Arabiya exists is because al Jazeera is making a difference. I do not accept the argument that it is al Jazeera that is inspiring the terrorists and this is what your argument is all about.

So it is not about audiotapes that we get from bin Laden and the other guy. It is actually about who has the right to get hold of the tapes; when, where, and how. Al Jazeera is not perfect, but we try. It is not by accident that it is talked about amongst most of the Arabs. If you acknowledge this fact, maybe, but maybe it is so popular because Arabs think it tries to tell them what actually takes place.

A. SALAMEH NEMATT: I write for a newspaper called *Al Hayat*. It is an internationally respected newspaper. It so happens that one of the owners is a Saudi, but it is not Saudi government money. It is a private individual. I won't be bought by anybody. I am a Jordanian and I was imprisoned in my own country because of my writings. I didn't let my own country buy me and I would not let any other country buy me. When you talk about the freedom of al Jazeera, yes, it is free to incite to murder. This is what it is doing. I think you know why a very, very big story for the Qataris, the people of Qatar, the owner of al Jazeera, cannot have an interview with the deposed Emir of Qatar whose son overthrew him and spent so many years in exile in Geneva. If al Jazeera is about freedom, why is it that the people of Qatar cannot see this interview?

Q. SCOTT WALLACE [Freelance writer and producer]: This question is for Michael Scheuer. Earlier today, someone in the first panel raised the notion of counterinsurgency and insurgency. Since then, I haven't heard anything more about it. I would be interested to know from you whether the wars in Iraq and Afghanistan are being conducted as counterinsurgencies, specifically if the military doctrine that is being used is a variation on the counterinsurgencies that we are familiar with from Vietnam and Central America. More broadly, do you think the proper response is a more global counterinsurgency response to rising Islamic militancy and what would that look like?

A. **MICHAEL SCHEUER:** It would look like a mess, but I think clearly the forces we are fighting are insurgent forces. They are not terrorists, rather the most effective al Qaeda methods are modeled after the Afghan insurgent forces that fought the Soviets. One of the reasons they are so good at replacing leaders is that they are always expecting to fight an organization that is much more powerful than they are.

We very seldom wait more than one or two days to find out who succeeded Khalid Sheikh Mohammed or any other senior al Qaeda lieutenant. They are very adept at replacing them. What we are fighting at the moment is, I think, a kind of "insurgency-lite." We clearly let al Qaeda get out of Tora Bora because we didn't use our own troops and instead employed people who were Osama's sidekicks during the war against the Soviets. I think the important thing is whether we really want to be involved in fighting this insurgency and to what extent. It will bleed us to death in terms of lives and money. Do we want to go to the Philippines and southern Thailand, which appear to be boiling at the moment? Of course, surely, the beginning of wisdom is to understand that this is an insurgency.

The other point I would like to make is why it was interesting this morning when someone mentioned Guantánamo. The reason Guantánamo has been such an abject failure is that there are no terrorists down there. Those folks were rounded up in Afghanistan fighting as an insurgency. What they could have done, had it been treated correctly, was to give us for the first time a controlled group that we could have talked about order of battle. For example, what were they trained on? What were their skills? What weapons did they have? How big were their units? Instead, we thought we were going to find the guy that bought the blueprints for the World Trade Center. Similarly, those gentlemen who were killed in Mazar-e-Sharif were not terrorists. That prison was full of insurgents. They could have asked them for the next one hundred years what terrorist plans they knew of. They simply did not know of any. So it is not a satisfactory answer but I think it is an insurgency, and until we come to grips with that fact, we are not going to know how to fight it. I think Iraq is an example of that at the moment.

Q. AUDIENCE PARTICIPANT: A couple of times during earlier discussions, the idea of an information operations campaign was brought up by some of the speakers. In terms of the previous successes that were alluded to during World War II and other conflicts, what role could an information operations campaign play in today's society where our messages are longer than a sound bite and our videos are not as horrific as the ones being discussed for news value?

A. SALAMEH NEMATT: I agree with you that this is a very, very important component in the war on terror. This is one of the reasons why I said Osama bin Laden would rather keep al Jazeera on his side than win Saudi Arabia. It is also one of the reasons why his number three, his head of operations, was at the same time head of the media operations. This shows that Osama bin Laden was giving it the same importance. It is not only the acts themselves, but the media exposure of these acts that is very, very important for him. Now I am not saying not to go around reporting acts of terrorism. That would be ridiculous. What I am saying is that you do not portray these acts as if they are heroic and glorify them. In so doing, these Arab television stations are basically increasing the number of recruits all over the world.

One thing Mike Scheuer actually brought to my attention is that Arab leaders have never condemned Osama bin Laden by name. Never. No fatwa was issued against suicide bombings or against Osama bin Laden and these terrorists. In Arab states, whenever the leader wants a fatwa, he just has his secretary give him a call and he tells him what kind of fatwa he wants and they will issue it. They will issue any fatwa that the leaders want. But they have not issued a fatwa against Osama bin Laden, which means that these Arab leaders do not want to condemn such acts. In other words, their media and they themselves support such acts. They just cannot say it openly, and this is where we have a problem. You have to delegitimize terrorism in the Arab world before you can defeat it. Otherwise we are going to have a continuous supply, but the media is serving in exactly the opposite direction. What can you do here? Not much. Most of the Arab world is not watching American media and hence will not be affected by it.

A. **MICHAEL SCHEUER:** I certainly agree with much of that. I think that the dependence on public diplomacy and the conclusions of *The 9/11 Commission Report* as an answer or even *the* answer is just whistling past the graveyard. In an odd sense we control both the message and the context, and the context at the moment is ours to control. The context in which the message is received is a hatred for our policies and not for who we are. If we should change a policy and do change it, we may be able to use public diplomacy to greater effect. But right now that is not going to happen. I know there are professional military men in the audience and I will yield to their criticism if it is deserved.

But I think we are in a really unusual position when we talk about the enemy's center of gravity. I think for al Qaeda, in many ways, American foreign policy is their center of gravity. We are their only indispensable ally. As long as we are there with those policies, the potential for Osama bin Laden or bin Ladenism to grow, the support for him to grow around the world, particularly in the Muslim world, is virtually unlimited. So every dollar that you put into public diplomacy at this moment is probably a dollar wasted.

Q. **TONY SCHWARTZ [U.S. Navy Lieutenant, Naval War College]:** My question is for both of you because I think there may be different answers given in response to this question. But Salameh, you have mentioned explicitly United States foreign policy as a reason for terrorism, specifically backing oppressive regimes or perceived oppressive regimes. Obviously the United States has been seen as taking sides with Israel over Palestine. There are issues with Saudi Arabia. You've mentioned specifically Egyptian and Jordanian backing of the government. My question is this: is it too idealistic to think that a democracy in Iraq could give the United States a footprint, for lack of a better term, from which to be more objective with their foreign policy in the region, and if so, would that reduce terrorism?

A. SALAMEH NEMATT: Yes, I absolutely agree with you. If, and this is a big if, we end up with a democracy in Iraq then the biggest claim that enemies of the Americans have against them is gone. Until now it hasn't happened. Afghanistan is not significant in the context of the Arab Middle East, as I said. It is still too early to judge. Until now, we have only statements about democratization in the region. No actual action has taken place to change the status quo. Now, with Iraq a factor, it will also depend on how everybody around Iraq reacts, meaning we must consider the question of whether or not you are going to have the Arab states claiming that these elections coming up are illegimate and are such because the Sunnis did not participate. Then the government that is going to come out from the national assembly will be seen as illegitimate. Of course, the media will again play a role. And I can already bet you that even if all Iraqis participated and we had elections similar to those we have in Sweden, the Arab media would nonetheless delegitimize any government that comes from America.

This is why: America's problem in the region is that the declaration of the democracy initiative has basically alarmed every single regime in that part of the world. Now America is not only fighting insurgents in Iraq, but America is fighting insurgents *and* almost every single dictatorship and authoritative regime there as well. I have no doubt that intelligence services of countries that are considered allies in Washington are basically recruiting people, smuggling weapons, and trying to do as much as they can to undermine the democracy project in Iraq. Because if Iraq succeeds this is the beginning of the end for the others.

A. MICHAEL SCHEUER: I think Salameh hits on an extraordinarily important point. As a great power we sometimes have geopolitical interests. In Afghanistan, for example, our leaders told us that all the countries bordering Afghanistan want a peaceful, stable country and that is certainly true, but only insofar as they can get it on their own interests. Iran's interests are not the same as Pakistan's, and Pakistan's are not the same as ours. The Russians certainly have a different view, and the Indians have yet another view. Certainly in Iraq, we have unleashed the birth of a new cockpit of international rivalry. The Iranians are never going to tolerate a Sunni-dominated state. Whether it would be a war, I doubt it, but it may certainly bring unending insurgent-type activities or terrorist activities supported by the Iranians. And on the other hand, the Saudis, the Jordanians, and the Kuwaitis are never, ever going to tolerate another Iran, another Shi'a-dominated state right there.

We tend to focus on national entities while forgetting that the countries around them are very, very important. The other point I would make is that the whole idea of exporting democracy, I think, is one of the most destabilizing things in the world today. I think we can forgive American leaders for not knowing the tenets of Islam or how it affects statecraft or how it affects the lives of Muslims.

One would hope that we grow more educated over the years, but certainly the major reclamation project for Mrs. Bush's program to reinvigorate the teaching of American history lies in the mentality of the neoconservatives. They cannot be forgiven for not knowing the history of their own country. American democracy is a project that started, to pick an arbitrary date, in a place called Runnymede in England in 1215. Eight hundred years later, we are still a little short of being perfect. We have only had a voting rights act for forty years. We fought a civil war 140 years ago and lynching, although in the back of an automobile instead of in front of a tree, has occurred in the last decade.

My point here is not to condemn America, but to remind those people that conduct our foreign policy how much blood, war, struggle, and sacrifice has been entailed in the last eight hundred years. To believe that you can put that on a CD-ROM, hand it to Ahmed Chalabi, and send him to Iraq and say, "Hey do this in about six weeks. We have to go to another country to save it," is really ludicrous and speaks very poorly of the knowledge of American history among some of our leadership.

A. PETER BERGEN: Actually it has sort of worked in Afghanistan. There are free and fair elections where Hamid Karzai scored fifty-five percent of the vote against seventeen candidates, a better record than President Bush. The Taliban was a dog that didn't bark. We see that the so-called democratic domino effect obviously has not occurred in Iraq. But this sends a huge signal to Pakistan, Uzbekistan, Tajikistan, and Iran, who think that Afghans are sort of neanderthals and couldn't possibly have a free and fair election. They proved them wrong.

A. MICHAEL SCHEUER: I think they could have an election every third day, Peter, and it wouldn't make a damn bit of difference. It doesn't send a message to anyone except that they are going to have to work harder to undermine Karzai's government. And at the end of the day, Afghanistan remains a tribally dominated, ethnically diverse country which will sort itself out along lines that have been established for the past two thousand years. The message it sent to Pakistan is that they are going to have to work much harder to get an Islamic government in Kabul, which is their only interest and a national security interest. So we differ on that. I think that in the long term it doesn't mean a whole lot but I hope I am wrong.

Q. AUDIENCE PARTICIPANT: Mr. Scheuer, earlier in your comments and again just recently in response, you said that the Islamists hate America not for what we are and who we are but for what we do. But another theme running through your comments is that this is a holy war, and that your history determines who you are and how you do things. So I wonder if it is realistic to create this dichotomy that you have between policy and identity. In other words, is it possible for America to change its policy in a way that is going to be satisfactory to the jihadist without fundamentally changing who we are?

A. MICHAEL SCHEUER: My opinion is that we do not have to change our policy to satisfy anybody. But I do think for survival purposes that we have to understand what effect our policy has and how it motivates other people. I thought surely one of the saddest statements made today was that American policies are immutable, which suggests that we don't even need to talk about them.

My argument is not that we should change policies but that we should understand how they motivate the enemy. More than that, with a shot of democracy in the United States, these policies would be debated and we would see if there is still a consensus of American opinion that these policies serve U.S. interests. Then at least we would know what we're doing. The American people would have an idea. If we had a debate on these six policies and we said, "This is just what we want," that's fine. Then the American people, with their eyes open, would know we are going into a war that is virtually endless, and is going to be terribly bloody and terribly costly. But at least it will be fair. This way, Americans would know what the end-game is. Right now, there is just this continual litany of, "They hate our elections and they hate us because we drink Budweiser and because women are in the workplace." I don't think there are a lot of you in America that really know what kind of enemy we are up against and why we are fighting him. I don't think we should change our policies to suit anybody unless it's to suit ourselves.

Q. MARK NUTURNO [Interactivity Foundation]: I guess I am picking up on the same idea. I was very much struck by your notion that American policies are offensive to Islam. I am wondering about the idea that the presence and behavior of Americans are offensive to Islam, and in particular, I wonder whether there is the possibility of changing the way we behave as Americans and still have any sort of interaction with Islamic culture in a way that would not be offensive?

A. MICHAEL SCHEUER: Salameh should certainly comment on this, but my own view is that our behavior has very little to do with it. Muslims may not like it but not many people are going to go out and die for it. We saw Ayatollah Khomeini rant and rave for a decade about debauchery, degeneracy, X-rated movies, alcohol, and all of that kind of behavioral stuff. Nobody died for that. Even if Hezbollah blew up our embassy in Lebanon and destroyed the Marine barracks in the Khomeini name with the aura of religion, they were really motivated by nationalist reasons. They wanted us out of their backyard and it worked.

I do not think that this war is at all about our behavior in the sense of social behavior or values. It is about visceral policies that are tangible and can be seen every day. One point Salameh makes that is exactly right is that as long as al Jazeera and Al Arabiya are televising everyday from Fallujah, from the West Bank, from Gaza, and from Southern Thailand, there is nothing we can say that is going to make a difference. Because the Arab world is seeing Muslims killed. I really do think it is policy. It is not behavior.

A. SALAMEH NEMATT: Just one further comment. We know that Saddam Hussein's regime buried three hundred thousand people in mass graves.

We have not seen a single picture of the act of doing it. The Syrians killed twenty thousand in twenty-four to forty-eight hours in Hamat. There is no picture. Why do you think Arab public opinion is more concerned with freedom for the Palestinians and now freedom for the Iraqis and less concerned for their own freedom? The Iraqis were living under Saddam, and Saddam's regime was worse than what the Americans are doing now in Iraq. Yet there was no outrage in the Arab world. You know why? Because the media was on Saddam's side and continues to be today. The problem is that there is no level playing field between America and the Arab world in which to talk about the efficiency of public diplomacy.

I am not defending American policies in the region, mind you. I think that the most dangerous policy is the continued dependence on autocratic regimes and dictatorships in the Middle East to conduct regional policies. They continue to do it until this very day. The U.S. receives the leaders of these dictatorships who are responsible for producing this brand of extremist militant Islam and terrorism. These people are being received in Washington as friends until this very day. And we talk about democracy. So I think there is not one thing that you can do to solve the problem. It is a combination of things. The primary thing is to put your money where your mouth is. If you talk about democracy and backing democrats, you better start doing it so that people can believe you.

Q. DAVID ENSOR [CNN]: I would ask both of you to be more specific. In your case Salameh Nematt, when you critique al Jazeera and the Arab media in the way you have, I wonder what you think that the U.S. government, for example, ought to do in response. In your case Mike Scheuer, you say that this is a war about the foreign policy of the United States. But with the exception of saying you don't like the war in Iraq, I would just ask you to be more specific. What foreign policies should we change? What things that are perhaps quite popular in the American foreign policy would you say people ought to start thinking about changing?

A. SALAMEH NEMATT: What should the U.S. response be? I think I already said. The U.S. response should be to really push forward for democracy in the Middle East so that you have a more balanced media. This is very important. Not to set up your own Arabic-speaking media which cannot function in the Arab world because they cannot cover any more stories than those al Jazeera and the others are covering. Why should you go for them when you cannot reach the people?

You can only reach them if you open up the Arab media, which is currently fully controlled. I'll give you a close example. I am a Jordanian and I have a weekly column in *Al Hayat* newspaper, which is based in London. I cannot publish my weekly column that appears in *Al Hayat* in my own national Jordanian newspaper. Why? Because I am calling for a democracy. People who speak for al-Zarqawi, support terrorism, and were on Saddam Hussein's payroll write columns in my own national newspaper today. And this is the closest Arab ally alive for the United States. I cannot publish stories while bin Laden and al-Zarqawi have a field day with the media in Jordan. So what do you do? You will have to have democracy, otherwise there is no way you can win. As I told you, even if you turn Iraq into a Scandinavian-style democracy you are not going to win.

A. MICHAEL SCHEUER: Concerning the war in Iraq, I do not think it is so much whether I like it or not. The point is that the Iraq war has broken our back in terms of terrorism. It was a bad decision, and that is a fact we have to deal with. And again, I repeat, I do not know what the policy should be but I do know that we are in this war because of them. The answer in a democratic society is to have a discussion. Certainly it is absurd that we continue to let the Israeli tail lead the American dog. That is a killing notion in the Muslim world and it is getting Americans killed.

Would we have a single strategic interest on the Arabian peninsula if it weren't for oil? Should there not be a debate in this country on developing more natural resources, fossil fuels here, but especially going toward alternative energies? And I think Ralph Peters has made the point that we make a mockery of our heritage and our history every day by supporting the al Sauds, the Kuwaitis, and the Mubaraks of the world.

Maybe all of those policies at the end of the day are what Americans want. But I don't know that. I have not in my lifetime heard much of a debate over that, and as Steve Simon said, those are immutable policies. So I am A.A. Milne's typical bear of little brain. I just wonder if those policies still suit U.S. interests, and there's no better way to find out than a public debate with our leaders.

Q. AUDIENCE PARTICIPANT: A lot of Arabs, in fact, have a problem with al Jazeera because they thought, before bin Laden's appearance on it, that it was actually the voice of Israelis in the Arab world. Secondly, a lot of things which appear on al Jazeera cannot be published in our Arab media, independent or otherwise. Of course, there is only a small number of independent newspapers anyway. But concerning al Jazeera, we need twenty al Jazeeras. A lot of Arab journalists in this town represent secular media. There is no voice for other media in the Arab world. You want to hear your echo in them, and that is why we see them repeatedly in all channels.

Q. AVI JORISCH [Author, *Beacon of Hatred: Inside Hizballah's al-Manar Television*]: I suspect that most of the non-Arabic speakers in this room will still walk away thinking that al Jazeera is terror television. And that is not exactly the case. It is not a perfect station, but you know they bring on Israeli officials, American officials, and there is room for debate. Why haven't we actually moved towards identifying terrorist media outlets such as al Manar Hezbollah television, that poison the minds of Middle Easterners daily? Mr. Scheuer, what kind of media policy do you think we should establish in general towards al Jazeera and towards al Manar?

A. MICHAEL SCHEUER: None. It is counterproductive for us to censor free speech anyplace in the world. It is not just about facts, if you suppress free speech, it becomes violence.

Q. AVI JORISCH: Even after they call for the killing of American soldiers, support insurgents, and basically bust on our foreign policy and who we are?

A. MICHAEL SCHEUER: The point is we are in a war and we ought to get on with it and stop whining about what people say. The one thing we should certainly get through our heads is to stop worrying about Hezbollah. They haven't attacked us since 1983. If anyone has a problem with them, it is the Israelis and not the Americans. There are so many people in this town who think that Iran and Hezbollah are somehow the most dangerous thing. Senator Graham said they were the A-team of terrorism. Well, that is phooey. I don't mean to dismiss your argument or your concerns. We should be concerned with what's said about us. We should certainly know what it is. But at the end of the day, we could shut up every one of these media outlets in the world and we would still have Americans being killed. So we need to stop whining and get on with the war.

Q. CHRISTINA DAVIDSON [Editor, *Imperial Hubris*]: I will direct my question toward Salameh, but Mike can feel free to back me up on this. Salameh, I just wanted to say that one complaint that has a lot of traction in the Middle East is, when it comes to freedom and democracy, the United States has one set of rules that applies to Muslims and one set of rules that apply to the rest of the world. Now you have mentioned that what the U.S. media does is okay, but that something needs to be done about al Jazeera. But don't you think that if the United States were to flex its power and to try to exercise any kind of control or influence over what al Jazeera was reporting, it would just underscore the impression that speech is only free when it supports interests? And wouldn't that, in fact, ultimately worsen our position in this war?

A. SALAMEH NEMATT: To start with, I am not here defending U.S. policy. What I am saying, however, is that we do not have a balanced picture of reality in the Middle East as a result of the fact that the media in the Arab world is totally dominated by these governments. I have a problem with the failure to establish an alternative media in the Arab world. When I criticize al Jazeera or al Manar or anyone else, these people say I am criticizing them because they are not giving the other point of view. They are not seeing it as it is. How can you accept it as journalism when someone equates legitimate resistance with terrorism? You are basically dealing a blow to legitimate resistance when you lump it together with murder.

This is what I am talking about. I am not saying America should go and shut down these stations, but America can tell these governments, especially friendly governments that run these satellite centers, "If you don't mind, since you say you have freedom of the press, why don't you allow somebody from the private sector to open another station to compete?" I tell you, they are not going to issue a license. In Iraq, under the American occupation, there are five television channels established without a license from the government, along with 200 newspapers throughout the Arab world. I cannot go on publishing newspapers in my own country because the government controls the licenses and they will give licenses only to those who support and work with the government.

Nobody is saying that we should shut down the media, but we should support democratization so that there will be the pluralism we have in America. In America, for example, you have the rightist media and you have the leftist media. You end up having multiple sources of information from which anybody can make a judgment. Some people tend to go to the right and they like the rightist media. Some would go to the left so they go to the liberal media. But the point is, you have the choice here in America. In their boat, there is no choice except the choice offered by the autocratic, nondemocratic regimes. This is the problem and this is what we are talking about.

Q. AUDIENCE PARTICIPANT: I have spent the past three years, since 9/11, in the Middle East, where I had to watch al Jazeera or BBC. That was my only choice in my hotel in Egypt. I will never forget that during the major Iraqi combat, al Jazeera played over and over again the shots of these dead American soldiers with flies buzzing around their heads, very disgusting footage. And while they played it over and over again, at the same time, the U.S. media would never play such things. And I wonder, do you think that people in this country would have reacted differently to the realities and the horrors of war; namely, all the dead American soldiers and the way in which their bodies have been paraded?

A. MICHAEL SCHEUER: I don't recall but I think they televised some dead American soldiers. I really do not know.

A. SALAMEH NEMATT: Well I think that yes, you have a point. You are right, the more you expose the ugliness of war, the more you will have anti-war feelings. That goes without saying. This is why I am making the argument. The more you legitimize acts of mass murder as legitimate jihad, the more recruits you will have, and the more people are going to join the so-called jihad, which basically has nothing to do with God because Islam never allows people to go and commit suicide and kill innocent people.

A. MICHAEL SCHEUER: I would just make one quick comment on that point. I really think that Salameh is a bit too general in terms of saying that all of this is not allowed within the Islamic religion. There are certainly philosophers and scholars who have provided rules of war which allow things very similar to what is going on today. Even al-Qaradawi has come very close to letting suicide be authorized. So I think it's a much bigger issue and a much more differentiated one.

Q. MAYER ZADI [*The Daily Jung,* Pakistan]: I will start with a question and make an observation. First, I appreciate your comments Michael because you said that you know that Western civilization and the political systems we have evolved over hundreds of years and that you just cannot introduce them in six weeks. But my question is that if you are asking for democracy, which version of democracy do you want? Is it the democracy in which only property owners could vote, the democracy in which slaves, human beings, were considered a property, the democracy that did not allow women the right to vote until 1920 or the democracy where the majority winner in Florida lost in spite of the greatest number of votes?

For a democracy that is in Turkey, for example, my observation is that when the United States is using countries as allies in a war or a military campaign, it doesn't want democracy. If they go to the Army Chief of Staff, he will say, "Gee, I can't do anything unless I talk to the President." The President will say, "I can't do anything until I go to the Parliament." The U.S. Central Command doesn't like that. They want a one-window operation. So please specify which version of American democracy you are advocating at this time.

A. MICHAEL SCHEUER: I understand the point and I have sympathy for it in the sense that our country was founded on the idea of democratic representative government. Our founders thought the idea should take hold and should serve as an example for the rest of the world. We should never go abroad and try to install democracy, and I think we have forgotten that. There's a lot of people in town who think the word *founder* is kind of a misstatement of the word for a fish rather than Alexander Hamilton and his like. Democracy takes a long time. It takes a lot of struggle and I entirely agree that we Americans should wish everyone could vote and do what they wanted to do, but we should have no interest in building democracies that will create more instability in the world.

5 The United States vs. al Qaeda

A Progress Report

MODERATOR: **Karen J. Greenberg,** Executive Director, Center on Law and Security. PANELISTS: **Daniel Benjamin,** Senior Analyst, Center for Strategic and International Studies; **Colonel Pat Lang,** former Chief of Middle East Intelligence, Defense Intelligence Agency, Department of Defense; **Reuel Gerecht,** Resident Fellow, American Enterprise Institute.

KAREN GREENBERG

There is a metaphor for the current circumstances in which the United States finds itself. And that is this: when someone takes a photograph of you and you see it and say, "I don't like that photograph." Then, six months later, you look at it and you say, "Oh, you know, I actually looked a little younger then. I looked much better than I do now!" That is how I would describe the sensibility of living in the U.S. right now. However unpleasant the picture looks to me in any given moment, subsequent facts turn out to be even less palatable, less something we want to associate with ourselves and our culture.

Every three or six months, if you stop and ask where we are, we know one thing – we're in a less good place. We are finding out more about the failures in Iraq, more about the widespread use of torture, more about the secrecy and deception on the home front. What we are left with is the question, "Wasn't it better back then, before we knew?" In terms of thinking about today, the real question in our minds ought to be, "What will it look like in a year?" Will this be a snapshot that will cause us to say that we should have listened more carefully to ourselves and tried to change things? Or will we perhaps be able to say that things are better than they were a year ago, that we have made some progress?

PAT LANG

In the United States, a whole generation of officers, like myself, were trained to go out and fight wars of insurgency and counterinsurgency around the world. There were many very complex ways in which we were sure that we understood what the mix should be between nonmilitary and military action in the effort to defeat the rising aspirations of various peoples around the world. And in those days it had as much bite as it does now, because in those days it was the radiological opponents who were our enemies.

So we did this in South America in, for example, the Andes. We had a good deal of success in Latin America and in various places in Central America. The reason I think our strategy worked in these places was that the level of commitment was not terrifically high on the part of the Indian populations. They were just very unhappy with their state of life and with the divisions of wealth in their country. So, if you offered them something in return and if you tried to sponsor some kind of reform in their country, they often turned away from the path they had been following. Now, when we ran into the really tough guys in Vietnam, people who were deeply committed, we ended up waging two wars at the same time. One was the war of counterinsurgency in which we essentially engaged in nation building. For example, we acted as local security and carried out counterguerilla activities around villages, small towns, and places like that. At the same time, we discovered that there was a full-size enemy army in the field so we ended up fighting them as a conventional army.

The two things worked in tandem, side by side, for a long time and it is beginning to look more and more as though this is what we are doing in Iraq. So the relevance of our previous experience in this matter, in spite of our natural ahistoricity as Americans, is that the experience of Vietnam begins to seem more and more relevant to the situation we face in Iraq.

But I wasn't just in the HUMINT [Human Intelligence] business, I was the head analyst for the DIA [Defense Intelligence Agency] for the Middle East for a long time. The fact is that there is a certain consistency in our inability to understand these situations which I find to be particularly frightening. When we go to these places and look at them, we always end up looking through a peculiar lens of our own, a view based on our national experience.

To some extent this affects the Europeans too, but America does have a rather exceptional history, particularly in regard to our beliefs about humanity. We hold a conviction that all men and women are essentially the same and have all the same desires, hopes, and fears. We believe that everybody is firmly in line with the idea of progress as we understand it to be embedded in our material life and in the evolution of our political institutions. There is a whole set of such beliefs that we bring to these situations. This is the lens through which we tend to see things and often this lens poses a severe problem for us, as it does, for example, in the case of Iraq.

When we went into Iraq, we went into the Islamic world with the basic belief that our culture was exportable in regard to political forms, participation, and the like. At the same time, we seem to have a very difficult time seeing the people who actually live there for what they are in their own terms.

We have been seeing a massive deconstruction of our previous beliefs about what the war was all about, an attempt to see that maybe, in fact, the Iraqis and the Afghans and the Egyptians and the Jordanians have some other idea of how life ought to be organized. I think Iraq is the perfect example of this. We went into Iraq with the belief that the government there had to be enormously unpopular. It had to be that people here are just waiting for us to liberate them from their previous state of servitude and that they would greet us joyously. Our belief was so firmly held that we did not make any preparations for dealing with any alternate situation.

It is not just the American government that did that. It is also one of the most popular news networks in this country, FOX news. I used to appear on FOX occasionally and I used to talk about this to a lot of their consultants – military officers of some seniority – before the war occurred. I used to ask them, "Well, what are you going to do now if you get into this place and you find out they don't welcome us?" and "What if, for example, there is guerilla resistance? What are you going to do?" The answer was, "Well that is not going to happen. That is not going be the case. There is not going be any of that kind of stuff. In fact, we are already taking in too many troops."

It is hard to remember that now, but before the war actually occurred the general position in the government, and in the media as well, was that the smaller the force, the better. This was going to be a liberation and not an occupation. This seems absolutely ludicrous now, but that was the position. Everybody believed that firmly. I went and visited various armed forces headquarters before the war and the staffs – quite senior and quite responsible officers, thoughtful people, but with no experience in the Middle East – would say to me, "You know, we are being given guidance from above that says that we don't have to concern ourselves with certain aspects of security in the country's reconstruction afterwards. It is just not going to be a problem. What do you think about that?" And I answered, "Well, I think that is absolute rubbish. I think it is nonsense. I think it is going to be bloody chaos in fact."

In Iraq, you had a country that was cobbled together out of the detritus of the wrecked Ottoman Empire for the imperial reasons that the British had at the time. In fact, they put together peoples that had nothing to do with each other except that most of them were Muslims of one kind or another. They drew borders on the map, and they said, "This is a country," and they brought in a foreign prince to run the place. And guess what happened? You had to hold this country together by force of arms and police action for fifty or sixty years. So if you make all that disappear, what do you think is going to happen? All these pieces are going to go in all different directions. The armed forces staff replied, "This is not what we are being told."

The reason the above exchange happened is the reason that I have seen these things happen in South America, in Indochina, in Africa, in Saudi Arabia, and every place else I served in my long and checkered experience in the government. The problem is that we just do not accept the reality of these other cultures. We have a tendency to believe that everybody is destined to be like us and is waiting to be liberated in order to be like us. So this warps our expectations of what is going on. And we are still doing this.

If you look at Iraq right now, or at any of the other episodes in our experience over the last few years of the jihadi phenomenon in the world, you will see that we tend to assign personal responsibility for whatever is really going wrong to some individual, whether it is Saddam Hussein or Osama bin Laden or Abu Musab al-Zarqawi. We pick somebody out and we say that the reason things are not going correctly is because there is some bad person who is causing these natural forces of history not to move things along. So we remove that person and guess what? Things don't remarkably improve. This is because, in fact, what we have missed is what has been revealed here today very well; the fact that what we are dealing with is not an organization, as in al Qaeda, with a top and little branches and items on the bottom with a reporting secretary over here and a fundraiser. That is not what we are dealing with. Nor is it a social movement as has been claimed. It is, rather, a phenomenon of history. And if you look at Islamic history over the last six hundred to seven hundred years, you will see that every once in a while people get the idea that they ought to do something serious about the fact that the West has too much power.

There has been a lot of talk here today about feelings of humiliation. I have spent most of my adult life now living and working with Muslim Arabs, Turks, Iranians, etc., and I speak Arabic. It is certainly true that they do feel humiliated. They do. But what humiliates them is not a specific thing. What really humiliates them is the fact that they do not think that it is right that we should be so strong and so wealthy and so dominant in the world and that they should not be.

In fact, when you look at specific things like the existence of Israel, the imposition of colonial regimes, the fact that all too many Arabs are running around wearing expensive business suits and not enough of them are wearing robes, you know that the kind of domination they find humiliating concerns the basic relationship between them and us. That is what really lies at the basis of this phenomenon in which periodically you have this uprising of Islamic hostility toward the West. It has never been everybody in the Islamic world. It is just some people in the Islamic world who feel that way enough to do something about it. To say to ourselves that we are programmatically going to eliminate this relationship is probably an illusion. What we have to do is to get on with the process of defeating the jihadis. They are reconcilable. At the same time we have to work for the betterment of the Islamic peoples. This is the way we do it.

But we are not doing a good enough job fighting the war. I spent a long, long time in the intelligence business. I did that as a kind of cowardice, basically, because I decided I never wanted to be involved in the policy business. I didn't mind carrying a gun in the woods; that was all right. But I did not want be in the policy business because that meant I would have to take responsibility for what I thought people were probably going to do. Whatever I saw around town here was not very encouraging in this regard, so I figured I would do the job of describing the reality. And that is what I have always tried to do.

There has been a lot of talk now in the context of intelligence reform, about what caused 9/11 in terms of intelligence failures. There was a failure, I think, involving the intelligence community with regard to 9/11. But it was not the kind of failure which is apt to be fixed by the kind of structural reform they are talking about now. What we are talking about, really, is moving boxes around on charts and lines and things, reshuffling who reports to whom, how the budget is divided up, and who gets to have the biggest piece of turf. But, in fact, that kind of intelligence is not the key to what you need to do to defeat the jihadis. The kind of intelligence you have to have is clandestine HUMINT. You need espionage which penetrates these groups. They have no photographic signature to speak of, just a few trucks and a bunch of guys walking around in robes. They do not have much of a signal intelligence signature because they are getting more and more clever all the time about this, and although they are good at using computers, they are very, very careful about it.

What we need is to be able to recruit agents and put them into their apparatus, to increase our strategy of penetration. That has been our single greatest failing and, as far as I know, remains our single greatest failing. If that was not the case, Osama bin Laden and Ayman al-Zawahiri would not be running around out in the woods somewhere. In fact, they would be in custody. So that is what we need to do, that was where our failure was, and that is where our failure continues to be. People want to talk about how we could not connect the dots; they see this as an analytic failure. But that is not the case. The problem was that there were not enough dots. You have to have many dots for a decent analyst to connect them, even allowing for intuitive leaps by analysts. The problem is leadership in the intelligence community. It is not the responsibility of any of several political administrations. It is the responsibility of the leadership of the HUMINT managerial community and of the intelligence business in general. They have been afraid to run the kind of operations necessary because of risks to their careers and to their reputations should they fail. Because of that, we have never had the kind of penetration in these groups we should have had. That remains a signal failure, and I do not see anything in any of the intelligence reform bills that is going to fix that, and that is what we need to have to beat the jihadis. Until you can change the culture of risk avoidance in the management of HUMINT, you are never going to be able to defeat the jihadis.

REUEL GERECHT

If good intelligence is the answer to the war on terror and to Islamic extremism, we are all dead. By contrast, I am fairly optimistic on the battle against al Qaeda and Islamic extremism. I am optimistic for two reasons. To begin with the second, it involves the Bush administration and the way it has responded to 9/11. I am largely in agreement with the way it has responded and part of it has to do with things that are beyond their control.

The first reason for my optimism involves the real unsung heroes of the post-9/11 world, the members of the American Muslim community. If the American Muslim community had been susceptible to the toxic call of al Qaeda and bin Laden, blood would be running in the streets. We would have more 9/11s. We would certainly have 3/11s everywhere.

That has not happened. In some ways this is actually surprising because if you look at the superstructure of the Muslim community in the United States, if you look at where the money has come from, you will see that it is overwhelmingly Salafi. It has been funded primarily by Saudi Arabia. If you take that and use it as a European parallel, and I do think Europe still remains the primary platform for an attack against the United States, then you would think that bin Laden would have had more luck. And if you go back to the early days of jihad, you can see these goals. If you look at the first, most important document that they put out, *The Encyclopedia of Afghan Jihad*, it is very clear that the objective there is to create cells in the West; it is not to have cells in the Islamic world. That is a secondary or tertiary issue. The primary goal is to have cells in the West. You have to kill Americans. Al Qaeda exists to kill Americans. That is its primary motivation. If it cannot do that, it will not survive. And it has not done that in the United States. The primary reason, and this is simply a guess on my part, is that the process of integration in the United States is significantly different from that in Western Europe. The absorption of the Muslim community in the U.S. is more or less successful and healthy. I look forward to the days of actually going into a mosque in the United States. I have gone to many in Western Europe and when you go into the radical mosques in Western Europe you get the distinct feeling of "uh-oh," of danger. I suspect that I would not have that same "uh-oh" feeling as much in the United States.

Another important fact is that we are going to do well because millenarian extremism in the Islamic world is not unknown. It has been there for some time; it recurs. My favorite millenarian movement of all times – I think it is certainly the most successful one in Islamic history – is the movement of the Qizilbash, the holy warriors or Sufi warriors that led to the foundation of the Safavid dynasty in Iran. If you think that al Qaeda is a tough group of individuals, of suicidal holy warriors, I suggest you go back and read about the Qizilbash movement in the 15th and 16th centuries, and then you will have a good idea of what true, hard-core holy warriors are like. By the way, they lost after they established their state. Millenarian movements always die out.

Now, the other reason for my optimism, and this has more to do with the Bush administration, is that I think they have responded to 9/11 reasonably well. I have certain problems with the way they have handled certain things, but I think the way they moved about in Afghanistan was alright. I wish they had fought the battles a little bit differently, but I suppose that, at this time in the game, these are peccadillos. As I said before, I think the response was correct. I think that people in the Middle East in particular, and beyond the Middle East, have gotten the idea that at least under the Bush administration the United States is willing to use military force and strike you if you establish terrorist camps. The age of the passive American reaction is over. The weakness which was a strong feature of the Clinton administration is over.

It is possible for 9/11 to recur but I am skeptical. I think that because of 9/11, the United States, whether you have Republicans or Democrats, now has a greater willingness to use force abroad. I think that is all for the good, because without those training camps, I am very skeptical that you can have a successful globalized movement.

What is happening with al Qaeda now is what happened with Islamic extremism before. It is falling into its component parts. That really doesn't scare me all that much; we have seen that before. It certainly would be worrisome if I lived in Indonesia. It would be worrisome if I lived in Saudi Arabia, and it may be worrisome in Egypt.

There were many, many good things about the war in Iraq. I still think there are many, many good things about the war in Iraq. I am very happy the Bush administration started it. For the purposes of Islamic extremism, I am particularly happy. When President Bush gave his speech before the National Endowment for Democracy, he understood something, something which particularly the Left in both the United States and Europe understood well before, and that is that there is a nexus between tyranny and Islamic extremism. If you go back and look, for example, at the thoughtful French critiques of Algeria, it is evident there was a nexus between the state of the Algerian regime after independence and the growth of FIS [Islamic Salvation Front], GIA [Armed Islamic Group], GSPC [Salafist Group for Preaching and Fighting], and a host of other people in the alphabet soup of Islamic militancy. The administration understands that, and I think that is an enormous step in the right direction.

The best works on this issue have been done by Bernard Lewis and Fouad Ajami, and I would suggest to Michael Scheuer that if he thinks these individuals do not know Islamic history, he needs to go back to school. You have to break that nexus. Now I am in favor of what the administration calls the democratic transformation in the Middle East. We will see just how forceful the administration wants to be in this process. Everyone knows that there is a great deal of opposition within the administration on this policy, as there would be in any administration. First and foremost, the State Department will fight it tooth and nail because the State Department, by its very nature, is about maintaining the status quo. But I suggest to you that any administration would continue in the direction of democratization, not just because Americans believe in democracy, and historically in exporting democracy, but also because Muslims themselves are moving in that direction.

What surprises me is what I would call discrimination against Muslims and the Muslim mind that is evident when people believe that Muslims cannot absorb Western ideas. The last two hundred years of Islamic history have been about the absorption of Western ideas, for example, in Iran. If you do not think the ideas of democracy have been penetrating Iran since the definitive moment of modern Iranian history, the 1905 and 1911 revolutions, that means you do not read Persian or even Persian translations. The Sunnis, for whatever reasons, are not as politically evolved. I would argue and suggest to you that, in fact, Sunnis have been on the receiving end of Western ideas as much as Shiites, or even more so. What we have going on now is in fact the absorption of a whole variety of different ideas. We have already seen that the Muslim Middle East can absorb socialism well. It absorbs nationalism well. It absorbs communism well. It has even absorbed fascism well. What we are going to see is how well the Middle East can absorb the democratic idea and move it forward. I would argue that, in fact, amongst the Shi'a and the Kurds in Iraq, it has been absorbed fairly well. And I remain reasonably optimistic that in Iraq you will see the Shi'a community drive forward the democratic process, and the small Sunni community, which I believe is divisible, will not succeed in bringing it down.

Further, I think the movement behind Grand Ayatollah Sistani is going to have a profound effect to the extent that, if Iraq goes off the rails, it is going to have an enormously bad effect on the United States. If it in fact succeeds, I believe Iraq will have an enormous effect on the rest of the Middle East. I think it will make it very, very difficult for other antidemocratic regimes, which is why those regimes will work strenuously to defeat the American project in Iraq. I do not think they can do it because I think that mainly the Shi'a community, but also the Kurdish community, are sufficiently committed to this enterprise, making very difficult for outside powers to bring it down. If you look at al Jazeera, if you look at the Arab press, it is striking to see the conversation about democracy now in the Middle East. It has penetrated into the blood system. Look also at Salafi Web sites. The vehemence that often is expressed about the idea of democracy is a reflection of the extent to which it has actually been absorbed into the Arab body politic. Now they are going to have the great debate.

The United States is also going to have a great debate, but we are not there yet. That debate will be about the extent to which we are going to run away. We are not going to do what the first Bush administration did. You might call that the "Djerejian Doctrine," named after the former assistant secretary of state for the Near East, who said, "We are not going to take the risk and support one man, one vote, one time." This was said also in relation to FIS in Algeria in 1991 when the military cracked down and annulled the election process. I hope we do not go in that direction again because what is essential is that fundamentalists become involved in this enterprise. Ultimately, it is going to be Shiite clerics and Sunni fundamentalists that defeat the phenomenon of Islamic extremism, and particularly bin Ladenism. They will destroy it; we will not.

I am not at all in favor of spending money and winning hearts and minds. I do not think it makes much sense. Whatever money the United States government has for public diplomacy should be used and spent in Europe where, in fact, public diplomacy does matter. They should not spend it in the Middle East where actions will speak louder than words. We may see this soon in Egypt, where Hosni Mubarak is not going to live forever. Egypt is going to be a very interesting country. I would keep a laserlike focus on it. I think that is where we are going to see the greatest chance of fundamentalists moving forward, demanding more open democratic representation. What they will do with it, I don't know. It is entirely possible that they will abort the democratic process. I am skeptical of that because I actually think there is in the heart of the Muslim political philosophy, the religious idea that every Muslim is a rational actor and accepts God voluntarily. This is one reason why Islamic extremists, the old version of Islamic extremists, certainly always wanted to take the state by a coup d'état. If you take the state by a coup d'état, you do not introduce the ideal voluntary association which has a profound track record in Islamic history. I think if you come into power democratically, it will be very difficult for fundamentalists to abort the process. But I say to you, even if they do abort the process, it is worth it because the evolution has to start.

Look back at Iran. In 1978 and 1979, there was no more anti-American country in the Middle East. There was no country in the Middle East which had a greater and more vigorous holy warrior culture. That holy warrior culture is now dead as a doornail. Iran is also probably the most pro-American country in the Middle East. You need to have that same evolution start in the Sunni Arab world. The sooner it starts, the better, because in the end that is what is going to finally kill off bin Ladenism and the Islamic extremism that hit us on 9/11.

DANIEL BENJAMIN

Let me try to go for a more pedestrian and schematic approach to what we are doing right and what we are doing wrong, beginning with what we are doing right. I think that at the level of tactical counterterrorism – which I would define principally as the intelligence and law enforcement operations that we use to wrap up terrorist cells and find leading al Qaeda operatives or other jihadists around the world – we are doing things the right way. True, there are a lot of questions about numbers, whether it is seventy-five percent of the leadership of al Qaeda that we have killed or captured or another figure. But I will take it on some faith that we have done pretty well, and certainly the fact that Khalid Sheikh Mohammed, Abu Zubaydah, and Ramzi Binalshibh are out of action is a very good sign.

I would add that one thing we ought to regain sight of now is the most effective way to conduct tactical counterterrorism. If you look at all the top al Qaeda people who have been wrapped up, all but two were taken in intelligence and law enforcement operations, and only two were actually killed through what I would call semi-military means. Both were killed by hellfire missiles fired from drones, a drone that was developed as a counterterrorism tool. None of them were killed on the battlefield. Quite frankly, I think you would have to ask whether any of our operations on the battlefield – and I'm a wholehearted supporter of what we did in Afghanistan – have made much difference in the war on terror beyond depriving al Qaeda of its sanctuary in Afghanistan. On the contrary, I think one can make a very strong argument that military means are, by definition, too violent and nonsurgical to advance the cause and that, more often than not, they will create more terrorists than they will remove. I cite as my source on this one Secretary Rumsfeld and his famous "snowflake" memo, which asked whether the harder we work the more behind we get.

But we should also look at other levels as well. First of all, we should look at the strategic level. How are we doing against the threat? Too often we define the threat as al Qaeda. Maybe we are doing well against al Qaeda, but it is hard for me to believe that we are doing well against the broader jihadi threat.

And there are a number of different ways of measuring this. What is the ideology and where do we find it? How much has it spread? It seems that al Qaeda's idea of using 9/11 as a kind of Roman candle to light up the sky, to enlighten the entire Ummah that al Qaeda was the sole true defender of Muslim dignities, worked pretty well. We have seen, first of all, that all or most of the ancillary groups, the satellite groups that bin Laden worked so hard to tie into his network, did in fact begin by carrying out follow-up attacks, whether it was in Indonesia or Riyadh or Istanbul. And we also saw that groups that hitherto had little or no relationship with al Qaeda were also motivated to accept the al Qaeda ideology and also the strategy of attacking the far enemy, attacking the United States, instead of carrying on these self-defeating efforts to attack the apostate governments of the Muslim world. We saw that in Casablanca. We seem to have seen that to some extent in Madrid, and my guess is that, as time goes on, we will see more of this.

Now is that a big danger? I think that the sort of galvanizing and splintering that we have seen in the jihadi world is a good news–bad news story. A lot of those groups are never going to constitute a very powerful threat. They are not going to have the technical sophistication, or the resources, or the know-how to carry out al Qaeda–type attacks. But that is a statistical matter, and it is only going to be most of them; never will it be all of them. It is entirely possible that in places such as Europe where there has been a pronounced trend towards radicalization, particularly among young Muslims who are alienated from the ambient society and not particularly happy with the accommodationist ethic of their parents, this trend will continue. We could see a lot more radicalism and we could see some very dangerous terrorism. In fact, one should never say that we cannot see anything worse than al Qaeda. We certainly can. The availability of high-class education and of very sophisticated technology in a place like Europe ought to concern us all.

I think we also see the failings of our strategy in the general viewpoints that exist in the Muslim world. The unpopularity of the United States right now is historic. Frankly, it is hard to see how Iraq bought us much in terms of fighting the terrorist movement. I am hopeful that Reuel is right, and that this is going to be one of the great dialectical turns in human history. But I guess I am just not all that convinced yet. When you look at the numbers of people who hate us in the populations of our very best friends in the Muslim world – to wit, Turkey, Jordan, Morocco, Pakistan – it is quite astonishing. It is hard not to believe that these people have not in some ways imbibed the bin Laden message. And the bin Laden message, if you really want to make it crude and short, is that the United States wishes to occupy Muslim lands and destroy Islam.

One of the interesting polls that came out after 9/11 was a poll that asked whether you thought that the United States posed an imminent threat of invasion to your country. In nine out of ten Muslim countries, they thought so or at least the majority of those polled said yes. The one exception was Nigeria which was just under 50 percent. This seems to me to be deeply worrisome and it suggests that even if the large majority of those people do not decide that they want to rush out and join their nearest cell, nonetheless, a number of people within that group are going to feel that, "Yes, al Qaeda is correct," and, "Yes, we ought to join up," and, "Yes, this is the only time to stand up for Muslim dignity and to make our lives better." This, after all, is what al Qaeda claims it will do through the removal of the United States from the region and the abolition of these apostate governments.

I think that we are doing poorly at the strategic level and we have not yet come up with something that is going to change the profile of the United States in the region. The Bush administration tried this with the Greater Middle East Initiative or Broader Middle East Initiative, but that died. The administration did not consult in the region nor in Europe. It was seen, I think appropriately, as not being the right way to go. Nonetheless, we do need something to put in that space. We need something that resembles strategic counterterrorism. We need something that is going to make Muslims in the world recognize that the United States is not the enemy and that we should not be the proxy punching bag for what is, ultimately, a civil war within Islam. We do not have such a strategy and I am deeply concerned that a strategy of democratization, which relies principally on the use of military force in Iraq and declaratory rhetoric in the United States, ultimately encourages the despots of the region to spurn our wishes and to manipulate us. I think we have seen plenty of that and you only have to look at the way some of the Central Asian states, more notable success stories, deal with the United States to recognize that our zeal for democratization is rather limited in its geographic scope.

There is one final bit of bad news, I would say, and that is that we have not really reckoned with the consequences of Iraq beyond those that have already been discussed in terms of our own interests, our own ability to preserve the lives of our troops and to put together a stable country. We may see a stable Iraq come out of the Kurdish and the Shiite zones, but it is very hard for me to believe that we are ever going to remove what is going to be a terrorist enclave in western Iraq for a long, long time to come. I think we have lost that battle. We can burn Fallujah and then we can wait for the rebels to come back, and they will indeed come back or they will move on to a half dozen other cities. And frankly, we are just not going to have the heart for urban warfare in all of these places. This is going to be a real problem.

We know that Islamist radicals around the world are focusing on Iraq. It is interesting to note, for example, that Pakistani jihadis now view Iraq as the big show and not Kashmir. This is quite extraordinary. It is depressing to think that decapitation videos have now become more popular than pornography in many parts of the Muslim world.

This is deeply disturbing. This means that a lot of people are experiencing the jihad vicariously. And what starts with vicarious enjoyment may ultimately evolve into a desire to do it in the flesh. I think that we need to recognize that the war on terror is not going to be best conducted through military means. We do need to find something to put in that hole where the Greater Middle East Initiative was. We need to change our profile in the region fairly dramatically and we need to build our own tactical counterterrorism capacity by working with others.

One of the great mistakes, I think, that has been made is that we have not seen this as an opportunity to build. There needs to be much greater capacity in the countries that want to fight terror. We have an anti-terrorism assistance program that was once very successful. It was increased after 9/11, but it has not gone very far since. We are only going to beat the jihadis if we act in tandem with allies who are prepared to work with us. Let's face it, we are going to need European allies over the long haul as we are going to need the cooperation of a lot of other countries that have not been particularly thrilled about the conduct of our foreign policy.

THE UNITED STATES VS. AL QAEDA: A PROGRESS REPORT

Question and Answer Session

Q. **KAREN GREENBERG:** What about the war against al Qaeda in the United States, which until March 11th was seen as an internal domestic question? Is there still a war against al Qaeda here?

A. **REUEL GERECHT:** I think the quick answer to that is no. If there was a war against al Qaeda in the United States, it would be all over the media. And the FBI certainly would not be prepared not to leak it, so no. I think it is a great, you might even say a miracle, blessing that we do not have a domestic front. If that were the case, we would be in a completely different situation.

A. **PAT LANG:** However much we may resent and dislike the kind of internal security measures that have been carried out here since 9/11, I think it has had a great effect indeed. If you look around at some of the things that were going on previous to the Great Calamity, there was a potential there for serious action in the United States and it has been dealt with quite severely, in some cases more severely than I like to contemplate. But I think it has been effective.

A. **DANIEL BENJAMIN:** I am a little more skeptical having, first of all, been through the law enforcement efforts of the late nineties. I am not particularly confident that we would have found the terrorists if they were here. We did not find them then. The vast majority of people who have been arrested have been wannabes and not members of al Qaeda.

Now, I do believe that if there is a presence, it is a small presence, but I think it is important to remember that al Qaeda has an extraordinary amount of patience and tends to carry out its operations at great intervals. The other thing to realize is that, from a jihadist perspective, and this is assuming that it is not necessarily core al Qaeda that we are talking about in the U.S., the show right now is Iraq. Yes, there is a lot of value to carrying out attacks elsewhere, but it is not like they think that they are losing and need to carry out that attack in the United States.

A. REUEL GERECHT: I disagree with that. I think that if al Qaeda exists to hit the United States, Iraq is a sideshow. And if it could hit the United States, it would. Now that is not to say that they might have developed or will develop a cell here. But that institution exists to kill Americans on American territory and that is far more magnetic than the battle in Iraq.

A. PAT LANG: I think the distinction which needs to be made here between al Qaeda as an organization and other forms of jihadi activity or potential jihadi activity is entirely artificial. They just do not organize themselves in a way that can be called an organization in fact. Islamic societies and Arab societies generally operate on the basis of a networked pattern of groups of varying sizes built around leaders and varying principles that seek consensus amongst each other and that support each other mutually in a kind of grand network. So to think that there is one organization called al Qaeda which could be a danger to you in the United States does not really reflect the reality of the opposition.

A. DANIEL BENJAMIN: Pat is absolutely right about the nature of the movement and we make big mistakes when we are overly schematic about the organization. We like to draw organizational charts. They like to bomb things. So I agree with him on that.

I guess I would just come back to my point vis-à-vis rules that, first of all, they are enormously patient to the extent that the people we may be rightfully worried about are jihadists. They may also be prepared to watch and let Iraq unfold for awhile. I don't agree that al Qaeda exists only to attack Americans. Ayman al-Zawahiri, for example, says it quite clearly. One of the top goals of al Qaeda's jihadist movement has to be the seizure of a state. And, frankly, I think that is what is going on.

Q. JEFF STEINBERG [*Executive Intelligence Review*]: Based on your opening remarks, the question that comes to mind is whether you anticipate that the next cakewalk is going to be in Iran?

A. REUEL GERECHT: No, I would not anticipate that, though I do think that the issue of the clerical regime's quest for nuclear weaponry is going to produce a very serious debate. It already is now finally producing that debate inside the American government and, eventually I think, we will get down to the pinch test and that will offer two options. One option is to allow Rafsanjani and Khomeini to develop a nuclear weapon. The second option is to try to preempt and delay it. I think that is the great debate and I would suspect that we will allow the clerical regime to develop nuclear weaponry. However, I do believe the president and the vice president really do wake up most mornings thinking about weapons of mass destruction being used against the United States. So I would not rule out a preemptive military strike against Iran.

A. PAT LANG: I would have to say from my previous experience with the Iranians that they have been, in fact, the major state sponsor of terrorist organizations against the United States over the period since the Iranian revolution. And if you look at Lebanon and the hostage-taking, the Iranian government was squarely behind that. They use a group of people recruited out of Hezbollah as cats' paws for the Iranian Ministry of Intelligence. They do not seem to have reformed much. You know, we keep looking for the moderate Iranians and we haven't quite found them yet.

I think that we are going to try every conceivable thing we can to prevent Iran from acquiring nuclear weapons. But, in the end, if they are obdurate in this and persist, we will be forced into the position in which military action will become unavoidable.

A. DANIEL BENJAMIN: It is hard to predict what the administration is going to do about Iran. I think Reuel's instincts are right. I do think, however, that we are not going to occupy Iran. We simply do not have the troops to do it, nor do we have the desire. But I do think that covert means might be used to try to disrupt their nuclear program.

Q. PHILLIP SMUCKER [Journalist, author of *Al Qaeda's Great Escape*]: How do you see the use of U.S. military power projected abroad? In Afghanistan, we did not throw the full force of the U.S. military into the battle. Many senior leaders of al Qaeda escaped. They went out of the country. In Iraq, we went in with 150,000 troops. Now al Qaeda is in there. An American cannot walk the streets of Baghdad without being kidnapped or killed. So how does the U.S. military project its force fighting al Qaeda?

A. REUEL GERECHT: I had disagreements with the way the Bush administration handled the military campaign in Afghanistan. However, I would say that I think bin Laden had a private retinue of somewhere between seventy-five and one hundred and twenty people in Afghanistan. To my knowledge, not one of them has been caught. That means bin Laden had a defensive plan for egress from Afghanistan. You could have tripled or quadrupled the number of soldiers and deployed them down in the region and border regions. But if you miss by a few hundred yards, you miss by a thousand. It is incredibly difficult terrain. I would have been in favor of the American military deploying a lot more force at Kandahar. They should have done it early on. Would we have been able to catch more of them? I don't know. I hope so, but that is water under the bridge now.

In Iraq, there are several things which the administration did that I would disagree with, but certainly a big one is that we did not view the former members of the former regime and the Sunni forces as a possible guerilla force. If you make a comparison to Nazi Germany, it is striking to see how many people we put into prison camps in Nazi Germany and how few we put into prison camps in Iraq. There were large communities of Iraqi intelligence officers who were left untouched.

A. DANIEL BENJAMIN: I think that the administration, through its advocacy of shock and awe, fell victim to a kind of messianism of its own, in terms of the efficacy of military power, and came to the belief that if we hit hard enough everyone would fall into line. That simply didn't happen. And we did not have the people on the ground. In this case, the United States is a victim of its own illusions, and I think military force is simply a very limited instrument when you are dealing with terrorists.

Q. MICHAEL SCHEUER: I would just like to make two quick points. The one point that Mr. Gerecht didn't mention on Iran, of course, is that the policy is no longer in our hands. It is in the Israelis' hands. The question is whether or not they will hit the reactors before we decide to invade. It is a question that has to be discussed, and I think that is the third option about your pinch theory. One more thing on al Qaeda: Osama bin Laden's goal is not in the first instance either to attack us or to attack anybody else. His first goal is to incite the Islamic world and instigate it to fight against us. So the idea that somehow attacking us is his first goal, I think, is incorrect.

My comment is this: whenever someone says democracy probably will not work in the Muslim world, you immediately get slapped back with the idea that you are saying Muslims cannot accommodate Western ideas or democracy. That is a kind of analysis by assertion. What we are saying is that, until you get over the hurdle of the separation between church and state, the idea of a democracy resembling the United States occurring in any Muslim country is absurd. And the history of American democracy has never been about exporting democracy except for the bloody-handed fantasies of Woodrow Wilson. There are very few Americans who are going to let their sons die to build a democracy in Iraq. Where we have exported democracy is to places with a common heritage – i.e., the Renaissance, the Reformation, and the Counter-reformation – like Eastern Europe and the Spanish countries of Latin America. It is not working in Russia where we have no shared heritage. So the idea that democracy is an exportable commodity is, I believe, a little madness.

A. PAT LANG: I would join you in feeling resentful. Every time I hear statements that the negative-minded SOBs in this country do not believe that Muslims or Iraqis or Arabs can govern themselves, or that they do not understand what democracy is and that they have never had democratic government anywhere, I see a really profound ignorance of history. If you look at the truth of this matter, these countries and regions have been self-governing for a very, very long time. A great many of these people who are educated in the West and have a deep understanding of our institutions and our societies know exactly how our system works.

The question is whether or not they want to get themselves together enough to apply it to their own governance. That is the big question. I am not sure what the answer is. You get Arab liberals, and we have heard some of that here today who say, "Well, you know, all you have to do is support the good guys and everything will fall into place." I do not think it is as easy as that. If it was that easy, you would have seen a whole lot more in the way of revolt and struggle inside these places.

A. REUEL GERECHT: The crux is whether you can have a recognized force higher than that of the holy law, and I think you actually are beginning to see that. This debate has been much more vigorous amongst the Shiite clergy than among the Sunni. But on the Sunni side, the clerical structure does not allow for the debate. This is one of the reasons why the Sunnis, I think, can actually sustain this because inside the Sunni world you do not have a higher authority that can dictate to you.

Actually you see that with al Qaeda. There is this constant grab-bag desire to try to find some religious authority to support this view, or that view, or another view. And you have this huge competition of trying to find support for your idea. In Algeria, you began to see fairly serious people challenging the idea that the holy law was in fact supreme over the popular vote. Now you have had those individuals who completely disagree, people like Ali Bin-Hajj, who thought the other way.

That is why you want the competition to evolve. You want fundamentalists screaming at each other. I suggest to you that, indeed, the absorption of these ideas is much more profound than people credit and that the old understanding that had people operating in isolation is erroneous now. If you go to Najaf and you talk to the senior clergy there, these individuals are not liberals. If you start seriously talking to them about the idea of maroof, about whether or not something is Koranically approved and has the weight of holy law, and if you ask them, "Is democracy maroof?" they say, "Yes, absolutely."

Now is there going to be a huge argument about whether there are some things that democracy cannot approve? Absolutely. But what I would suggest is that we do not want a democracy. For the battle against bin Ladenism, you do not necessarily want a democracy in the Middle East that is liberal in the Western sense. I do not think it is going to have a lot of traction. What you want to have there is something much more organic that may not be terribly liberal. You may have a lot of women, for example, who have grown up under the secular tyrannies of the Middle East who feel distinctly uncomfortable living in what may come in the Middle East, in what may come in Iraq. But all I suggest to you is that Western ideas have penetrated there much more profoundly than people think.

6 Al Qaeda's Media Strategy

MODERATOR: **Peter Bergen,** Fellow, New America Foundation, and terrorism analyst, CNN. PANELISTS: **Henry Schuster,** Senior Producer, CNN; **Octavia Nasr,** Senior Editor, CNN's Arab Affairs; **Paul Eedle,** former Middle East Correspondent, Reuters, and expert on al Qaeda's use of the Internet.

HENRY SCHUSTER

I want to start with a story that took place about four months ago. I was in front of the house at number five Momir Asma bin Mohammed Street. A week before, even a few days before, this was an unremarkable house on an unremarkable short side street near the Sahara Mall in the King Fahd neighborhood of Riyadh. But on this day, the houses in the street looked like they belonged in Baghdad, not Riyadh. There were literally thousands of pockmarks from bullet holes up and down the streets.

As for the house itself, number five, half of it stood looking normal on the outside. The other half was twisted as if in a half grimace. The heat, the intensity of the 120-degree heat from what must have been an explosion, had melted half of the front gate. As you walked up to the house as I did – I had tried to get there two nights before that when there had been a shootout between Saudi security forces and members of Saudi al Qaeda – the first thing that you noticed was that underfoot there were still hundreds of rounds that had become embedded in the asphalt.

The second thing that was noticeable was the smell. As you walked up to the front gates, you could smell from several houses away the smell of blood, literally boiling in the heat because it had not been cleaned up. And then, as you walked up to the front gate and peered inside, what you saw was the result of what had been a very brutal search, a brutal and efficient search after the shootout. There were mattresses. There were sheets. There were papers lying in the front courtyard.

What had been removed already were what I would call the standard accoutrements of the modern terrorist cells. There were Kalashnikovs – three dozen of them, I think. There were thousands of rounds of ammunition. There were plastic explosives. There were other sorts of explosives. There were RPGs. There was even a SAM-7 missile. But that is not all that was there. What the Saudi security forces had also taken away were the other things that have become essential accessories for any terrorist group, any al Qaeda–related terrorist group. And that was computers, video cameras, and editing equipment as well as a high-speed Internet connection.

If you went through the house, and if you looked at the weaponry, you could match up different scenes in the house and different pieces of weaponry with three very slick "documentaries" that had been put out by the Saudi branch of al Qaeda earlier in the year. These three videos showed a progression, beginning with footage as well as suicide statements from an attack at the al-Muhaya compound in November of 2003. There were cell phone calls as the attackers were driving up to the compound. There were statements, mostly in Arabic, from the suicide bombers. There were even a few lines from some of the suicide bombers in English, which were duly played over and over again on our network, CNN, and on NBC and on the BBC and in the Western media. I guess they were sophisticated enough to know that Western media would play this.

These three videos, if you went by them alone, had come at a time when they filled a void, a propaganda void. And these three videos seemed to chart the progression of an ever-growing and startlingly powerful movement in Saudi Arabia. There were shots of rooms full of people training. There were shots of vehicles being prepared for what was supposed to be the mission to attack the housing compound. And it was not just these three videos that were there. It was the weaponry that was shown. It was the online magazines. There were two different online magazines which showed everything from how to field strip an AK-47 to offering news digests and editorial commentary, increasingly about Iraq.

As you walked up to this house, you saw that this was in many ways the word made flesh. It was from here that the bricks and mortar of terrorism were being conducted against housing compounds, against individuals. This was also the place that Paul Johnson's head was discovered inside the freezer. This was the place where he had likely been killed. Just literally days before the raid on this house, there was a video that had been circulating in cyberspace that showed his execution. And, in fact, what had triggered the whole shootout was a Saudi police car patrolling down the street. One of the people inside saw it and began firing, and within an hour there were hundreds of Saudi security forces surrounding the building, rather ineptly shooting at it. And in the ensuing firefight, the most recent head of Saudi al Qaeda was killed and his family was captured.

But what the house and its contents – its modern accessories and its "documentaries" – served to underscore was the difficulty involved in discerning how much of this was propaganda and how much was reality. For example, the Saudi government actually found itself on the defensive after the attacks on the Oasis compound in Khobar because, as part of the propaganda campaign, the al Qaeda people who were writing online said that it had been an inside job, that they had received help from Saudi security forces. Now, in retrospect, this was probably untrue. Nevertheless, there was the intent to project the idea of a certain amount of force to create the image that Saudi al Qaeda was in many ways much more powerful than they actually were.

At this house there were visible, physical, tangible, and gruesome reminders that there was an intersection between the propaganda campaign – the media strategy, if you will – and the actual acts of terrorism. But what it also served to underscore was that the modern terrorist cell, or the more recent al Qaeda cell, has the bullets. It has the cameras. It has the bombs. In one sense, it has the studio. We saw that apparently taking place in Fallujah, Iraq, where U.S. forces discovered what they called a chamber of horrors, inside of which they felt that several videos of executions had been recorded.

The larger point to take away from this house was that at number five Momir Asma bin Mohammed Street, al Qaeda, both the group and the movement, used twenty-first-century technology in pursuit of fourteenth-century aims. That this should be so is hardly surprising because, almost since al Qaeda's founding, it has had an obsession with the media. When al Qaeda classic – that which pre-dated 9/11 – was formed, it had a very elaborate structure. They formed four committees, and one of those committees was a media committee. The person that ran the media arm of al Qaeda, even during the early 1990s, had the name Abu Musab Reuter. So they were sophisticated.

If you think about it, there was not much point in bin Laden or any of his inner circle, including Ayman al-Zawahiri or Mohammed Atef, declaring war on the West if they could not get the West to pay attention. It was not enough to fax their fatwas to the Pakistani media or to some segments of the Arab media. They sought to do interviews with Western media. It is worth remembering that before al Qaeda and al Jazeera, Osama bin Laden did interviews with the Western media. Peter Bergen, Peter Arnett, Scott McCloud, Robert Fisk, John Miller, and others interviewed him. It was only in May 1998, when al Qaeda declared its war, that it went public with its war against the West. It called a press conference. It escorted members of the Pakistani media across the border and in front of them declared its fatwa.

It was not until the end of 1998, then, that we saw the most profound shift in the al Qaeda media strategy, and that shift came about because of al Jazeera. It didn't come about because they deliberately targeted al Jazeera. The irony here was that at the end of 1998, Peter Bergen and I were talking about another interview that we had hoped to conduct with Osama bin Laden. We were sitting in our offices in Washington and we got a call from somebody in Pakistan who had been helping us try to pave the way for this interview. The person said, "I'm sorry, it's too late, so-and-so went in and is doing it with al Jazeera and that's where this interview is going take place." Bin Laden had gotten his message out to the West, but not to what in al Qaeda terms would be called the "near enemy," the Arab and Muslim world. So al Jazeera offered a chance for bin Laden to speak, if not uninterrupted, then certainly untranslated and fairly unremediated. This was important because it quickly became apparent that CNN and others would be getting their video from al Jazeera. The word could first get out in the Arab media and through satellite television. The Arab media now offered a venue for bin Laden to get his message out. That was really what had happened up until 9/11.

There was another aspect that showed al Qaeda's sophistication, and that was the fact that, even in Sudan and certainly in Afghanistan, al Qaeda – that is, bin Laden and his high command – had a satellite dish and a VCR wherever they went. What they did was record newscasts from the BBC, from CNN, from al Jazeera and from any other networks that they could. They were inveterate tapers. Some of this was for their own edification and some of this was to record the interviews that had been done with the Western media. Some of this was to play to the recruits in the training camps. In my office I have a chart from one of the training camps. It basically told new recruits about how they could come and watch this bin Laden interview with CNN or that bin Laden interview with ABC.

These tapes were required viewing inside the camps, but they were doing something else with the tapes that became apparent at the beginning of the summer of 2001. That is when al Qaeda formed its own production company, called al Sahab. They took footage that they had recorded off of CNN. They took footage that they had recorded off of al Jazeera. They mixed it in with their own footage of Osama bin Laden, and they put out videos. The first video that appeared was a video CD that made the rounds, especially in the Gulf area in the summer of 2001. It was this video CD more than anything that had Peter Bergen calling me on the morning of September 10th, saying, "You know, I think there's going to be something and I think it's going to be somewhere in Saudi Arabia." That's where the U.S. intelligence community and most of us thought that something was going to happen, primarily because al Qaeda was spreading its message through video CDs.

After 9/11, things changed and accelerated. We saw a rapid regression. First there was a fax. Then there was the Internet with al-nida.com, which was for all intents and purposes an official al Qaeda Web site. And then, fairly quickly after that, there was a series of video and audio messages. Twenty-eight, I think, at last count. Most of these messages went to al Jazeera. In a couple of instances they went to other Arab networks, and in two instances they were posted directly to the Internet. So things accelerated at a rapid rate.

Al Qaeda did not have a home base, it did not have a place to record its videos, yet twice in 2002 it was still able to put out very sophisticated, very well-edited videos with Osama bin Laden in them. We never saw his face at that point, but we heard his words. In 2003 we saw some fresh video of him, though it was unclear where that was shot. But there was the same pattern: the video went to al Jazeera. It is worth listening to what an al Qaeda spokesman himself said about why they were doing this. He wrote:

> Sheikh Osama knows that the media war is not less important than the military war against America. That's why al Qaeda has many media wars. The Sheikh has made al Qaeda's media strategy something that all TV stations look for. There are certain criteria for the stations to be able to air our videos, foremost of which is that it has not taken a previous stand against the mujahideen. That maybe explains why we prefer al Jazeera to the rest.

The spokesman added another purpose for the media strategy which was that the Sheikh wanted to give out news that would make the Muslims feel proud and thus give him a moral boost, to help attract followers who would be able to sacrifice their lives for God at any moment. That was their media strategy. Create the appetite. Use al Jazeera primarily. The sophistication of the media strategy seemed to multiply with the availability of the technology. So you had the faxes, the video CDs, the Internet postings, and the videos themselves that were being delivered.

Now various permutations have taken place since 9/11. We have talked about how al Qaeda has transformed itself, to put it in Coca-Cola terms, from "al Qaeda Classic" to "Diet al Qaeda" or "al Qaeda Lite." Al Qaeda has transformed itself from an organization to an ideology, to what Osama bin Laden's brother-in-law recently called the *idea* of Osama. So we have seen a proliferation of al Qaeda–related and sympathetic groups using the same media tactics as al Qaeda central. Everybody has a Web site. Everybody has their own production unit producing video documentaries. Just a few weeks ago, for example, my colleagues and I got a video CD from a group in South Waziristan. Again, it had a production company branding on it. It was not al Jazeera, it was a local production company, and the video was about local tribesman. They edited and produced a very sophisticated CD video that they sent to us. It was an hour long. And to make it perfectly clear at the beginning and end what the point of the video was, there was a picture of President Musharraf and bullet holes kept appearing on his face. So these offshoots from al Qaeda have added one horrible twist – which they got from the Chechens, who have been no slouches themselves over the years when it comes to video production – and that is the showing of executions.

It is a much more crowded house now on the Internet, and it is hard sometimes to even keep your sanity, just watching some of the material that is out there. So in one sense, that brings us back to number five Momir Asma bin Mohammed Street or its equivalent in Iraq. Because, as well as being their exercises and propaganda, these are the studios of the terrorists, their execution chambers for hyperreality TV. And this is just the latest twist in al Qaeda's media strategy.

The irony of all of this is that you might think that bin Laden himself risks having his own message lost in what has become an increasingly crowded spectrum as it fills up with all these messages. But that is not the case at all, as we saw the weekend before the 2004 presidential election. The Saudi videos themselves show how eager these offshoots are to embrace the idea and image of Osama bin Laden. He is the brand. His face is in many ways as ubiquitous as the Nike swoosh or McDonald's golden arches. And when he chooses to speak his words, and now with his reappearance on videotape his face, gets spread across the Internet in a way that would make any savvy marketer envious.

Osama bin Laden's media strategy has succeeded in two ways. One, it spreads fear in the West. And secondly, it garners support in the Arab world. It has also failed in one very important way. If his aim is to reach the public in the West, no one is listening to his message. When you kill 3,000 people, you have a hard time getting your audience to care about anything that you are actually saying. He gets the fear and he gets the anger. But he is not getting people in the West to actually listen to him.

OCTAVIA NASR

On the 20th day of September 2001, exactly nine days after 9/11, I went on a mission to the small emirate of Qatar in the Arabian gulf. My mission was to visit a tiny but daring station that would soon become one of the most famous, some will say infamous, television names around the world. Al Jazeera had the only correspondent working in Kabul at the time and we were interested in cooperating with the network in Afghanistan.

I had no idea what was waiting for me. It never crossed my mind that the events of the next five weeks would shape not just my world forever but the entire universe, including the future of my children and of their children. The trip, which lasted a good twenty-nine-plus hours, went by like a flash in my mind because I was buzzing with ideas. My adopted country, which I had just left, was mourning the loss of thousands of lives. Families were searching for their loved ones through the rubble at Ground Zero, and people were searching for answers to questions they never thought they would ask. The whole world was in shock. The nation was planning its next move, which seemed very obvious to many of us, namely attacking Afghanistan, where Osama bin Laden was enjoying the generous hospitality of his comrades-in-arms. The Taliban were then the rulers of Afghanistan.

I was headed to a world that was not too sure about how to feel about what had just happened. Arabs first thought the attacks were too sophisticated for al Qaeda to undertake. Conspiracy theories surfaced, mixed with shock. They were also mixed with a bit of gloating as they saw America "tasting a little bit of its own poison," as many at that time believed. The Middle East seemed to be on pause waiting for someone to announce the next move. Most Arabs and Muslims I spoke with seemed to support bin Laden, not so much for his killing of innocent people, but more for the way he stood up to the "tyrant" called America. I was moving in between two different worlds, two very different worlds. And for the first time in my life I could not bring them together.

I witnessed first hand the switch al Qaeda made from paper statements to video statements, and was able to see how they shaped their message to fit the medium. I will share with you my impressions from listening to hundreds of hours of bin Laden and al-Zawahiri tapes, and translating some of them in real time. I have seen how bin Laden and his deputies have used the media to their advantage and have kept us all on our toes waiting for what's coming next.

As my plane approached Doha International Airport in Qatar, I checked the local newspaper that was available on board. The headline that day said that the Sultan of Oman has sent a telegram to the Emir of Qatar as he flew through Qatar air space, thanking him and the people of Qatar for their short air hospitality. That was the headline! I asked myself, "Where is the news of the terror attacks and the repercussions? Why isn't there any reporting this morning on the thousands of innocent people killed and the most diabolic act of terror in history? How can a greeting from the Sultan be more important than all that?" This is the Middle East, I reminded myself, where old monarchies dictate policy and control the media, using them as mouthpieces and propaganda machines.

Then it occurred to me that only a few years back, the Emir of Qatar had sent his father to Europe for his summer vacation and while his father was gone, took over the country in a bloodless coup. The old Emir never returned to Qatar. "Isn't this part of the reason why bin Laden enjoys a following in the Arab world?" I asked myself. Ask anyone who reveres bin Laden, and he or she will tell you that bin Laden's al Qaeda started as a rebellion against Arab regimes that do nothing other than live in luxury while at the same time they say that their Muslim brothers face persecution in Palestine, Chechnya, Afghanistan, Bosnia, and elsewhere around the world.

Though I did not know it at the time, my first Monday at the all-news Arab network would serve as my first real introduction to Osama bin Laden and his terror network, al Qaeda. On the morning of September 24th, as we were discussing with much intensity how we would coordinate our coverage in Afghanistan, the director general of al Jazeera took a quick call from the office of Mullah Omar in Kandahar. Later, during the same meeting, the assistant came in with a paper which she handed over to the boss and said, "We just got this from Afghanistan." The director general gave it to the editor-in-chief, who left the meeting room for a few minutes and returned as if nothing happened.

A few minutes later my phone rang. It was CNN. Well, I thought, it can't be urgent. My boss is new. I'm in meetings all day, I thought, so I did not answer. Then my phone rang again, as we were wrapping up the meeting. My phone kept ringing incessantly, so I excused myself and took the call. My boss was on the phone saying very calmly but intensely, "Al Jazeera just aired a statement from al Qaeda. Can you find out if it's authentic?" I put my boss on hold and turned around and repeated the same thing to the group. "It is signed by Osama bin Laden himself. Of course it's authentic," the director general said. "Do you want a copy of it?" I said, "Well, I'd rather have it faxed to Atlanta, if it's not too much to ask." "Oh, no problem at all," he replied. The fax was on its way to Atlanta within minutes. At that moment a relationship was born, not only between our two networks – al Jazeera and CNN – but also between bin Laden and the West.

In its archives, CNN had a copy of bin Laden's signature on an affidavit, and as I am sure many of you know, it was a perfect match with the signature that came to al Jazeera's office in Doha. While Western news rooms were busy reporting on the al Qaeda fax statement calling on Pakistan to resist a U.S. attack on Afghanistan, the al Jazeera bosses were having lunch at the diplomatic restaurant in Doha. Al Jazeera aired what it had. End of story. They did not need to authenticate the statement. They did not have to match signatures to know that this was bin Laden. They did not need to bring in the experts to analyze what was in the message. And from this point forward al Jazeera's name would be linked to bin Laden's, and the whole world would start taking notice of what happened on al Jazeera.

This was the beginning of a new era. A terror network was lifting itself up from the dark ages by adapting itself to the most sophisticated technologies. This terror network would provide its audience with the elements that defined the biggest networks. They would broadcast the story, analyze it, invite guests to comment on it, and monitor it. "Bin Laden dead. Bin Laden injured. Bin Laden on 9/11. Bin Laden on the U.S. elections. Bin Laden wants Bush. No. He wants Kerry." We became an obsessed nation. And that is exactly what bin Laden wanted and still wants: i.e., a terror network that uses some of the best technologies that Western culture can offer, from the Internet to video clips, to propagate its message and keep us all on our toes. It makes you wonder how much of this is al Qaeda's strategy and how much of it is our own doing. Did you ever think of the moment when we all became obsessed with bin Laden?

Henry Schuster told us earlier that we were always interested in hearing what bin Laden had to say because, more often than not, an attack followed. But what happened since 9/11 deserves to be looked at closely, as bin Laden's popularity among Muslim extremists and militants has soared. He became a terror mastermind, an idol with many wanting to be him, beginning with al-Zarqawi.

Let's look at one of bin Laden's recent video clips. It pictured bin Laden taking a walk up mountains and down hills. This did not look like a man on the run or a man in hiding. This was the picture of a man enjoying nature and posing for the camera. The last tape from bin Laden came just two days before the 2004 U.S. presidential elections – proof that the man was well. He was wearing his golden robe, the one you save for a special occasion. Al Qaeda was using the media here to project a statesman-like image of its leader. There were no machine guns around. Bin Laden was calm and poised, elevating himself to the level of the U.S. presidential candidates. The man left no room to doubt that the video was recent, and he spared no effort to show us that he was alive and well.

When you have a message and you intend to deliver it effectively, you need to understand your recipients. Bin Laden knew who was listening to him, and he shaped his message to their liking. He made himself a hero in their eyes. He gave them what they wanted and what he thought they needed. He turned them into an audience while he delivered hour-long speeches which he disseminated using his known improvisational skills and his deep knowledge of the Koran. As a Muslim cleric once told me, bin Laden has "the unprecedented genius to manipulate the interpretation of the Koran and turn some of the most popular verses into vehicles of evil and diabolic intention."

One other important al Qaeda media moment came earlier, on October 7, 2001. As the U.S. strikes on Afghanistan began, al Jazeera aired what many consider to be the first al Qaeda TV production meant for the world to see. I was still at al Jazeera, and I remember that night being summoned to the control room for something big. Al Jazeera's control room had always been off limits during live broadcasts, but it was not off limits to me that night. I walked into a full control room. Al Jazeera's bigwigs were all there. There was also the cameraman documenting the coverage. The anchor talked to Tayseer Alouni in Kabul.

Tayseer rolled the tape live as we all watched a bearded man speaking. All those present in the control room tried to guess the identity of that person. When the shot showed the whole group sitting in a cave-like setting, someone suggested this was Suleiman Abu Gheit, the number three man in al Qaeda. Next to him was Osama bin Laden and Ayman al-Zawahiri. The control room told the anchor, who repeated the information, seemingly unable to assimilate either the impact and scope of such a tape or its timing. That moment seemed like one from an absurdist Samuel Beckett play. The sound got mixed up in my head, and all I could hear was "Bin Laden will speak. Bin Laden will speak." I looked at my phone. It did not have any reception. I ran outside the control room, back to my station and sent a message to my boss at CNN headquarters in Atlanta, "Bin Laden will speak on al Jazeera next."

I hurried back to the control room. Instead of bin Laden, al-Zawahiri spoke next. I remember him explaining to the American people that it was their country's foreign policy that brought the 9/11 attacks on them. Just as a well-planned performance would go, bin Laden spoke last and went straight to the point. He said, "There is America hit by God in one of its softest spots. Its greatest buildings were destroyed. Thank God for that. There is America full of fear from its north to its south, from its west to its east. Thank God for that."

For the next three weeks there would be more tapes from bin Laden, more drama, and even an invitation to CNN to submit questions for the man to answer. And for the next three years, listening, translating, and analyzing al Qaeda would become an important part of my job. When I sit in the translation booth waiting for bin Laden or al-Zawahiri to speak, I feel my heart racing, not so much because I am worried about the translation, but because I know how many millions of people will get a glimpse of the terrorists through my very voice and the very words I will say. It is a huge responsibility, but one that is most certainly exciting and rewarding. When I translate bin Laden I have the advantage of hearing him, hearing his intonation, and hearing the kind of nuances that indicate whether he's feeling down or feeling energized.

Unlike our viewers, who hear al Qaeda through a translator, I hear it raw. Raw, it has a much stronger impact. As I listen in the quiet of a translation booth, my first job is to identify the voice and determine if it is bin Laden or al-Zawahiri. Over the years I have become very aware of how bin Laden and other al Qaeda leaders speak – their enunciation, their sentence construction, their breathing patterns, even their favorite lines and stories, and of course, their message. But I am still not sure al Qaeda has a clear media strategy. What I do know is that al Qaeda, by which I mean Osama bin Laden and Ayman al-Zawahiri, has stayed on message regardless of the medium they have used. They have proven over the past three years that they are versatile and able to shape their message to fit the medium they are utilizing and the audience they are interested in.

PAUL EEDLE

If we want to understand how al Qaeda has survived and adapted since the war in Afghanistan, how it has transformed itself from the organization that carried out the 9/11 attacks to the dispersed social movement of today, then the most important single factor to look at is its use of the Internet. The Internet is a weapon of great power in twenty-first-century warfare. Let me just look at one recent example that shows the effectiveness of this weapon in the hands of one of the most recent al Qaeda affiliates, al-Zarqawi's group in Iraq.

For the whole of 2003, Abu Musab al-Zarqawi was known to the public only through leaks from American and Jordanian intelligence. Then, in little more than a month, during April and May of 2004, he rocketed to worldwide fame, infamy if you will, by a deliberate combination of extreme violence and Internet publicity. It began in early April, when al-Zarqawi issued a half-hour audio recording which explained exactly who he was, what he had done, and why he was fighting. It was a comprehensive, branding statement. And it showed, incidentally, just how differently from Osama bin Laden he viewed the world, yet still stayed on message. He said he was fighting a jihad to defend Islam against an American-led crusader campaign. America had invaded Iraq to steal its wealth, to block the expansion of Islam, and to protect Israel.

But in Iraq, al-Zarqawi said that the real enemies were the Shiites and the Kurds. The Kurds were in league with the Israelis. The Shiites were not Muslims and throughout history had fought to undermine true Islam. America, he said, wanted to set up Kurdish and Shiite statelets to prevent the forces of true Sunni Islam from reuniting. So he claimed responsibility for bombing the headquarters of the UN, America's puppet, and for bombing the Shiite shrine in Najaf, an attack that killed the most popular Shiite politician, the man who would probably have been elected president in January if he had lived, Ayatollah Mohammed Baqir al-Hakim. The reformed Iraqi police and army, according to al-Zarqawi, were would-be targets because they had become platforms for Shiite power. He said,

> The hissing of these snakes – that's the Shiites – has begun to rise again and they have lifted their heads to draw them out of the region where their allies, the Americans, and the dregs and mad among the Sunni Muslims [are]. Through their military brigades and their secret and public organizations, they have penetrated sensitive positions and taken control of the police and army. They are preparing to inherit the earth and control the country to establish a rejectionist – that means Shiite – state stretching from Iran through Iraq, esoteric Syria, Lebanon and the party of gods and the cardboard kingdoms of the Gulf.

That was published on the Internet. It was not given to al Jazeera. I'm not sure al Jazeera would have seen the news value in it. The Internet gave Zarqawi the means to build a brand very quickly. Suddenly this mystery man had a voice, if not a face, and a clear ideology to explain his violence. But what is the point of an insurgent group building a brand and establishing a public profile in that way? The answer is, they want to magnify the impact of their violence. In 2003, the bombings of the UN and in Najaf and of the Red Cross headquarters and of many Iraqi police stations certainly did send messages. But those messages were open to different interpretations, and al-Zarqawi needed to kill a lot of people to get noticed. By using the Internet, al-Zarqawi was able to control the interpretations of his message and to achieve his impact with smaller operations, even with failed operations.

Before the end of April, his group started to issue communiqués on a message board on the Internet called "The Lansar." The first communiqué claimed responsibility for a suicide speed boat attack on Iraq's off-shore oil export terminal in the Gulf. The operation failed. No exports were affected, but it still shook oil markets because al-Zarqawi publicized it through the Internet. In May, using this force multiplier effect to the maximum for the first time, al-Zarqawi personally cut off the head of Nicholas Berg live on video and had the footage posted on the Internet. I rode the London underground in central London the next day, and every single front page down the carriage had the image of Nick kneeling in his orange jumpsuit before the man who was about to kill him. The entire purpose of the beheading was to videotape it to create images that would grip the imaginations of friends and enemies alike. And it worked. Al-Zarqawi risked almost nothing in that operation. What does it take to capture an unarmed man and cut his head off in a secure safe house and dump his body? There were no suicide operations involved. There was no risk at all. Yet that moment started a withdrawal of foreign contractors which, with repetition, has paralyzed reconstruction work in Iraq and done as much if not more to undermine U.S. plans. He planned the bomb that killed 100 people in Najaf, and he made himself a hero to jihadis across the world.

In that short month, we saw several of the features of the Internet that have made it such a powerful weapon. First, the Internet has a global reach, especially when the Net plugs into relatively free broadcast and print media, not just in the West but increasingly in the Arab world. It can reach a global audience almost instantly. Second, the Internet can sustain physically scattered networks of people through message boards such as The Lansar, through email lists, and through instant messenger voice chat. The jihadis are scattered in scores of countries, pursued by security services, so they continue to collaborate and reinforce their identity through the Net. This is how the Net has underpinned the resilience of al Qaeda and its ability to replicate itself, as we have seen in Iraq and Saudi Arabia.

Third, the Internet is resilient and secure. Throughout the recent crisis in Iraq over the British hostage Ken Bigley and the U.S. offensive in Fallujah, al-Zarqawi's group was able to continue to publish communiqués and videos, even if satellites and mobile phones were too dangerous for the insurgents to use. As long as they have access to a single landline, they can talk to the world. The group's media spokesman, who uses the handle Abu Maysara al-Iraqi, felt secure enough to post his messages at the same time every night during the Bigley crisis. Even with all of the fighting, and with everything that has happened in Iraq over the last six weeks, I was able yesterday to download a beautifully produced one-hour video praising the effective number two person in al-Zarqawi's group, Sheikh Abu Anas al-Shami, who was killed by an American rocket during an abortive attack on Abu Ghraib prison in September.

Lastly, the Internet is two-way, unlike al Jazeera. This is not just a matter of publishing. This is a matter of research. We all know the experiences of colleagues of ours who have been Googled when they have been held by insurgents in Iraq, their lives depending on what showed up. Al-Zarqawi's audio recording in April quoted *The New York Times*, which I don't think has a delivery service in Fallujah, so this guy is absolutely in touch with the Internet.

But it is not just Abu Musab al-Zarqawi, it is the whole broad al Qaeda movement. The core al Qaeda affiliates have all been using the Internet since 9/11, particularly since the war in Afghanistan, to pursue their very consistent goal of destroying American power in the world. Thousands of pages of text, tens of hours of audio recordings and video productions, hundreds of thousands of postings on message boards have been published to try to persuade people across the world that Islam and the West are at war and that the West is the aggressor.

Now what is the impact of all this? We cannot prove cause and effect, but a number of people have mentioned some of the opinion surveys in America and in the Arab world which have produced data that I think should be of great concern to Americans. The surveys may by familiar to you but you need to think about them in the context of this media effort. If you were the chairman of a major corporation, say Chairman of GM, and you had been running a multimillion dollar campaign for some new concept in SUVs and you saw numbers like these, whether you could prove cause and effect or not, you'd give a bonus to the marketing department.

Interestingly, the Pew Research Center's findings in August showed that liberal and young Americans increasingly agree with the proposition that U.S. wrongdoing may have motivated the 9/11 attacks. More than half of Democrats and nearly half of people under thirty take that view, up from forty percent and less than thirty percent three years ago. However, the opposite is true of older people and conservatives. Only seventeen percent of Republicans and nineteen percent of people over sixty-five say that U.S. wrongdoing played a part.

When we turn to the Arab world, however, the survey data are stark. The two best known polls, the Pew Research Center and Zogby International, both show overwhelming hostility to the United States. One country to look at in this context is Egypt, where I used to live. I think Egypt has been the biggest single recipient of U.S. aid in the last twenty years. Ninety-eight percent of people polled in Egypt, however, view America unfavorably. That is a staggering return on investment. Contrast this with the Ukraine, for instance, where I'm not sure very much was spent at all and yet people seem to be demonstrating in the tens of thousands for what are essentially our concepts of liberal democracy.

The reason for the lack of support for the U.S. is clear. It is about policy. Above all, it is about the invasion of Iraq. It is about support for Israel. We found negative views of U.S. policy towards the Palestinians running at eighty-nine to ninety-five percent, negative views of policy on Iraq between seventy-eight and ninety-eight percent, and on terrorism, on the war on terrorism, negative views ran at seventy-five to ninety-six percent. Many Arabs also even support violence, at least against certain types of targets and in certain circumstances. In March, the Pew Center found support for suicide bombings against Americans in Iraq and against Israelis by Palestinians. Seventy percent of those polled in Jordan support attacks in Iraq. Eighty-six percent support attacks on Israelis.

There is no evidence one way or the other that al Qaeda's media machine has produced these attitudes, but what is certain is that when al-Zarqawi or Osama bin Laden or al-Zawahiri talks about fighting back against the American-led crusader campaign, they are tapping into a view of events that is shared by an overwhelming majority of people in the Arab world, as well as a considerable number of Muslims in this country and in Europe. This has big implications for the future of the conflict with al Qaeda.

The information campaign, or as some still would have it, the war of ideas or the struggle for hearts and minds, is important to every war effort. In this war it is an essential objective because the larger goals of U.S. strategy depend on separating the vast majority of nonviolent Muslims from the radical militant Islamist jihadists. But American efforts have not only failed in this respect, they may also have achieved the opposite of what is intended. American policy makers may feel that these attitudes are so deeply entrenched that there is no point in trying to change them. This is a defeatist policy. Winning Arab hearts does not mean reversing

U.S. policies. It is, after all, U.S. policy that there should be a Palestinian state alongside the State of Israel.

It is U.S. policy that Iraq should be free and democratic. As others have said, deeds need to match words. These policies may not need to be torn up and started again, but they need to be pursued in dramatically new ways with imagination, courage, and a much better understanding of how al Qaeda's media strategy exploits deeply held views across the world. Let me leave you with just one question. If you were Condoleezza Rice, and Mustafa Barghouti won a mandate from his prison cell as President of Palestine, what would you do?

AL QAEDA'S MEDIA STRATEGY

Question and Answer Session

Q. AMY IBRAHIM [CFI International]: My experience in working with both al Qaeda on the Web and U.S. media organizations is that sometimes, when a new video or audio statement comes out, it is not deemed to be newsworthy by U.S.-based networks until al Jazeera wants to air it. In recent months there have been a few statements directed at al Jazeera by al Qaeda saying that if the network does not air the video or the audiotape in its entirety then al Qaeda will stop releasing that media directly to al Jazeera. Do you have any comments on that, or have you seen that in your experience, and what do you think will be the outcome of that?

A. OCTAVIA NASR: I am not aware of the al Qaeda threat to al Jazeera that you talked about. One thing I will say about Western media and al Jazeera and how each deals with material from al Qaeda is that al Jazeera just puts the stuff on air, end of story. The Western networks sometimes carry the footage for a whole week. Even through the weekend, we are still talking about the same thing that al Jazeera aired a few days ago. So I do see an obsession. On the one hand, we complain that al Jazeera airs this stuff. On the other hand, we run it a lot more than they do. So this is definitely something for all of us to think about.

Q. PAUL CRUICKSHANK [CSIS]: How do you counter this ideology on the Internet? Should there be a proactive attempt to win the hearts and minds of Muslims? Isn't it maybe more important for moderate Muslims to go on the Internet and to make their presence felt? I think there hasn't been enough moderate Muslim presence on the Internet, making their sites attractive to young Muslims all around the world.

A. **PAUL EEDLE:** I think moderate Muslims find themselves in an impossible bind. Whenever anything happens, they are expected to roll out condemnation and yet at the same time, they are expected not to criticize U.S. policies which they see as extremely damaging to people they care deeply about. I think moderate Muslims across the Middle East are crippled by being unable to speak out in favor of democracy and in favor of Western values, because they are then tainted by their association with America.

Q. **AUDIENCE PARTICIPANT:** My question is about designing and conveying a message to Arab rulers. How can we convey the message to Arab rulers that unless they show some respect for human life or regret for the killing of innocent people, they are contributing to Islamic terrorism and its killing of those innocent people?

A. **OCTAVIA NASR:** I don't think it is our role to tell the Arab governments what to do or to tell the U.S. government what to do, for that matter. Our job is to report the news.

Q. **MATTHEW LYONS [Counterterrorism analyst]:** Al Qaeda has largely succeeded in what I think is one of the core components of its message which is directed to the Ummah, namely that the West is an aggressor. The follow-up to this is that there needs to be a response, listeners need to join the jihad. Clearly the messages have resonated. Is there any chance that they might actually succeed in the strategic goal behind that message, which is to incite some sort of uprising or holy war?

A. **HENRY SCHUSTER:** Having just spent some time in Saudi Arabia, I think the answer is that if anybody succeeds in inciting uprisings, it will be the respective governments more than al Qaeda. I don't think that there is evidence there of huge organizations on the ground. One of the paradoxes of the Internet is that it creates a virtual community. The question is, how much of it is the Wizard of Oz effect, where you pull back the curtain and see how much of it is actually real?

Q. SHAUN WATERMAN [UPI]: My question is for Octavia Nasr and Paul Eedle. You have both heard bin Laden speaking in Arabic. I have been told that he actually speaks quite beautifully and is a great orator. Is that true? Could you talk a little bit about his rhetorical style, the kind of Arabic he speaks, etc.?

A. OCTAVIA NASR: He is eloquent, very eloquent. He uses classical Arabic, which makes him one of the toughest people to translate. He also has an extraordinary knowledge of the Koran. He has memorized the Koran. He chooses his quotes. He also improvises his speeches. This is someone who does not read speeches. In all of the videotapes that I have seen and translated, he does not even look at a script, and he can go on for hours nonstop, staying clear and on message. He doesn't get tired. You can say he's one of those top public speakers.

A. PAUL EEDLE: I agree.

Q. MARIA RESSA [CNN]: My question is about the verification process and the differences between the Western sensibility and the Muslim sensibility of deciding what is news. Have you seen that change over the last three or four years as you have gone through hundreds of these messages on the Internet? Has the verification process been affected by the different perspectives?

A. PAUL EEDLE: I think that the Western media has been far more worried about verification and indeed has been encouraged to be worried about verification by their governments. They are nervous to say, "This is bin Laden," until they have had somebody in government say it is bin Laden. I think the Western media has fallen into worrying about authentication. Yet, when I look on the Web, I see an overwhelming audience in the Muslim world believing this stuff. That is what I go on, rather than the judgment of somebody with the voice analysis box in some computer lab.

Q. YOSRI FOUDA: I want to comment on the survey that was done in Egypt proving that something like eighty percent of Egyptians do not favor America. I do not really think that they meant America as a country. People in Egypt or in the Middle East make the distinction between four concepts when it comes to America: America as a country; the American people; the current administration; and the extreme right wing within the current administration. So I think this is a misleading statistic.

My second point is directed to Octavia Nasr. I very much enjoyed her fairy tale about her visit to al Jazeera. I thank her on behalf of myself as a member of al Jazeera and on behalf of al Jazeera in general that she has just proven how transparent al Jazeera is. We even allow everybody to go into our control room at the most critical times. And then we are generous enough to take them to the diplomatic club for dinner, yet we never leave any machine to play any tape by itself. Tell me about a single time that al Jazeera broadcast anything that had to do with bin Laden or any of his people without calling somebody from the United States to comment on it. And if there is an Islamic argument in it, we always bring in a mainstream Islamic cleric to refute it.

May I just remind you that at one point in time, the Taliban foreign minister offered both al Jazeera and CNN equal access to the story. CNN did not see much in the story. We did. And ever since, we have been paying the price for our vision that one day this might be a big story. Al Jazeera and our man there, our correspondent, was the working news agency of the world. And when Octavia arrived in Doha, al Jazeera willingly decided to share its exclusive with its most obvious rival because we believed that we were both in this together.

I don't think that most of the talk is now about al Jazeera. Al Jazeera just happened to be there as a medium. I was at the very heart of deciding on certain tasks and whether or not to air them. I will remind you about a certain tape that came to al Jazeera. It was immediately after the American strike in Afghanistan. Bin Laden sent for our man there, our correspondent, for an exclusive, a moment any news organization would just dream to have an exclusive on. Our correspondent goes to bin Laden and interviews him for about an hour. He sends the tape to Doha, and our people in Doha look at the tape. They do not find it very newsworthy. They decide not to air a minute of it. Guess what happens next? It appears on CNN. I do not want to make this out to be al Jazeera versus CNN. But once again, I think we are very much trying to prove the fact that we don't have horns on our heads and that we are transparent.

PETER BERGEN

Just a comment actually, I hate to get into the middle of this, but if bin Laden was reading from the phone book after 9/11, it would be a newsworthy tape. It was a curious decision on al Jazeera's part. I don't know what the details were, but al Jazeera never aired this hour-long interview with bin Laden. We at CNN eventually aired it many months later, much to al Jazeera's chagrin, and there was a huge bust-up and now it's all fine. But on that videotape, actually, bin Laden was asked two very interesting questions. One was, "How do you justify attacks on civilians in the United States?" Bin Laden answered, "Well they pay American taxes, therefore they're complicit in American foreign policy." The other thing Tayseer Alouni asked bin Laden, which was fascinating, was "What about this clash of civilizations?" And bin Laden said, "Of course there is a clash of civilizations. The Jews and the Christians are drugging us, pretending there isn't one."

I think, as Jessica Stern said earlier, the biggest fans of Samuel Huntington's work are people like bin Laden, because the clash is inevitable, and in their view, they are going to win.

7 The Real Twin Towers

Al Qaeda's Influence on Saudi Arabia and Pakistan

MODERATOR: **Arif Lalani,** Director, South Asia Division, Department of Foreign Affairs, Government of Canada. PANELISTS: **Hamid Mir,** Anchor, GEO television, Pakistan; **Lawrence Wright,** Writer, *New Yorker*; **Anatol Lieven,** Senior Associate, Carnegie Endowment for International Peace.

ARIF LALANI

I think it is fitting that we are ending with a focus on something concrete, namely Pakistan and Saudi Arabia. We have spent most of the day talking about issues across the globe: transnational issues, theories, and trends. But at the end of the day, what matters, in fact, is what is happening on the ground. And the topic before us, al Qaeda's influence on Pakistan and Saudi Arabia, could be reworded to ask, "How successful has the campaign against al Qaeda been?"

To answer the question of what al Qaeda's influence is at the moment in places like Pakistan and Saudi Arabia is really to answer that question about everything we've been discussing today.

HAMID MIR

Preliminarily, I want to share something with you. Some days ago, a Pakistani newspaper published a story about this conference. That story was filed by Mr. Khalid Hassan, who is a very senior and well-respected journalist based in Washington. I did not read the story because on that day I was in the tribal area where the Pakistan army is fighting against al Qaeda. In the evening when I came back, I received a call on my cell phone and somebody was saying, "You are going to Washington and there is a big controversy. You are going to speak against us there and if you go, you must be ready to face the consequences." I did not take it seriously, but two days later my flight was cancelled due to bad weather and I went back home. But that night, when I went to bed, I thought about this conference and I realized that if I didn't come, the people who had threatened me, who had called me, would be very happy that Hamid Mir was such an obedient journalist. I could hear them thinking, "We just make a phone call and threaten him and he doesn't go." They would have been very happy. So, I decided that they should not be so happy and I tried my best to catch flights to Washington. After I have attended this conference, they will not be so very happy.

I have learned a lot. I appreciate most of the views expressed here. I have differences of opinion, especially with the idea that al Qaeda is no longer a dangerous organization and has lost its operational capacity. If al Qaeda is dead, then why have hundreds of Pakistani soldiers lost their lives in just the last six months in the tribal areas of Pakistan? If al Qaeda is dead, then why has Ayman al-Zawahiri criticized George W. Bush and praised Musharraf in his latest radio message? Because he is angry and he knows that they are after us and we are after them. So I think that al Qaeda is still a threat and we should not underestimate al Qaeda. I think that many people underestimated the threat of al Qaeda and that is why 9/11 happened.

Nobody can understand al Qaeda without understanding the situation in Pakistan and Saudi Arabia. Pakistan is the only Muslim country which was created in the name of Islam and it is the only nuclear power in the Islamic world. Saudi Arabia is the center of the Muslim holy lands and the biggest, as well as the largest, oil producer. These two countries played a large role in the war against the Soviet Union from 1979 to 1989. Also, these two countries are at the moment allies of the United States of America. They came into international focus after 9/11 because fifteen out of nineteen attackers of 9/11 were from Saudi Arabia, and all the important leaders of al Qaeda were arrested from Pakistan after 9/11. So that is why I think that these two countries are very important for understanding al Qaeda.

Al Qaeda was created in the city of Peshawar in Pakistan in 1988 by bin Laden. At that time, Osama bin Laden wanted to use Pakistan as the base camp for an international jihad, since the jihad against the Soviet Union was over. He wanted to start a new kind of jihad. Pakistan was the country used as a launching pad against the Soviet Union by the U.S., and Osama bin Laden wanted to use that launching pad against Israel after 1989. He tried to destabilize the democratically elected government of Pakistan through money, which is something that very few people know. Some Pakistani politicians who were rivals of Benazir Bhutto got big amounts of money from Osama bin Laden. But thank God they were not ready to cooperate with him politically. They just got the money and used it against the government and that is all. Still, whenever I interviewed him, bin Laden expressed his displeasure over the attitude of the Pakistani politicians who got the money. They never used that money for his objectives.

It was 1990 when Saddam Hussein attacked Kuwait, and Osama bin Laden tried to exploit that opportunity for reorganizing his fighters in Saudi Arabia. He approached the Saudis and volunteered to mobilize veterans of the 1979 to 1989 Afghan jihad against Soviet occupation to defend Saudi Arabia from Iraq. The Saudi government declined his offer, preferring to rely instead on the U.S.-led coalition assembled by President George H. W. Bush, Sr. It was then that Osama bin Laden started speaking against Americans openly.

He started speaking openly about his resentment over the presence of the infidel troops in the holy lands. It was then that he left Saudi Arabia and went to Sudan. He came back to Afghanistan in May 1996. You must understand that when Osama bin Laden came back to Afghanistan in May 1996, Kabul was not controlled by the Taliban. Kabul was controlled by Mr. Rabani, who is now an ally of Mr. Hamid Karzai, which means that he is the ally of President Bush and President Musharraf.

In October 1996, I wrote a critical column about the Taliban's policies. Some Saudis reacted to my column and they contacted me in Islamabad. They protested and said that Radio Tehran was using my column to defame the Taliban and to defame them. They claimed that I was playing into the hands of the Iranians, and they explained their opposition. So I asked why they were closing down girls' schools in Afghanistan and I also asked why, on the other side, Pakistani officials and the U.S. officials say they are supporting them. And they said, "Okay, we will prove that we are not playing any games with the Pakistani establishment or the U.S. establishment. You must come to Kandahar and you will meet Mullah Omar, our leader, and then you can realize the situation." So I went to Kandahar in December of 1996. I met Mullah Omar for thirty minutes, because it was very difficult to understand his Pashto. But I still remember that Mullah Omar asked me, "If I am an American ally, why have I given refuge to Osama bin Laden?" So I asked him, "Where is he?" And he answered, "He's in Afghanistan." So I said, "Oh, I'm not ready to believe you. If he's here, please set up my meeting with him." And that is how Mullah Omar set up my first meeting with Osama bin Laden, which took place in 1997.

I interviewed bin Laden and the interview got a full page of coverage in my newspaper. It was not a big hit. My editor asked me, "Why have you invested so much time and space in a person who is not known in Pakistan?" So because he was a nobody in 1997, my first interview with him was a flop. He confessed to the killing of the American and Pakistani soldiers in Somalia and that he had spoken against the presence of American troops in Saudi Arabia, but that is all. The people of Pakistan were not aware of bin Laden.

He started getting lots of coverage in the Western media in early 1998 when he issued an edict to kill Americans. That year, in 1998, I interviewed bin Laden a second time in Kandahar. This time I confronted him for hours about his edict in the light of Islamic teachings. I disagree with one of the speakers here who claimed that he has a lot of Koranic knowledge. I am not a religious scholar, and I do not have a command of Islamic law, but when I confronted him, I asked him a simple question. "Convince me. How can you justify the killing of the innocent non-Muslims in the light of Islamic teachings? You have issued a fatwa. You have issued a statement to 'kill the Americans.' How can you justify this through the Koran?" He took five hours. His plan was to convince me. After five hours, I said, "You cannot make your point." So then he asked for help from Dr. Ayman al-Zawahiri. He said, "You can convince him." Then he started speaking to me in English.

After lunch, they invited me to another meeting where Osama bin Laden was delivering a speech to fifty or sixty boys. In that speech, I noticed that he was not talking religion. He was talking politics. He was trying to exploit the situation in the Middle East like he has tried to exploit the situation in Bosnia, in Chechnya, in Kashmir. So that is why I think that he is not representative of a religion. I realized it in 1998. When he talks about religion in front of young boys, I do not see motivation. I do not see big slogans. I see nothing. He cannot convince them, because his case is very weak. But when he talks politics, suddenly there is a lot of motivation among the angry youth, the angry boys. They repeat the slogans, "We are ready to die!" So he is doing politics in the name of religion.

In May 1998 I interviewed him, and after that interview he extended an invitation to me. He said, "I am going to address a press conference and I am going to make a very important announcement." After some weeks, somebody contacted me. I thought, "This is a very dangerous game and now he's going to address a press conference with more than a dozen journalists." And at that time, I thought that the Americans, being very smart, might bomb his press conference. So I decided not to attend. Was there was a problem at that press conference? More than twenty journalists belonging to different international organizations, including some U.S. organizations, attended that press conference, and only myself and Peter Bergen were missing. I was fearing that somebody would attack that press conference, but attacks in Kenya and Tanzania took place some days after it. After the attacks in Kenya and Tanzania, the place where he addressed the press conference *was* bombed.

Over the next few years I visited Afghanistan again and again and I came to know that al Qaeda had set up training camps in eastern and southern Afghanistan and had provided training to thousands of Arabs, Pakistanis, Afghanis, Bengalis, Indonesians, Malaysians, Turks, and African-Americans. I have met at least two African-Americans in bin Laden's hideout speaking excellent English with an American accent as well as Muslims from different parts of this world.

Many people confuse the Taliban with al Qaeda. The training of al Qaeda was different from that of the Taliban. Al Qaeda trained ex-fighters for urban warfare while the Taliban trained their fighters for guerilla warfare in the mountains, hit-and-run style. The motive was very clear. Al Qaeda was planning to organize big attacks against U.S. interests in the big cities and they were also trying to organize an armed revolt in

Saudi Arabia to overthrow the kingdom. One recently captured Pakistani operative of al Qaeda, Qari Saifullah Akhtar, who was arrested in Dubai, was part of an armed revolt and a conspiracy unearthed in 1995, in which some high-ranking members of the Pakistani army in his cell were also arrested. They were convicted; he was part of that conspiracy also. So it is proof that al Qaeda is trying to organize some kind of armed coup with the help of some army officers, not only in Saudi Arabia, but also in Pakistan.

When I visited Afghanistan in November 2001, I spent at least three days in the al Qaeda network. They blindfolded me and transferred me from one hideout to another. They had information, the information which I had obtained from different al Qaeda sources in 2001. They told me not to publish that information. They said that they had just been sharing it in a conversation, and that a clever journalist could get that kind of information. They told me that more than thirty-five hundred trained al Qaeda fighters left Afghanistan between July and October 2001. Out of those thirty-five hundred fighters, fifteen hundred were sent to Saudi Arabia and the rest of them were sent to Europe and America with different passports and different names. Most of them used Italian, Portuguese, Dutch, and Japanese passports with Christian and Jewish names.

Pakistan was not a target of al Qaeda before 9/11. The changes in Pakistani policy after 9/11 were a great surprise for the al Qaeda leadership. Pakistan banned some terrorist organizations just three weeks before the 9/11 attacks but al Qaeda was not expecting a big U-turn in Pakistani policy towards Afghanistan. When I interviewed Osama bin Laden in Afghanistan for the third time in November 2001, he mainly criticized President Musharraf and asked the people of Pakistan to overthrow his government. Dr. Ayman al-Zawahiri expressed hope that there would be a coup in the Pakistani army against Musharraf. But his hope never materialized. When Afghanistan was attacked, thousands of people in all the big cities of Pakistan came out onto the streets in protest against the U.S. But Musharraf played the India card very cleverly. He gave the impression that he was cooperating with the U.S. to prevent a possible alliance between India and the U.S. against Pakistan. After spending a difficult two years, he explained to the people of Pakistan that we were not fighting that war for the U.S.; we were fighting that war in our interest. Because terrorism is not good for the U.S., terrorism is not good for Pakistan, and that is why we are fighting that war.

In the next year, Pakistan became a target of al Qaeda terrorism. Dozens of innocent Muslims were killed, but the Musharraf regime never faced any major political attack from anti-American religious parties. Then came the general election of October 2002, in which the six parties played the anti-American card openly and got a majority in two out of four provinces of Pakistan which border Afghanistan. It was true that a big, silent part of the Pakistani population was not happy with the U.S. and Musharraf. The leaders and voters of the religious alliance never supported al Qaeda openly, but some of them had had meetings with Osama bin Laden and Mullah Omar in the past. They never criticized al Qaeda directly like Musharraf did. President Musharraf used military power against al Qaeda in tribal areas, and is still using military power in tribal areas. This last year proved that these al Qaeda militants and some of the leaders were not fighting a just war. Now it has been proven to the population of the tribal areas because the Pakistani army has arrested some children, some Tajik and Uzbek children, twelve-year-old children, fourteen-year-old children, who were imported from Afghanistan. Al Qaeda was using those small children for suicide attacks and for organizing remote-control bomb explosions in the Pakistani army. So when those children were presented in front of the media, it was a big surprise for the Pakistani people that these champions of Islam could use twelve-year-old kids for their fight against the Pakistani army.

On the other hand, we have to admit that the Musharraf regime has not been very successful. He has launched many operations against al Qaeda. He has tried his best to break the backbone of al Qaeda in the tribal areas. But there is no political opposition against his war on terror in Pakistan because he has not engaged the moderate and liberal political parties in Pakistan. There is opposition between President Musharraf and the liberal and moderate political parties, and this is one of the points which has to be addressed by President Musharraf. He is trying his best to overcome the problem. The governments in Pakistan and Saudi Arabia are the new Twin Towers for al Qaeda. Al Qaeda is striking again and again on these towers to destroy them. In Pakistan, Musharraf is trying his best to eradicate al Qaeda from Pakistani society. He has introduced the idea of enlightened moderation. In Saudi Arabia, the Saudi regime is also trying to do its best as well. But I do not think that they have been very successful. I spoke to many Saudi youngsters when I visited Saudi Arabia recently. They are very happy. They said, "We don't know what the problem between bin Laden and Bush is. We are not bothered about Bush. We are very happy that he is criticizing our leaders because they have not given us democracy. They have not given us freedom of expression and that's why we are happy with bin Laden because he's exposing them." So their thinking is different. They are not supporting Osama bin Laden because he is fighting against George Bush. They are supporting Osama bin Laden because he is fighting against corrupt regimes and some dictators in the Middle East. And I must say that if the U.S. is not ready to withdraw its support for these kinds of corrupt regimes, you cannot address this problem properly.

Osama bin Laden, then, is a hero for many disgruntled Muslims not because of religion but due to some political issues. If these issues are not resolved on the basis of justice, the world will become a more dangerous place in which to live in the future.

LAWRENCE WRIGHT

I would like to talk about the effect of al Qaeda on Saudi Arabia, a country that I spent three months in last year, teaching young journalists at a newspaper called the *Saudi Gazette.*

When I was a boy I went to visit my cousins in Kansas on this family farm. And one of my cousins asked, "Have you ever hypnotized a chicken?" I'm a city slicker so I said, "Well no. I don't think that's possible." And he said, "Well, come here, I'll show you." As I learned, chickens like to roost up on top of the roof of the barn. So we climbed up on top of the barn and snuck up on the chickens. My cousin grabbed one of the chickens and stuck its head under its wing and then he hurled it around ten or fifteen times. Then he very carefully set it back down on the edge of the roof. And it was the strangest thing: the chicken just sat there for the longest time.

The reason that I bring this up is that sometimes the existence of Saudi Arabia in the modern world reminds me of that hypnotized chicken. It's unlikely, it's improbable, it's unnatural – but there it is!

Single-family rule is an incredible anachronism, in this day and time. This is a family that not only runs the country but essentially owns it, that has, according to Saudi economists, stolen thirty to forty percent of the country's vast natural wealth. It is a country where even very minor princes in this enormous family allow themselves to build $40 million palaces, where they set a standard for debauchery around the world that will probably never be equaled, even at a time when poverty in the kingdom is increasing and the disparity of income, of wealth, is so noticeable.

There are a lot of troubling trends in the kingdom. Prince Alwaleed bin Talal says that the majority of Saudis weren't even born during the 1991 Gulf War. Like most statistics in Saudi Arabia, this one is anecdotal, and it may or may not be true. There are no reliable statistics in a country that hypothesizes all of its information. So, when we come to a question like joblessness, officially it is eight or nine percent. But in truth, it is more like thirty or forty percent. But no one that stands behind either of those statistics takes into account the underemployment of the Saudis who do have jobs. Nor do they take into account the ninety-five percent of women who, even the government admits, are unemployed, even though women in Saudi Arabia have more college degrees and more advanced degrees at every level of education than do the men. They comprise perhaps the most qualified pool of unemployed labor in the world.

Youth and idleness is a dangerous combination in any society. With joblessness, especially in Saudi Arabia, comes also boredom. Let me describe what life is like in Saudi Arabia, especially for young people like my reporters. There is no music. There are no movies. There are no plays. There is no theater. There are very few parks. There is one significant museum I went to in Riyadh, and there was only one other family going through the museum at the time that I was there. It has a very impoverished literature, a very impoverished art. There is no political life. There are no parties. There are no unions. There is nothing between the government and the mosque. That entire space that we call civil society doesn't exist. Alhough, Jeddah *does* have the world's largest Chuck E. Cheese pizza parlor. Recently as well in Jeddah, the Ikea furniture store opened its first branch. It was such a thrilling event that fifteen thousand people showed up and two people were trampled to death.

One of my reporters did a story about a survey on depression that was done at King Abdul Aziz University in Jeddah. All of my reporters were very depressed. Some of them couldn't sleep at night. They bit their nails down to the nubs. But this was a scientific survey of two thousand students in Saudi Arabia. Sixty-five percent of the boys and seventy-two percent of the girls showed symptoms of depression. Seven percent of the girls admitted that they had attempted suicide. Five percent of both sexes admitted to chronic drug use and alcoholism – this in a kingdom where alcohol is strictly forbidden. And I can tell you, it is very difficult to get a drink in the Kingdom of Saudi Arabia! So one has to appreciate how stark those figures are.

One of the political facts of Saudi Arabia is that there are a lot of idle, bored young men. And this is made worse by the fact that the separation of sexes has gotten more extreme than it was in the past. So these young men are unsocialized. They are unexposed to the civilizing influence of the female sex and the companionship and solace that that kind of relationship provides.

So let's add up all of these elements, each one of which is so dangerous by itself that any political scientist would say Saudi Arabia is overripe for revolution, especially when you throw in the religious fanaticism that has long been a part of the culture. The pressures for explosive, total change in the Kingdom seem irresistible. But still the hypnotized chicken stands on the barnyard roof, unmoved by the predictions of journalists and social scientists. Why? What force is greater than the anger, the despair, the frustration, the hopelessness that everywhere else in the world has led to revolutions, coups, and civil wars, but in Saudi Arabia has resulted in a kind of social coma that justifies my tortured metaphor of the hypnotized chicken?

Fear is that force. I'm not speaking exactly of the fear of the government. Saudis don't fear their government, although they hate it. Their government is not nearly as cruel to its citizens – or its subjects to use the correct word – as for instance Egypt is. What they fear is the alternative. So let's look at Saudi Arabia from the point of view of the chicken. How did it come to be hypnotized?

The unification of Saudi Arabia in the 1920s and 1930s was far bloodier than even most Saudi historians have allowed themselves to say. I will give you an example. The city of Taif was the gateway to the conquest of the kingdom of Hijaz. The city surrendered to King Abdul Aziz's shock troops, who were known as the Ikhwan. They were a precursor of modern-day al Qaeda in many ways, and they believed in purifying the peninsula of any kind of extraneous elements. So the city surrendered, and the Ikhwan entered the gates of the city and found every able-bodied man they could find, cut him to pieces and threw him down into the well. Eventually this group turned on their sponsor, King Abdul Aziz, and he was only able to subdue them with the help of the British RAF bombers.

As a result, among most of the Saudis that I know, there is an internalized fear that this fanaticism that is so indigenous will be unleashed again, and even worse in their opinion, the country will devolve into tribal warfare. The al Saud family represents a bulwark in their minds against total chaos, and this is true even in the minds of a lot of liberal reformers that I talk to. Why would that be true? Look at the neighborhood that the Saudis live in. Then look around at where revolutions have taken place in Egypt, where you have an enduring autocracy. This regime is far less liberal than the monarchy it replaced. Look at Iran, which produced the mullahs. Look at Iraq, where Saddam Hussein came to power. Look at Somalia, where you have tribal chaos. Looking at these examples, you would say to yourself that change does not necessarily equal progress.

It is often said that the Saudis are conservative and slow to change. But when I hear that, I think about Mohammad Shoukani, who was my editor at the *Saudi Gazette*. He is a man about my age. Mohammad was born in Aseer in the southern part of Saudi Arabia, where many of the hijackers came from. And like many Aseeri boys, he was a shepherd. He wore flowers in his hair. He did not see an automobile until he was ten years old, when he moved to Jeddah. Eventually, he got a scholarship, went to the University of Texas, and got a degree in Comparative Literature. He became a professor at King Abdul Aziz University, and became the editor of that paper. His life encompasses all the technical and social change that the world has endured since the industrial revolution. It's worth keeping in mind when we talk about Saudi Arabia and change, that it has changed more rapidly perhaps than any other society.

So what would wake the chicken? In real life, to wake a hypnotized chicken you push him off the barn. His wings open up. His head comes out. He finds himself in mid-air . . . and that's how you wake a chicken. Now, can al Qaeda push the chicken off the barn? No, I don't believe it can because the fear of fanaticism and social chaos are the greatest friends that the al Saud family has. Bin Laden, who calls for the overthrow of the royal family, paradoxically helps keep them in power. So do we. It is my theory that the chicken is not really hypnotized. He is standing there with his head under his wing, thinking, "If I don't do anything, I won't get whirled around any more." If you want the chicken to wake from his fearful slumber, you have to provide him with a positive model for social change. That is where Iraq becomes so important to Saudi Arabia and to other countries in the region. For now, Iraq embodies exactly what the Saudis fear the most: chaos, tribal warfare, a descent into barbarism. So my forecast is the same as Lubna Olayan, that wonderful Saudi businesswoman who encapsulated the Saudi idea of governance: reform without change. In other words, the chicken stays hypnotized.

ANATOL LIEVEN

I would not say that Pakistan is a hypnotized chicken. It is a pretty depressed chicken, and you could say that it has a lot to be depressed about. In the case of Pakistan, I think that the first thing you have to understand about people's attitudes, people's political behavior, and the very considerable degree today of political apathy, is the fact that so many different models over the past two generations – or really, in many ways, since the creation of the Pakistani state – have failed. Pakistan has experienced periods of developmental dictatorship, particularly under Ayub Khan. It experienced a period of quasi-democratic or pseudo-democratic socialist, populist development under Bhutto. It experienced a not very extreme but rhetorically quite extreme Islamist military, authoritarian rule under Zia-ul-Haq. In the 1950s, in the 1970s, and then again in the 1990s, it experienced several periods of what was supposed to be democratic rule by democratic political parties. And as far as the mass of the population is concerned, they have seen, at least relatively when compared to other countries, very little come out of any of this.

This lack of progress has been dramatized more recently by the fact that, whereas previously Pakistan was at least growing faster economically than India (which is the most important index in Pakistan itself of course for relative development), in recent years even that has failed, and Pakistan has begun to grow at a markedly slower rate than India. This occurred after India itself moved to more free market economics beginning in the late 1980s.

So there is a feeling that a very wide range of different regimes and different approaches have all failed. From the point of view of democratization, the most important period at present is of course the 1990s in which there were two periods of rule by the Pakistan People's Party under Benazir Bhutto, and two periods of rule by a kind of Islamist party, a conservative alliance of urban Baathist businessman and rural landowners with links to the military. Each of these periods came to an end in a welter of corruption and mismanagement.

One hears a lot, particularly in America, about America's responsibility for backing Zia in the 1980s, for not backing Pakistan in the 1990s, and particularly for not backing Benazir Bhutto. Sometimes you hear that America today is, in some sense, responsible for Musharraf's authoritarian rule and for the continued dominance of the military in Pakistan. While there is a certain amount of truth in this, I think it can be exaggerated. The phrase in Pakistan is, admittedly, that the country is governed by the three As: Allah, Army, and America. But it is also worth pointing out that America is the third of these, not the first. America could have done much more over the years. In particular, I think the way in which America walked away from Pakistan, and even more strikingly, from Afghanistan after the Soviet expulsion from Afghanistan, was extremely negative. But I think in Pakistan and in the Muslim world more widely, that there are considerable dangers in making it all come back to America. It encourages a kind of narcissism that places all the emphasis on American decisions.

If one looks at the failure of democracy in Pakistan in the past, I think any serious analysis has to begin with the nature of Pakistani society and the Pakistani economy, and the failure of that economy and that society to generate modern mass political parties. The Pakistan People's Party (PPP) is the most striking example of that. Benazir Bhutto once told me that the PPP was a Scandinavian-type social democratic party. Since I had a considerable regard for self-preservation and I was a very, very junior journalist, I didn't reply that I entirely agreed: it was a Scandinavian-type social democratic party of the type Sweden had in 1000 A.D.! That is what the PPP is to a very great extent. If not Sweden in 1000 A.D., maybe sometime a bit later in the Middle Ages when it was a coalition of big landowners. Feudalism is a mistaken term, but their ancestors were in many cases feudal. Like their equivalents in many other parts of the world – the Philippines would be one example – they employ populism as a means of extending their own power and of gaining control of the government. Given the class they come from – they tend to come from more westernized backgrounds and sometimes originally from a British background – they do have certain aspects of secularism. But in terms of a serious socioeconomic program, they have never actually displayed that in practice, at least not since Zulfikar Ali Bhutto in the 1970s, and that turned into a disaster because it became completely mixed up with the looting of the state.

You are not going to get democratic development in Pakistan until you have mass political parties with a serious modernizing agenda. And in my view, you are not going to get mass political parties until you have a very different kind of society in Pakistan. It is not something that we can create with the flash of a wand. At present, it must be said that in many ways, the most effective genuine mass political parties today in Pakistan are: first, an ethnic party in Karachi, the MQM [Muttahida Quami Movement], representing the Mohajir minority of people who originally emigrated from India; and second, the Islamist Jamaat, the best organized, and also to some degree, the most moderate of the Islamist alliance. So I would just enter a very strong caution – which I think we also heard with regard to Saudi Arabia to some extent – against the view that we should push the chickens off the roof and that they will then learn to fly, to fly in a democratic manner. I do not think that in most cases that is so.

We must also be very cautious when people there blame America and Britain. When people blame us for having supported and for still supporting corrupt, authoritarian regimes, we need to ask the question, "Does that mean that you would favor direct interventions by us, much stronger interventions to change your government, to shape your society?" Now if you read, for example, the latest Zogby poll, the answer in the vast majority of cases is no. Our past record does not lead to a demand for us to change our policy radically. It only leads to distrust of whatever we do, distrust of our motives. It leads to the feeling that whatever policy we pursue will not be motivated by idealism or genuine concern for the well-being of these countries, but instead will be motivated by other agendas of American interest or Israeli interest, or in the case of the Pakistanis, of Indian interest. When it comes to the promotion of democracy, if it is to lead to the results that we want – stable, successful, democratic states – it needs to be preceded by long periods of socioeconomic transformation with very strong elements, both of developmentalism and of redistribution. This is something which one does not see very much of in the present Greater Middle East Initiative, for example.

That brings me very briefly to the nature of our radical Islamist enemies. Clearly on the one hand, in some ways, like the communists before them, there are two main strains that have popular appeal in different parts of the Muslim world. The first is that of social revolution or social radicalism. They obviously appealed enormously to sentiments stemming from the socioeconomic absence of opportunity, as we have so often heard among the educated youth in particular. On the other hand, there is nationalist resentment, ethnic resentment, or geopolitical resentment. On the socioeconomic level, it seems to me that as far as the Sunni-Islamists are concerned, this aspect of their appeal is an ambiguous one, and it can serve us in some ways because in a vague sense it does appeal to very large numbers of Muslims. But on the other hand, when they actually set out their whole agenda, even pretty conservative Muslims have a tendency to run away.

In the case of Afghanistan, the Afghan urban population, even in the Pashtun areas, is deeply conservative. They really did not like the kind of rigid totalitarian rule that the Taliban clamped on them. In the countryside, it was rather different because the countryside had always pursued its own ways, irrespective of what the government said. So it wasn't as if the Taliban were actually making much difference one way or another.

Even among the most conservative, there was this feeling that the form of Islam that had been clamped upon them actually did not correspond even to conservative Islamic traditions.

To a very considerable extent, the kind of Islam represented by al Qaeda is modernist. It is a modern creation based on extremely ancient roots. This reflects patterns in Islam which were analyzed by Haldoon and many others, some seven hundred years ago. Nonetheless, in its specific form, it is both modern and alien. To a very considerable extent, it comes from outside most of the Muslim countries where it is being applied.

Although we have to be very cautious as to our levels of interventionism in these societies, I think al Qaeda is facing many challenges in appealing to the mass population. When it comes to their nationalist or geopolitical appeal, unfortunately, their appeal is often very much stronger. The world of Sunni Islamist extremism – al Qaeda and its allies – is not an organization, it's a web or net with different nodes. We have seen how different nodes or groups in this web have been able to infiltrate and colonize ethnic resentments across the Muslim world, from the southern Philippines up. We now see very strongly in southern Thailand how local resentments are being given an Islamist shape by people who come in. We've seen this in Chechnya. We see it in Palestine to a considerable extent and, of course, in Kashmir. It seems to me that to some extent, it also reflects something that we saw during the Cold War, when there were all these rebellions, these movements which came up for local reasons and took on the form of communism and called themselves socialist liberation movements.

We saw that when the world appeal of communism faded at the end of the Cold War, many movements in Africa and Latin America immediately renamed themselves, abandoned the whole idea of communism, and adopted a completely different ideology. So it does seem to me that this ability of al Qaeda and its allies to colonize these movements is very menacing. That is what makes them pose the greatest danger to the West and other countries as well. This may in some ways prove to be of shallow appeal if we can find a way to actually appease or reduce the ethnic and national resentments which they have succeeded in colonizing.

THE REAL TWIN TOWERS: AL QAEDA'S INFLUENCE ON SAUDI ARABIA AND PAKISTAN

Question and Answer Session

Q. **ARIF LALANI:** It seems that in both Pakistan and Saudi Arabia, what you seem to be saying, in fact, is that you have extremism because the societies are dysfunctional in terms of the governance and economic development. It is those vulnerable societies that are incubating extremists. If that is the case, ought that not to be just as important a plank in the campaign against terrorism and al Qaeda as the so-called military hard end?

A. **ANATOL LIEVEN:** Yes, I would entirely agree with that. I think that the development of these societies is just as critical as the development of a number of societies was during the Cold War. What perturbs me, and once again Pakistan is a leading example, is that the economic development that the U.S. is putting into the region is very, very much less than the effort the U.S. put into supporting and developing South Korea or Taiwan or Thailand or Malaysia during the Cold War. Now when I say that, I am not advocating simply pouring large amounts of money into these places because much of it would be stolen anyway. But one of the most important aspects during the Cold War was the question of the American openness to trade, geopolitically driven openness to the exports of these countries. Free trade agreements with a number of Middle Eastern countries could constitute a useful development. But I have to say that, so far, they have been very much more open to the smaller countries, and the results have been on a relatively small scale. So I would like to see the Greater Middle East Initiative accompanied by the conscious commitment to socioeconomic development that we saw during the Cold War.

A. LAWRENCE WRIGHT: I had the opportunity last year to interview the American ambassador to Saudi Arabia at the time and I said, "You know, as an American, I am a little sick of having to defend the fact that we're always supporting these autocratic regimes. Can't we be promoting American values and projecting values as much as we project American power all around the world?" And he said, "Well, you know, we don't really want to have democracy here right now. We are in a position where if they had an election, the Islamists would win. They have a lot of money. They have a defense agreement with Pakistan. We don't want Saudi Arabia run by a bunch of people who hate America and might bomb us."

Right after I got back, Bush changed his policy and his ambassadors, and has begun espousing more work in the vineyards of democracy in the Middle East. Yet the ambassador's caution is worth taking into account, because you do also need to prepare civil society. It is very difficult to imagine the creation of a democracy in a country that does not have any other supporting institutions. So I think there is a whole lot of work to be done before we can imagine a functioning, self-regulating democracy in Saudi Arabia and a number of other countries there.

A. HAMID MIR: I think real democracy is the only solution to this growing transnational terrorism. I want to make the point very clearly that, whether it is Saudi Arabia or Pakistan, the United States of America has always supported dictators. The first dictator in Pakistan, General Ayub Khan, was supported by the United States. He was a liberal man. The second dictator, General Zia-ul-Haq, was Islamist. He was supported by the United States. And the third one is also supported by the United States. The first-ever democratically elected prime minister of Pakistan was Zulfiqar Ali Bhutto, a progressive man fighting against the Islamic extremists and the Pakistan army. When his government was toppled by Zia-ul-Haq, with the collusion of some corrupt judges, they hanged him because he opposed the mullahs. These same mullahs then became allies of the United States of America and the Pakistani army. All of them created bin Laden. So I am not ready to agree with some of those who say that the Pakistanis are not fit for democracy. Pakistanis are very much fit for democracy. Pakistan is the creation of a democratic process. The founder of Pakistan was a clean ship, a liberal and democratic man. But unfortunately you imposed dictators on us.

Q. **MARK SANTILLIS [Terrorism Research Center]:** My question is for Hamid Mir. I have a question about the western provinces of Pakistan such as Balochistan, Waziristan, and the northwest frontier provinces. I am wondering about the extent to which the people in those tribal areas support al Qaeda or Taliban remnants that have fled there.

Q. **RANDY COOK:** Could the commentators comment briefly upon the continuing involvement in and possible complicity between the Saudi and Pakistani governments and the al Qaeda networks or with other terrorist networks, specifically in relation to the Khan network in continuing relationships between Pakistani secret service agents in al Qaeda and then also with Saudi contributions to Wahabi types of ideologies?

A. **HAMID MIR:** The first question is a very important question. Nobody can deny the fact that the majority of the population in the tribal areas of Pakistan is very supportive of al Qaeda because they are Pashtuns and they are illiterate. This area was not open to Pakistani authorities. The British army tried their best to capture that area for eighty years, but they were not able to control or capture it. This is the first time in the history of that area that any army has established check posts there. The Pakistani army is fighting a very complicated war in that area because they are facing not only the local tribes, but they are facing fighters from Uzbekistan, from Tajikistan, and from Chechnya, and all of them are united against the Pakistani army, and the population is supportive to them. So there is a need for American journalists to visit that area to understand why bin Laden is surviving.

As far as Pakistan is concerned, I don't believe that there is any connection now between the Pakistani government as such and al Qaeda or other terrorist groups, because these terrorist groups have twice tried to assassinate Musharraf, they blew up the core command in Karachi, and they conducted other attacks within Pakistan as well. On the other hand, in 2002, I was talking to a senior Pakistani police officer, and he said that when he received the information leading him to plan an operation to try to capture either al Qaeda people within Pakistan or leading Islamist terrorists from some other group, he kept the planning of that operation within a circle of two, or at most three people until the last possible moment, when the police actually more or less left the door and set out. He did this because he was very well aware that the police force, including middle-ranking officers, was thoroughly infiltrated by extremist sympathizers.

Q. AUDIENCE PARTICIPANT: What are your thoughts on the perception that al Qaeda's new headquarters are in Pakistan? Why is it difficult to penetrate the upper echelons of the organization and what are your thoughts on the penetration or the level of penetration of the Pakistani security and intelligence apparatus?

Q. KHALID HASSAN [*Daily Times Lahore*]: My question is to Hamid Mir. The view in Washington among the academics and among officials is that, while Musharraf has performed creatively against al Qaeda, as far as the Taliban are concerned, they are alive and well and living in Pakistan. And to Mr. Wright: it is the fate of most chickens to end up in the pot. As the national poet, Muhammad Iqbal, said, the only permanence in life is change. So how do you think change will come to Saudi Arabia?

Q. AUDIENCE PARTICIPANT: My question is regarding the Saudi opposition in London. What are the chances that they could win some elections and de-hypnotize the chickens?

A. HAMID MIR: Briefly, the new al Qaeda Military Operations Chief, Saif al Adel, is not based in Pakistan. He is, according to my information, issuing directions while sitting in Iran and creating problems for Pakistan and Saudi Arabia. Mr. Khalid Hassan has asked me a question about the relationship between Pakistan and Taliban. Yes, there is a difference between al Qaeda and Taliban. The Taliban still enjoys a lot of respect and popularity in some tribal areas and also in the Pashtun-speaking areas of Pakistan. But there is the issue of all those pro–al Qaeda militants who were killed in Pakistan and who participated in assassination attempts against President Musharraf. They were actually part of the Taliban, not al Qaeda. So now President Musharraf has realized that the Pakistani chapter of the Taliban is actually al Qaeda. There is no difference between al Qaeda and the Taliban in Pakistan. But definitely in Afghanistan, al Qaeda and the Taliban are two different things.

A. LAWRENCE WRIGHT: The change will come to Saudi Arabia. It cannot be stopped. The men who run Saudi Arabia have been in power since before electricity. They dye their beards, but nobody denies the fact that change is stalking them. As for the women, they have been shut out of municipal elections. It is a tragedy, but at least they are voting in small things, like the elections in the Jeddah Chamber of Commerce. They are setting certain precedents, so one can only hope. But I don't have much hope for anything immediate.

A. ANATOL LIEVEN: As far as the Taliban and al Qaeda in Pakistan are concerned, as we have heard, they are largely in the Pashtun tribal areas which the British attempted to conquer and rule directly. Then after a number of, shall we say "unfortunate" experiences, they decided that they had to rule indirectly, and essentially let the Pashtuns rule themselves. That is a very problematic and unsatisfactory situation, but it may be the best that we and the Pakistanis can actually hope for.

PART TWO

In His Own Words

Statements by Osama bin Laden

AUGUST 1996

Ladenese Epistle: Declaration of War

This is the first of two religious edicts which justifies violence against Western interests in the Middle East. It was written in August of 1996 and published in the London-based *Al Quds Al Arabi*, a newspaper that Osama bin Laden has often used to impart his views. The epistle was translated by the Committee for the Defense of Legitimate Rights, an organization sympathetic to bin Laden's cause, and later distributed on the Internet in October of 1996.

A MESSAGE FROM OSAMA BIN MUHAMMAD BIN IN LADEN TO HIS MUSLIM BRETHREN ALL OVER THE WORLD GENERALLY AND IN THE ARAB PENINSULA SPECIFICALLY

Praise be to Allah, we seek His help and ask for his pardon. We take refuge in Allah from our wrongs and bad deeds. Who ever been guided by Allah will not be misled, and who ever has been misled, he will never be guided. I bear witness that there is no God except Allah-no associates with Him – and I bear witness that Muhammad is His slave and messenger.

{O you who believe! be careful of – your duty to – Allah with the proper care which is due to Him, and do not die unless you are Muslim} (Imraan; 3:102), {O people be careful of – your duty to – your Lord, Who created you from a single being and created its mate of the same – kind – and spread from these two, many men and women; and be careful of – your duty to – Allah, by whom you demand one of another – your rights –, and (be careful) to the ties of kinship; surely Allah ever watches over you} (An-Nisa; 4:1), {O you who believe! be careful – of your duty – to Allah and speak the right word; He will put your deeds into a right state for you, and forgive you your faults; and who ever obeys Allah and his Apostle, he indeed achieve a mighty success} (Al-Ahzab; 33:70-71).

Praise be to Allah, reporting the saying of the prophet Shu'aib: {I desire nothing but reform so far as I am able, and with non but Allah is the direction of my affair to the right and successful path; on him do I rely and to him do I turn} (Hud; 11:88).

Praise be to Allah, saying: {You are the best of the nations raised up for – the benefit of – men; you enjoin what is right and forbid the wrong and believe in Allah} (Aal-Imraan; 3:110). Allah's blessing and salutations on His slave and messenger who said: (The people are close to an all encompassing punishment from Allah if they see the oppressor and fail to restrain him.)

It should not be hidden from you that the people of Islam had suffered from aggression, iniquity and injustice imposed on them by the Zionist-Crusaders alliance and their collaborators; to the extent that the Muslims blood became the cheapest and their wealth as loot in the hands of the enemies. Their blood was spilled in Palestine and Iraq. The horrifying pictures of the massacre of Qana, in Lebanon are still fresh in our memory. Massacres in Tajakestan, Burma, Cashmere, Assam, Philippine, Fatani, Ogadin, Somalia, Erithria, Chechnia and in Bosnia-Herzegovina took place, massacres that send shivers in the body and shake the conscience. All of this and the world watch and hear, and not only didn't respond to these atrocities, but also with a clear conspiracy between the USA and its' allies and under the cover of the iniquitous United Nations, the dispossessed people were even prevented from obtaining arms to defend themselves.

The people of Islam awakened and realised that they are the main target for the aggression of the Zionist-Crusaders alliance. All false claims and propaganda about "Human Rights" were hammered down and exposed by the massacres that took place against the Muslims in every part of the world.

The latest and the greatest of these aggressions, incurred by the Muslims since the death of the Prophet (ALLAH'S BLESSING AND SALUTATIONS ON HIM) is the occupation of the land of the two Holy Places – the foundation of the house of Islam, the place of the revelation, the source of the message and the place of the noble Ka'ba, the Qiblah of all Muslims – by the armies of the American Crusaders and their allies. (We bemoan this and can only say: "No power and power acquiring except through Allah").

Under the present circumstances, and under the banner of the blessed awakening which is sweeping the world in general and the Islamic world in particular, I meet with you today. And after a long absence, imposed on the scholars (Ulama) and callers (Da'ees) of Islam by the iniquitous crusaders movement under the leadership of the USA; who fears that they, the scholars and callers of Islam, will instigate the Ummah of Islam against its' enemies as their ancestor scholars-may Allah be pleased with them – like Ibn Taymiyyah and Al'iz Ibn Abdes-Salaam did. And therefore the Zionist-Crusader alliance resorted to killing and arresting the truthful Ulama and the working Da'ees (We are not praising or sanctifying them; Allah sanctify whom He pleased). They killed the Mujahid Sheikh Abdullah Azzaam, and they arrested the Mujahid Sheikh Ahmad Yaseen and the Mujahid Sheikh Omar Abdur Rahman (in America).

By orders from the USA they also arrested a large number of scholars, Da'ees and young people – in the land of the two Holy Places – among them the prominent Sheikh Salman Al-Oud'a and Sheikh Safar Al-Hawali and their brothers; (We bemoan this and can only say: "No power and power acquiring except through Allah"). We, myself and my group, have suffered some of this injustice ourselves; we have been prevented from addressing the Muslims. We have been pursued in Pakistan, Sudan and Afghanistan, hence this long absence on my part. But by the Grace of Allah, a safe base is now available in the high Hindukush mountains in Khurasan; where – by the Grace of Allah-the largest infidel military force of the world was destroyed. And the myth of the super power was withered in front of the Mujahideen cries of Allahu Akbar (God is greater). Today we work from the same mountains to lift the iniquity that had been imposed on the Ummah by the Zionist-Crusader alliance, particularly after they have occupied the blessed land around Jerusalem, route of the journey of the Prophet (ALLAH'S BLESSING AND SALUTATIONS ON HIM) and the land of the two Holy Places. We ask Allah to bestow us with victory, He is our Patron and He is the Most Capable.

From here, today we begin the work, talking and discussing the ways of correcting what had happened to the Islamic world in general, and the Land of the two Holy Places in particular. We wish to study the means that we could follow to return the situation to its' normal path. And to return to the people their own rights, particularly after the large damages and the great aggression on the life and the religion of the people. An injustice that had affected every section and group of the people; the civilians, military and security men, government officials and merchants, the young and the old people as well as schools and university students. Hundred of thousands of the unemployed graduates, who became the widest section of the society, were also affected.

Injustice had affected the people of the industry and agriculture. It affected the people of the rural and urban areas. And almost every body complain about something. The situation at the land of the two Holy places became like a huge volcano at the verge of eruption that would destroy the Kufr and the corruption and its' sources. The explosion at Riyadh and Al-Khobar is a warning of this volcanic eruption emerging as a result of the sever oppression, suffering, excessive iniquity, humiliation and poverty.

People are fully concerned about their every day livings; every body talks about the deterioration of the economy, inflation, ever increasing debts and jails full of prisoners. Government employees with limited income talk about debts of ten thousands and hundred thousands of Saudi Riyals. They complain that the value of the Riyal is greatly and continuously deteriorating among most of the main currencies. Great merchants and contractors speak about hundreds and thousands of million Riyals owed to them by the government. More than three hundred forty billions of

Riyal owed by the government to the people in addition to the daily accumulated interest, let alone the foreign debt. People wonder whether we are the largest oil exporting country?! They even believe that this situation is a curse put on them by Allah for not objecting to the oppressive and illegitimate behaviour and measures of the ruling regime: Ignoring the divine Shari'ah law; depriving people of their legitimate rights; allowing the American to occupy the land of the two Holy Places; imprisonment, unjustly, of the sincere scholars. The honourable Ulamah and scholars as well as merchants, economists and eminent people of the country were all alerted by this disastrous situation.

Quick efforts were made by each group to contain and to correct the situation. All agreed that the country is heading toward a great catastrophe, the depth of which is not known except by Allah. One big merchant commented:" the king is leading the state into 'sixty-six' folded disaster", (We bemoan this and can only say: "No power and power acquiring except through Allah"). Numerous princes share with the people their feelings, privately expressing their concerns and objecting to the corruption, repression and the intimidation taking place in the country. But the competition between influential princes for personal gains and interest had destroyed the country. Through its course of actions the regime has torn off its legitimacy:

(1) Suspension of the Islamic Shari'ah law and exchanging it with man made civil law. The regime entered into a bloody confrontation with the truthful Ulamah and the righteous youths (we sanctify nobody; Allah sanctify Whom He pleaseth).

(2) The inability of the regime to protect the country, and allowing the enemy of the Ummah – the American crusader forces – to occupy the land for the longest of years. The crusader forces became the main cause of our disastrous condition, particularly in the economical aspect of it due to the unjustified heavy spending on these forces. As a result of the policy imposed on the country, especially in the field of oil industry where production is restricted or expanded and prices are fixed to suit the American economy ignoring the economy of the country. Expensive

deals were imposed on the country to purchase arms. People asking what is the justification for the very existence of the regime then?

Quick efforts were made by individuals and by different groups of the society to contain the situation and to prevent the danger. They advised the government both privately and openly; they send letters and poems, reports after reports, reminders after reminders, they explored every avenue and enlist every influential man in their movement of reform and correction. They wrote with style of passion, diplomacy and wisdom asking for corrective measures and repentance from the "great wrong doings and corruption" that had engulfed even the basic principles of the religion and the legitimate rights of the people.

But – to our deepest regret – the regime refused to listen to the people accusing them of being ridiculous and imbecile. The matter got worse as previous wrong doings were followed by mischief's of greater magnitudes. All of this taking place in the land of the two Holy Places! It is no longer possible to be quiet. It is not acceptable to give a blind eye to this matter.

As the extent of these infringements reached the highest of levels and turned into demolishing forces threatening the very existence of the Islamic principles, a group of scholars-who can take no more – supported by hundreds of retired officials, merchants, prominent and educated people wrote to the King asking for implementation of the corrective measures. In 1411 A.H. (May 1991), at the time of the gulf war, a letter, the famous letter of Shawwaal, with over four hundred signatures was send to the king demanding the lift of oppression and the implementation of corrective actions. The king humiliated those people and choose to ignore the content of their letter; and the very bad situation of the country became even worse.

People, however, tried again and send more letters and petitions. One particular report, the glorious Memorandum Of Advice, was handed over to the king on Muharram, 1413 A.H (July 1992), which tackled the problem pointed out the illness and prescribed the medicine in an original, righteous and scientific style. It described the gaps and the shortcoming in the philosophy of the regime and suggested the required course of action and remedy. The report gave a description of:

(1) The intimidation and harassment suffered by the leaders of the society, the scholars, heads of tribes, merchants, academic teachers and other eminent individuals;

(2) The situation of the law within the country and the arbitrary declaration of what is Halal and Haram (lawful and unlawful) regardless of the Shari'ah as instituted by Allah;

(3) The state of the press and the media which became a tool of truth-hiding and misinformation; the media carried out the plan of the enemy of idolising cult of certain personalities and spreading scandals among the believers to repel the people away from their religion, as Allah, the Exalted said: {surely – as for – those who love that scandal should circulate between the believers, they shall have a grievous chastisement in this world and in the here after} (An-Noor, 24:19).

(4) Abuse and confiscation of human rights;

(5) The financial and the economical situation of the country and the frightening future in the view of the enormous amount of debts and interest owed by the government; this is at the time when the wealth of the Ummah being wasted to satisfy personal desires of certain individuals!! while imposing more custom duties and taxes on the nation. (the prophet said about the woman who committed adultery: "She repented in such a way sufficient to bring forgiveness to a custom collector!!");

(6) The miserable situation of the social services and infra-structure especially the water service and supply, the basic requirement of life;

(7) The state of the ill-trained and ill-prepared army and the impotence of its commander in chief despite the incredible amount of money that has been spent on the army. The gulf war clearly exposed the situation;

(8) Shari'a law was suspended and man made law was used instead;

(9) And as far as the foreign policy is concerned the report exposed not only how this policy has disregarded the Islamic issues and ignored the Muslims, but also how help and support were provided to the enemy against the Muslims; the cases of Gaza-Ariha and the communist in the south of Yemen are still fresh in the memory, and more can be said.

As stated by the people of knowledge, it is not a secret that to use man made law instead of the Shari'a and to support the infidels against the Muslims is one of the ten "voiders" that would strip a person from his Islamic status (turn a Muslim into a Mushrik, non believer status). The All Mighty said: {and whoever did not judge by what Allah revealed, those are the unbelievers} (Al-Ma'ida; 5:44), and {but no! by your Lord! they do not believe (in reality) until they make you a judge of that which has become a matter of disagreement among them, and then do not find the slightest misgiving in their hearts as to what you have decided and submit with entire submission} (An-Nissa; 4:65).

In spite of the fact that the report was written with soft words and very diplomatic style, reminding of Allah, giving truthful sincere advice, and despite of the importance of advice in Islam – being absolutely essential for those in charge of the people – and the large number who signed this document as well as their supporters, all of that was not an intercession for the Memorandum. Its' content was rejected and those who signed it and their sympathisers were ridiculed, prevented from travel, punished and even jailed.

Therefore it is very clear that the advocates of correction and reform movement were very keen on using peaceful means in order to protect the unity of the country and to prevent blood shed. Why is it then the regime closed all peaceful routes and pushed the people toward armed actions?!! which is the only choice left for them to implement righteousness and justice. To whose benefit does prince Sultan and prince Nayeff push the country into a civil war that will destroy everything? and why consulting those who ignites internal feuds, playing the people against each other and instigate the policemen, the sons of the nation, to abort the reform movement. While leaving in peace and security such traitors who implement the policy of the enemy in order to bleed the financial and the human resources of the Ummah, and leaving the main enemy in the area-the American Zionist alliance enjoy peace and security?!

The advisor (Zaki Badr, the Egyptian ex-minister of the interior) to prince Nayeff – minister of interior – was not acceptable even to his own country; he was sacked from his position there due to the filthy attitude and the aggression he exercised on his own people, yet he was warmly welcomed by prince Nayeff to assist in sins and aggressions. He unjustly filled the prisons with the best sons of this Ummah and caused miseries to their mothers. Does the regime want to play the civilians against their military personnel and vice versa, like what had happened in some of the neighbouring countries?!! No doubts this is the policy of the American-Israeli alliance as they are the first to benefit from this situation.

But with the grace of Allah, the majority of the nation, both civilians and military individuals are aware of the wicked plan. They refused to be played against each others and to be used by the regime as a tool to carry out the policy of the American-Israeli alliance through their agent in our country: the Saudi regime.

Therefore every one agreed that the situation can not be rectified (the shadow cannot be straighten when its' source, the rod, is not straight either) unless the root of the problem is tackled. Hence it is essential to hit the main enemy who divided the Ummah into small and little countries and pushed it, for the last few decades, into a state of confusion. The Zionist-Crusader alliance moves quickly to contain and abort any "corrective movement" appearing in the Islamic countries. Different means and methods are used to achieve their target; on occasion the "movement" is dragged into an armed struggle at a predetermined unfavourable time and place. Sometime officials from the Ministry of Interior, who are also graduates of the colleges of the Shari'ah, are leashed out to mislead and confuse the nation and the Ummah (by wrong Fatwas) and to circulate false information about the movement. At other occasions some righteous people were tricked into a war of words against the Ulama and the leaders of the movement, wasting the energy of the nation in discussing minor issues and ignoring the main one that is the unification of the people under the divine law of Allah.

In the shadow of these discussions and arguments truthfulness is covered by the falsehood, and personal feuds and partisanship created among the people increasing the division and the weakness of the Ummah; priorities of the Islamic work are lost while the blasphemy and polytheism continue its grip and control over the Ummah. We should be alert to these atrocious plans carried out by the Ministry of Interior. The right answer is to follow what have been decided by the people of knowledge, as was said by Ibn Taymiyyah (Allah's mercy upon him): "people of Islam should join forces and support each other to get rid of the main "Kufr" who is controlling the countries of the Islamic world, even to bear the lesser damage to get rid of the major one, that is the great Kufr".

If there are more than one duty to be carried out, then the most important one should receive priority. Clearly after Belief (Imaan) there is no more important duty than pushing the American enemy out of the holy land. No other priority, except Belief, could be considered before it; the people of knowledge, Ibn Taymiyyah, stated: "to fight in defence of religion and Belief is a collective duty; there is no other duty after Belief than fighting the enemy who is corrupting the life and the religion. There is no preconditions for this duty and the enemy should be fought with one best abilities. (ref: supplement of Fatawa). If it is not possible to push back the enemy except by the collective movement of the Muslim people, then there is a duty on the Muslims to ignore the minor differences among themselves; the ill effect of ignoring these differences, at a given period of time, is much less than the ill effect of the occupation of the Muslims' land by the main Kufr. Ibn Taymiyyah had explained this issue and emphasised the importance of dealing with the major threat on the expense of the minor one. He described the situation of the Muslims and the Mujahideen and stated that even the military personnel who are not practising Islam are not exempted from the duty of Jihad against the enemy.

Ibn Taymiyyah, after mentioning the Moguls (Tatar) and their behaviour in changing the law of Allah, stated that: the ultimate aim of pleasing Allah, raising His word, instituting His religion and obeying His messenger (ALLAH'S BLESSING AND SALUTATIONS ON HIM) is to fight the enemy, in every aspects and in a complete manner; if the danger to the religion from not fighting is greater than that of fighting, then it is a duty to fight them even if the intention of some of the fighter is not pure i.e. fighting for the sake of leadership (personal gain) or if they do not observe some of the rules and commandments of Islam. To repel the greatest of the two dangers on the expense of the lesser one is an Islamic principle which should be observed. It was the tradition of the people of the Sunnah (Ahlul-Sunnah) to join and invade- fight- with the righteous and non righteous men. Allah may support this religion by righteous and non righteous people as told by the prophet (ALLAH'S BLESSING AND SALUTATIONS ON HIM). If it is not possible to fight except with the help of non righteous military personnel and commanders, then there are two possibilities: either fighting will be ignored and the others, who are the great danger to this life and religion, will take control; or to fight with the help of non righteous rulers and therefore repelling the greatest of the two dangers and implementing most, though not all, of the Islamic laws. The latter option is the right duty to be carried out in these circumstances and in many other similar situation. In fact many of the fights and conquests that took place after the time of Rashidoon, the guided Imams, were of this type. (majmoo' al Fatawa, 26/506).

No one, not even a blind or a deaf person, can deny the presence of the widely spread mischief's or the prevalence of the great sins that had reached the grievous iniquity of polytheism and to share with Allah in His sole right of sovereignty and making of the law. The All Mighty stated: {And when Luqman said to his son while he admonish him: O my son! do not associate ought with Allah; most surely polytheism is a grievous iniquity} (Luqman; 31:13). Man fabricated laws were put forward permitting what has been forbidden by Allah such as usury (Riba) and other matters. Banks dealing in usury are competing, for lands, with the two Holy Places and declaring war against Allah by disobeying His order {Allah has allowed trading and forbidden usury} (Baqarah; 2:275).

All this taking place at the vicinity of the Holy Mosque in the Holy Land! Allah (SWT) stated in His Holy Book a unique promise (that had not been promised to any other sinner) to the Muslims who deals in usury: {O you who believe! Be careful of your duty to Allah and relinquish what remains (due) from usury, if you are believers * But if you do (it) not, then be appraised of WAR from Allah and His Apostle} (Baqarah; 2:278-279). This is for the "Muslim" who deals in usury (believing that it is a sin), what is it then to the person who make himself a partner and equal to Allah, legalising (usury and other sins) what has been forbidden by Allah. Despite of all of the above we see the government misled and dragged some of the righteous Ulamah and Da'ees away from the issue of objecting to the greatest of sins and Kufr. (We bemoan this and can only say: "No power and power acquiring except through Allah").

Under such circumstances, to push the enemy-the greatest Kufr – out of the country is a prime duty. No other duty after Belief is more important than the duty of had. Utmost effort should be made to prepare and instigate the Ummah against the enemy, the American-Israeli alliance-occupying the country of the two Holy Places and the route of the Apostle (Allah's Blessings and Salutations may be on him) to the Furthest Mosque (Al-Aqsa Mosque). Also to remind the Muslims not to be engaged in an internal war among themselves, as that will have grieve consequences namely:

1 – consumption of the Muslims human resources as most casualties and fatalities will be among the Muslims people.

2 – Exhaustion of the economic and financial resources.

3 – Destruction of the country infrastructures

4 – Dissociation of the society

5 – Destruction of the oil industries. The presence of the USA Crusader military forces on land, sea and air of the states of the Islamic Gulf is the greatest danger threatening the largest oil reserve in the world. The

existence of these forces in the area will provoke the people of the country and induces aggression on their religion, feelings and prides and push them to take up armed struggle against the invaders occupying the land; therefore spread of the fighting in the region will expose the oil wealth to the danger of being burned up. The economic interests of the States of the Gulf and the land of the two Holy Places will be damaged and even a greater damage will be caused to the economy of the world. I would like here to alert my brothers, the Mujahideen, the sons of the nation, to protect this (oil) wealth and not to include it in the battle as it is a great Islamic wealth and a large economical power essential for the soon to be established Islamic state, by Allah's Permission and Grace. We also warn the aggressors, the USA, against burning this Islamic wealth (a crime which they may commit in order to prevent it, at the end of the war, from falling in the hands of its legitimate owners and to cause economic damages to the competitors of the USA in Europe or the Far East, particularly Japan which is the major consumer of the oil of the region).

6 – Division of the land of the two Holy Places, and annexing of the northerly part of it by Israel. Dividing the land of the two Holy Places is an essential demand of the Zionist-Crusader alliance. The existence of such a large country with its huge resources under the leadership of the forthcoming Islamic State, by Allah's Grace, represent a serious danger to the very existence of the Zionist state in Palestine. The Nobel Ka'ba, – the Qiblah of all Muslims – makes the land of the two Holy Places a symbol for the unity of the Islamic world. Moreover, the presence of the world largest oil reserve makes the land of the two Holy Places an important economical power in the Islamic world. The sons of the two Holy Places are directly related to the life style (Seerah) of their forefathers, the companions, may Allah be pleased with them. They consider the Seerah of their forefathers as a source and an example for re-establishing the greatness of this Ummah and to raise the word of Allah again. Furthermore the presence of a population of fighters in the south of Yemen, fighting in the cause of Allah, is a strategic threat to the Zionist-Crusader alliance in the area. The Prophet (ALLAH'S BLESSING AND SALUTATIONS ON HIM) said: (around twelve thousands will emerge from Aden/Abian

helping – the cause of – Allah and His messenger, they are the best, in the time, between me and them) narrated by Ahmad with a correct trustworthy reference.

7 – An internal war is a great mistake, no matter what reasons are there for it. the presence of the occupier – the USA – forces will control the outcome of the battle for the benefit of the international Kufr.

I address now my brothers of the security and military forces and the national guards may Allah preserve you hoard for Islam and the Muslims people:

O you protectors of unity and guardians of Faith; O you descendent of the ancestors who carried the light (torch) of guidance and spread it all over the world. O you grandsons of Sa'd Ibn Abi Waqqaas, Almothanna Ibn Haritha Ash-Shaybani, Alga'ga' Ibn Amroo Al-Tameemi and those pious companions who fought Jihad alongside them; you competed to join the army and the guard forces with the intention to carry out Jihad in the cause of Allah – raising His word – and to defend the faith of Islam and the land of the two Holy Places against the invaders and the occupying forces. That is the ultimate level of believing in this religion "Deen". But the regime had reversed these principles and their understanding, humiliating the Ummah and disobeying Allah. Half a century ago the rulers promised the Ummah to regain the first Qiblah, but fifty years later new generation arrived and the promises have been changed; Al-Aqsa Mosque handed over to the Zionists and the wounds of the Ummah still bleeding there. At the time when the Ummah has not regained the first Qiblah and the rout of the journey of the Prophet (Allah's Blessings and Salutations may be on him), and despite of all of the above, the Saudi regime had stunt the Ummah in the remaining sanctities, the Holy city of Makka and the mosque of the Prophet (Al-Masjid An-Nabawy), by calling the Christians army to defend the regime. The crusaders were permitted to be in the land of the two Holy Places. Not surprisingly though, the King himself wore the cross on his chest. The country was widely opened from the north-to- the south and from east-to-the west for the crusaders. The land was filled with the military bases of the USA and the allies. The regime became unable to keep control without the help of these bases. You know more than any body else about the size, intention and the danger of the presence of the USA military bases in the area. The regime betrayed the Ummah and joined the Kufr, assisting and helping them against the Muslims. It is well known that this is one of the ten "voiders" of Islam, deeds of de-Islamisation. By opening the Arab peninsula to the crusaders the regime disobeyed and acted against what has been enjoined by the messenger of Allah (Allah's Blessings and Salutations may be on him), while he was at the bed of his death: (Expel the polytheists out of the Arab Peninsula); (narrated by Al-Bukhari) and: (If I survive, Allah willing, I'll expel the Jews and the Christians out of the Arab Peninsula); saheeh Aljame' As-Sagheer.

It is out of date and no longer acceptable to claim that the presence of the crusaders is necessity and only a temporary measures to protect the land of the two Holy Places. Especially when the civil and the military infrastructures of Iraq were savagely destroyed showing the depth of the Zionist-Crusaders hatred to the Muslims and their children, and the rejection of the idea of replacing the crusaders forces by an Islamic force composed of the sons of the country and other Muslim people. moreover the foundations of the claim and the claim it self were demolished and wiped out by the sequence of speeches given by the leaders of the Kuffar in America. The latest of these speeches was the one given by William Perry, the Defense Secretary, after the explosion in Al-Khobar saying that: the presence of the American solders there is to protect the interest of the USA. The imprisoned Sheikh Safar Al-Hawali, may Allah hasten his release, wrote a book of seventy pages; in it he presented evidence and proof that the presence of the Americans in the Arab Peninsula is a pre-planed military occupation. The regime want to deceive the Muslim people in the same manner when the Palestinian fighters, Mujahideen, were deceived causing the loss of Al-Aqsa Mosque. In 1304 A.H (1936 AD) the awakened Muslims nation of Palestine started their great struggle, Jihad, against the British occupying forces. Britain was impotent to stop the Mujahideen and their Jihad, but their devil inspired that there is no way to stop the armed struggle in Palestine unless through their agent King Abdul Azeez, who managed to deceives the Mujahideen. King Abdul

Azeez carried out his duty to his British masters. He sent his two sons to meet the Mujahideen leaders and to inform them that King Abdul Azeez would guarantee the promises made by the British government in leaving the area and responding positively to the demands of the Mujahideen if the latter stop their Jihad. And so King Abdul Azeez caused the loss of the first Qiblah of the Muslims people. The King joined the crusaders against the Muslims and instead of supporting the Mujahideen in the cause of Allah, to liberate the Al-Aqsa Mosque, he disappointed and humiliated them.

Today, his son, king Fahd, trying to deceive the Muslims for the second time so as to loose what is left of the sanctities. When the Islamic world resented the arrival of the crusader forces to the land of the two Holy Places, the king told lies to the Ulamah (who issued Fatwas about the arrival of the Americans) and to the gathering of the Islamic leaders at the conference of Rabitah which was held in the Holy City of Makka. The King said that: "the issue is simple, the American and the alliance forces will leave the area in few months". Today it is seven years since their arrival and the regime is not able to move them out of the country. The regime made no confession about its inability and carried on lying to the people claiming that the American will leave. But never-never again; a believer will not be bitten twice from the same hole or snake! Happy is the one who takes note of the sad experience of the others!!

Instead of motivating the army, the guards, and the security men to oppose the occupiers, the regime used these men to protect the invaders, and further deepening the humiliation and the betrayal. (We bemoan this and can only say: "No power and power acquiring except through Allah"). To those little group of men within the army, police and security forces, who have been tricked and pressured by the regime to attack the Muslims and spill their blood, we would like to remind them of the narration: (I promise war against those who take my friends as their enemy) narrated by Al-Bukhari. And his saying (Allah's Blessings and Salutations may be on him) saying of: (In the day of judgement a man comes holding another and complaining being slain by him. Allah, blessed be His Names, asks: Why did you slay him?! The accused replies: I did so that all exaltation may be Yours. Allah, blessed be His Names, says: All exaltation is indeed mine! Another man comes holding a fourth with a similar complaint. Allah, blessed be His Names, asks: Why did you kill him?! The accused replies: I did so that exaltation may be for Mr. X! Allah, blessed be His Names, says: exaltation is mine, not for Mr. X, carry all the slain man's sins (and proceed to the Hell fire)!). In another wording of An-Nasa'i: "The accused says: for strengthening the rule or kingdom of Mr. X"

Today your brothers and sons, the sons of the two Holy Places, have started their Jihad in the cause of Allah, to expel the occupying enemy from of the country of the two Holy places. And there is no doubt you would like to carry out this mission too, in order to re-establish the greatness of this Ummah and to liberate its' occupied sanctities. Nevertheless, it must be obvious to you that, due to the imbalance of power between our armed forces and the enemy forces, a suitable means of fighting must be adopted i.e. using fast moving light forces that work under complete secrecy. In other word to initiate a guerrilla warfare, were the sons of the nation, and not the military forces, take part in it. And as you know, it is wise, in the present circumstances, for the armed military forces not to be engaged in a conventional fighting with the forces of the crusader enemy (the exceptions are the bold and the forceful operations carried out by the members of the armed forces individually, that is without the movement of the formal forces in its conventional shape and hence the responses will not be directed, strongly, against the army) unless a big advantage is likely to be achieved; and great losses induced on the enemy side (that would shaken and destroy its foundations and infrastructures) that will help to expel the defeated enemy from the country.

The Mujahideen, your brothers and sons, requesting that you support them in every possible way by supplying them with the necessary information, materials and arms. Security men are especially asked to cover up for the Mujahideen and to assist them as much as possible against the occupying enemy; and to spread rumours, fear and discouragement among the members of the enemy forces.

We bring to your attention that the regime, in order to create a friction and feud between the Mujahideen and yourselves, might resort to take a deliberate action against personnel of the security, guards and military forces and blame the Mujahideen for these actions. The regime should not be allowed to have such opportunity.

The regime is fully responsible for what had been incurred by the country and the nation; however the occupying American enemy is the principle and the main cause of the situation. Therefore efforts should be concentrated on destroying, fighting and killing the enemy until, by the Grace of Allah, it is completely defeated. The time will come – by the Permission of Allah – when you'll perform your decisive role so that the word of Allah will be supreme and the word of the infidels (Kaferoon) will be the inferior. You will hit with iron fist against the aggressors. You'll re-establish the normal course and give the people their rights and carry out your truly Islamic duty. Allah willing, I'll have a separate talk about these issues.

My Muslim Brothers (particularly those of the Arab Peninsula): The money you pay to buy American goods will be transformed into bullets and used against our brothers in Palestine and tomorrow (future) against our sons in the land of the two Holy places. By buying these goods we are strengthening their economy while our dispossession and poverty increases.

Muslims Brothers of land of the two Holy Places:

It is incredible that our country is the world largest buyer of arms from the USA and the area biggest commercial partners of the Americans who are assisting their Zionist brothers in occupying Palestine and in evicting and killing the Muslims there, by providing arms, men and financial supports.

To deny these occupiers from the enormous revenues of their trading with our country is a very important help for our Jihad against them. To express our anger and hate to them is a very important moral gesture.

By doing so we would have taken part in (the process of) cleansing our sanctities from the crusaders and the Zionists and forcing them, by the Permission of Allah, to leave disappointed and defeated.

We expect the woman of the land of the two Holy Places and other countries to carry out their role in boycotting the American goods.

If economical boycotting is intertwined with the military operations of the Mujahideen, then defeating the enemy will be even nearer, by the Permission of Allah. However if Muslims don't co-operate and support their Mujahideen brothers then, in effect, they are supplying the army of the enemy with financial help and extending the war and increasing the suffering of the Muslims.

The security and the intelligence services of the entire world can not force a single citizen to buy the goods of his/her enemy. Economical boycotting of the American goods is a very effective weapon of hitting and weakening the enemy, and it is not under the control of the security forces of the regime.

Before closing my talk, I have a very important message to the youths of Islam, men of the brilliant future of the Ummah of Muhammad (ALLAH'S BLESSING AND SALUTATIONS ON HIM). Our talk with the youths about their duty in this difficult period in the history of our Ummah. A period in which the youths and no one else came forward to carry out the variable and different duties. While some of the well known individuals had hesitated in their duty of defending Islam and saving themselves and their wealth from the injustice, aggression and terror – exercised by the government – the youths (may Allah protect them) were forthcoming and raised the banner of Jihad against the American-Zionist alliance occupying the sanctities of Islam. Others who have been tricked into loving this materialistic world, and those who have been terrorised by the government choose to give legitimacy to the greatest betrayal, the occupation of the land of the two Holy Places (We bemoan this and can only say: "No power and power acquiring except through Allah"). We are not surprised from the action of our youths. The youths were the companions of Muhammad (Allah's Blessings and Salutations may be on him), and was it not the youths themselves who killed Aba-Jahl, the Pharaoh of this Ummah?. Our youths are the best descendent of the best ancestors.

Abdul-Rahman Ibn Awf – may Allah be pleased with him – said: (I was at Badr where I noticed two youths one to my right and the other to my left. One of them asked me quietly (so not to be heard by the other): O uncle point out Aba-Jahl to me. What do you want him for?, said Abdul Rahman. The boy answered: I have been informed that he – Aba-Jahl – abused the Messenger of Allah (), I swear by Allah, who have my soul in His hand, that if I see Aba-Jahl I'll not let my shadow departs his shadow till one of us is dead. I was astonished, said Abdul Rahman; then the other youth said the same thing as the first one. Subsequently I saw Aba-Jahl among the people; I said to the boys do you see? this is the man you are asking me about. The two youths hit Aba-Jahl with their swords till he was dead. Allah is the greatest, Praise be to Him: Two youths of young age but with great perseverance, enthusiasm, courage and pride for the religion of Allah's, each one of them asking about the most important act of killing that should be induced on the enemy. That is the killing of the pharaoh of this Ummah Aba Jahl –, the leader of the unbelievers (Mushrikeen) at the battle of Badr. The role of Abdul Rahman Ibn Awf, may Allah be pleased with him, was to direct the two youths toward Aba-Jahl. That was the perseverance and the enthusiasm of the youths of that time and that was the perseverance and the enthusiasm of their fathers. It is this role that is now required from the people who have the expertise and knowledge in fighting the enemy. They should guide their brothers and sons in this matter; once that has been done, then our youths will repeat what their forefathers had said before: "I swear by Allah if I see him I'll not let my shadow to departs from his shadow till one of us is dead".

And the story of Abdur-Rahman Ibn Awf about Ummayyah Ibn Khalaf shows the extent of Bilal's (may Allah be pleased with him) persistence in killing the head of the Kufr: "the head of Kufr is Ummayyah Ibn Khalaf. . . . I shall live not if he survives" said Bilal.

Few days ago the news agencies had reported that the Defence Secretary of the Crusading Americans had said that "the explosion at Riyadh and Al-Khobar had taught him one lesson: that is not to withdraw when attacked by coward terrorists".

We say to the Defence Secretary that his talk can induce a grieving mother to laughter! and shows the fears that had enshrined you all. Where was this false courage of yours when the explosion in Beirut took place on 1983 AD (1403 A.H). You were turned into scattered pits and pieces at that time; 241 mainly marines solders were killed. And where was this courage of yours when two explosions made you to leave Aden in lees than twenty four hours!

But your most disgraceful case was in Somalia; where- after vigorous propaganda about the power of the USA and its post cold war leadership of the new world order – you moved tens of thousands of international force, including twenty eight thousands American solders into Somalia. However, when tens of your solders were killed in minor battles and one American Pilot was dragged in the streets of Mogadishu you left the area carrying disappointment, humiliation, defeat and your dead with you. Clinton appeared in front of the whole world threatening and promising revenge, but these threats were merely a preparation for withdrawal. You have been disgraced by Allah and you withdrew; the extent of your impotence and weaknesses became very clear. It was a pleasure for the "heart" of every Muslim and a remedy to the "chests" of believing nations to see you defeated in the three Islamic cities of Beirut, Aden and Mogadishu.

I say to Secretary of Defence: The sons of the land of the two Holy Places had come out to fight against the Russian in Afghanistan, the Serb in Bosnia-Herzegovina and today they are fighting in Chechenia and – by the Permission of Allah- they have been made victorious over your partner, the Russians. By the command of Allah, they are also fighting in Tajakistan.

I say: Since the sons of the land of the two Holy Places feel and strongly believe that fighting (Jihad) against the Kuffar in every part of the world, is absolutely essential; then they would be even more enthusiastic, more powerful and larger in number upon fighting on their own land – the place of their births – defending the greatest of their sanctities, the noble Ka'ba (the Qiblah of all Muslims). They know that the Muslims of the world will assist and help them to victory. To liberate their sanctities is the greatest of issues concerning all Muslims; It is the duty of every Muslims in this world.

I say to you William (Defence Secretary) that: These youths love death as you loves life. They inherit dignity, pride, courage, generosity, truthfulness and sacrifice from father to father. They are most delivering and steadfast at war. They inherit these values from their ancestors (even from the time of the Jaheliyyah, before Islam). These values were approved and completed by the arriving Islam as stated by the messenger of Allah (Allah's Blessings and Salutations may be on him): "I have been send to perfecting the good values". (Saheeh Al-Jame' As-Sagheer).

When the pagan King Amroo Ibn Hind tried to humiliate the pagan Amroo Ibn Kulthoom, the latter cut the head of the King with his sword rejecting aggression, humiliation and indignation.

If the king oppresses the people excessively, we reject submitting to humiliation.

By which legitimacy (or command) O Amroo bin Hind you want us to be degraded?!

By which legitimacy (or command) O Amroo bin Hind you listen to our foes and disrespect us?!

Our toughness has, O Amroo, tired the enemies before you, never giving in!

Our youths believe in paradise after death. They believe that taking part in fighting will not bring their day nearer; and staying behind will not postpone their day either. Exalted be to Allah who said: {And a soul will not die but with the permission of Allah, the term is fixed} (Aal Imraan; 3:145). Our youths believe in the saying of the messenger of Allah (Allah's Blessings and Salutations may be on him): "O boy, I teach a few words; guard (guard the cause of, keep the commandments of) Allah, then He guards you, guard (the cause of) Allah, then He will be with you; if you ask (for your need) ask Allah, if you seek assistance, seek Allah's; and know definitely that if the Whole World gathered to (bestow) profit on you they will not profit you except with what was determined for you by Allah, and if they gathered to harm you they will not harm you except with what has been determined for you by Allah; Pen lifted, papers dried, it is fixed nothing in these truths can be changed" Saheeh Al-Jame' As-Sagheer. Our youths took note of the meaning of the poetic verse:

"If death is a predetermined must, then it is a shame to die cowardly."

and the other poet saying:

"Who do not die by the sword will die by other reason; many causes are there but one death".

These youths believe in what has been told by Allah and His messenger (Allah's Blessings and Salutations may be on him) about the greatness of the reward for the Mujahideen and Martyrs; Allah, the most exalted said: {and – so far – those who are slain in the way of Allah, He will by no means allow their deeds to perish. He will guide them and improve their condition. and cause them to enter the garden – paradise – which He has made known to them}. (Muhammad; 47:4-6). Allah the Exalted also said: {and do not speak of those who are slain in Allah's way as dead; nay – they are – alive, but you do not perceive} (Bagarah; 2:154). His messenger (Allah's Blessings and Salutations may be on him) said: "for those who strive in His cause Allah prepared hundred degrees (levels) in paradise; in-between two degrees as the in-between heaven and earth". Saheeh Al-Jame' As-Sagheer. He (Allah's Blessings and Salutations may be on him) also said: "the best of the martyrs are those who do NOT turn their faces away from the battle till they are killed. They are in the high level of Jannah (paradise). Their Lord laughs to them (in pleasure) and when your Lord laughs to a slave of His, He will not hold him to an account". narrated by Ahmad with correct and trustworthy reference. And: "a martyr will not feel the pain of death except like how you feel when you are pinched". Saheeh Al-Jame' As-Sagheer. He also said: "a martyr privileges are guaranteed by Allah; forgiveness with the first gush of his blood, he will be shown his seat in paradise, he will be decorated with the jewels of belief (Imaan), married off to the beautiful ones, protected from the test in the grave, assured security in the day of judgement, crowned with the crown of dignity, a ruby of which is better than this whole world (Duniah) and its' entire content, wedded to seventy two of the pure Houries (beautiful ones of Paradise) and his intercession on the behalf of seventy of his relatives will be accepted". Narrated by Ahmad and At-Tirmithi (with the correct and trustworthy reference).

Those youths know that their rewards in fighting you, the USA, is double than their rewards in fighting some one else not from the people of the book. They have no intention except to enter paradise by killing you. An infidel, and enemy of God like you, cannot be in the same hell with his righteous executioner.

Our youths chanting and reciting the word of Allah, the most exalted: {fight them; Allah will punish them by your hands and bring them to disgrace, and assist you against them and heal the heart of a believing people} (At-Taubah; 9:14) and the words of the prophet (ALLAH'S BLESSING AND SALUTATIONS ON HIM): "I swear by Him, who has my soul in His hand, that no man get killed fighting them today, patiently attacking and not retreating, surely Allah will let him into paradise". And his (Allah's Blessings and Salutations may be on him) saying to them: "get up to a paradise as wide as heaven and earth".

The youths also reciting the All Mighty words of: "so when you meat in battle those who disbelieve, then smite the necks..." (Muhammad; 47:19). Those youths will not ask you (William Perry) for explanations, they will tell you singing there is nothing between us need to be explained, there is only killing and neck smiting.

And they will say to you what their grand father, Haroon Ar-Rasheed, Ameer-ul-Mu'meneen, replied to your grandfather, Nagfoor, the Byzantine emperor, when he threatened the Muslims: "from Haroon Ar-Rasheed, Ameer-ul-Mu'meneen, to Nagfoor, the dog of the Romans; the answer is what you will see not what you hear". Haroon El-Rasheed led the armies of Islam to the battle and handed Nagfoor a devastating defeat.

The youths you called cowards are competing among themselves for fighting and killing you. reciting what one of them said:

The crusader army became dust when we detonated al-Khobar.

With courageous youth of Islam fearing no danger.

If (they are) threatened: The tyrants will kill you, they reply my death is a victory.

I did not betray that king, he did betray our Qiblah.

And he permitted in the holy country the most filthy sort of humans.

I have made an oath by Allah, the Great, to fight who ever rejected the faith.

For more than a decade, they carried arms on their shoulders in Afghanistan and they have made vows to Allah that as long as they are alive, they will continue to carry arms against you until you are – Allah willing – expelled, defeated and humiliated, they will carry on as long as they live saying:

O William, tomorrow you will know which young man is confronting your misguided brethren!

A youth fighting in smile, returning with the spear coloured red.

May Allah keep me close to knights, humans in peace, demons in war.

Lions in Jungle but their teeth are spears and Indian swords.

The horses witness that I push them hard forwarded in the fire of battle.

The dust of the battle bears witnesses for me, so also the fighting itself, the pens and the books!

So to abuse the grandsons of the companions, may Allah be pleased with them, by calling them cowards and challenging them by refusing to leave the land of the two Holy Places shows the insanity and the imbalance you are suffering from. Its appropriate "remedy," however, is in the hands of the youths of Islam, as the poet said:

I am willing to sacrifice self and wealth for knights who never disappointed me.

Knights who are never fed up or deterred by death, even if the mill of war turns.

In the heat of battle they do not care, and cure the insanity of the enemy by their 'insane' courage.

Terrorising you, while you are carrying arms on our land, is a legitimate and morally demanded duty. It is a legitimate right well known to all humans and other creatures. Your example and our example is like a snake which entered into a house of a man and got killed by him. The coward is the one who lets you walk, while carrying arms, freely on his land and provides you with peace and security.

Those youths are different from your soldiers. Your problem will be how to convince your troops to fight, while our problem will be how to restrain our youths to wait for their turn in fighting and in operations. These youths are commendation and praiseworthy.

They stood up tall to defend the religion; at the time when the government misled the prominent scholars and tricked them into issuing Fatwas (that have no basis neither in the book of Allah, nor in the Sunnah of His prophet (Allah's Blessings and Salutations may be on him)) of opening the land of the two Holy Places for the Christians armies and handing the Al-Aqsa Mosque to the Zionists. Twisting the meanings of the holy text will not change this fact at all. They deserve the praise of the poet:

I rejected all the critics, who chose the wrong way;

I rejected those who enjoy fireplaces in clubs discussing eternally;

I rejected those, who inspite being lost, think they are at the goal;

I respect those who carried on not asking or bothering about the difficulties;

Never letting up from their goals, inspite all hardships of the road;

Whose blood is the oil for the flame guiding in the darkness of confusion;

I feel still the pain of (the loss) Al-Quds in my internal organs;

That loss is like a burning fire in my intestines;

I did not betray my covenant with God, when even states did betray it! As their grandfather Assim Bin Thabit said rejecting a surrender offer of the pagans:

What for an excuse I had to surrender, while I am still able, having arrows and my bow having a tough string?!

Death is truth and ultimate destiny, and life will end any way. If I do not fight you, then my mother must be insane!

The youths hold you responsible for all of the killings and evictions of the Muslims and the violation of the sanctities, carried out by your Zionist brothers in Lebanon; you openly supplied them with arms and finance.

More than 600,000 Iraqi children have died due to lack of food and medicine and as a result of the unjustifiable aggression (sanction) imposed on Iraq and its nation. The children of Iraq are our children. You, the USA, together with the Saudi regime are responsible for the shedding of the blood of these innocent children. Due to all of that, what ever treaty you have with our country is now null and void.

The treaty of Hudaybiyyah was cancelled by the messenger of Allah (Allah's Blessings and Salutations may be on him) once Quraysh had assisted Bani Bakr against Khusa'ah, the allies of the prophet (Allah's Blessings and Salutations may be on him). The prophet (Allah's Blessings and Salutations may be on him) fought Quraysh and concurred Makka. He (Allah's Blessings and Salutations may be on him) considered the treaty with Bani Qainuqa' void because one of their Jews publicly hurt one Muslim woman, one single woman, at the market. Let alone then, the killing you caused to hundred of thousands Muslims and occupying their sanctities. It is now clear that those who claim that the blood of the American solders (the enemy occupying the land of the Muslims) should be protected are merely repeating what is imposed on them by the regime; fearing the aggression and interested in saving themselves. It is a duty now on every tribe in the Arab Peninsula to fight, Jihad, in the cause of Allah and to cleanse the land from those occupiers. Allah knows that there blood is permitted (to be spilled) and their wealth is a booty; their wealth is a booty to those who kill them. The most Exalted said in the verse of As-Sayef, The Sword: "so when the sacred months have passed away, then slay the idolaters where ever you find them, and take them captives and besiege them and lie in wait for them in every ambush" (At-Tauba; 9:5). Our youths knew that the humiliation suffered by the Muslims as a result of the occupation of their sanctities can not be kicked and removed except by explosions and Jihad. As the poet said:

The walls of oppression and humiliation cannot be demolished except in a rain of bullets.

The freeman does not surrender leadership to infidels and sinners.

Without shedding blood no degradation and branding can be removed from the forehead.

I remind the youths of the Islamic world, who fought in Afghanistan and Bosnia-Herzegovina with their wealth, pens, tongues and themselves that the battle had not finished yet. I remind them about the talk between Jibreel (Gabriel) and the messenger of Allah (Allah's Blessings and Salutations may be on both of them) after the battle of Ahzab when the messenger of Allah (Allah's Blessings and Salutations may be on him) returned to Medina and before putting his sword aside; when Jibreel (Allah's Blessings and Salutations may be on him) descend saying: "are you putting your sword aside? by Allah the angels haven't dropped their arms yet; march with your companions to Bani Quraydah, I am (going) ahead of you to throw fears in their hearts and to shake their fortresses on them". Jibreel marched with the angels (Allah's Blessings and Salutations may be on them all), followed by the messenger of Allah (Allah's Blessings and Salutations may be on him) marching with the immigrants, Muhajeroon, and supporters, Ansar. (narrated by Al-Bukhary).

These youths know that: if one is not to be killed one will die (any way) and the most honourable death is to be killed in the way of Allah. They are even more determined after the martyrdom of the four heroes who bombed the Americans in Riyadh. Those youths who raised high the head of the Ummah and humiliated the Americans-the occupier – by their operation in Riyadh. They remember the poetry of Ja'far, the second commander in the battle of Mu'tah, in which three thousand Muslims faced over a hundred thousand Romans:

How good is the Paradise and its nearness, good with cool drink But the Romans are promised punishment (in Hell), if I meet them.

I will fight them.

And the poetry of Abdullah Bin Rawaha, the third commander in the battle of Mu'tah, after the martyrdom of Ja'far, when he felt some hesitation:

O my soul if you do not get killed, you are going to die, anyway.

This is death pool in front of you!

You are getting what you have wished for (martyrdom) before, and you follow the example of the two previous commanders you are rightly guided!

As for our daughters, wives, sisters and mothers they should take prime example from the prophet (Allah's Blessings and Salutations may be on him) pious female companions, may Allah be pleased with them; they should adopt the life style (Seerah) of the female companions of courage, sacrifice and generosity in the cause of the supremacy of Allah's religion. They should remember the courage and the personality of Fatima, daughter of Khatab, when she accepted Islam and stood up in front of her brother, Omar Ibn Al-Khatab and challenged him (before he became a Muslim) saying: "O Omar, what will you do if the truth is not in your religion?!" And to remember the stand of Asma', daughter of Abu Bakr, on the day of Hijra, when she attended the Messenger and his companion in the cave and split her belt in two pieces for them. And to remember the stand of Naseeba Bent Ka'b striving to defend the messenger of Allah (Allah's Blessings and Salutations may be on him) on the day of Uhud, in which she suffered twelve injuries, one of which was so deep leaving a deep lifelong scar! They should remember the generosity of the early woman of Islam who raised finance for the Muslims army by selling their jewelery. Our women had set a tremendous example of generosity in the cause of Allah; they motivated and encouraged their sons, brothers and husbands to fight – in the cause of Allah – in Afghanistan, Bosnia-Herzegovina, Chechenia and in other countries. We ask Allah to accept from them these deeds, and may He help their fathers, brothers, husbands and sons. May Allah strengthen the belief – Imaan – of our women in the way of generosity and sacrifice for the supremacy of the word of Allah. Our women weep not, except over men who fight in the cause of Allah; our women instigate their brothers to fight in the cause of Allah.

Our women bemoan only fighters in the cause of Allah, as said:

Do not moan on any one except a lion in the woods, courageous in the burning wars.

Let me die dignified in wars, honourable death is better than my current life.

Our women encourage Jihad saying:

Prepare yourself like a struggler, the matter is bigger than words!

Are you going to leave us else for the wolves of Kufr eating our wings?!

The wolves of Kufr are mobilising all evil persons from every where!

Where are the freemen defending free women by the arms?!

Death is better than life in humiliation! Some scandals and shames will never be otherwise eradicated.

My Muslim Brothers of The World:

Your brothers in Palestine and in the land of the two Holy Places are calling upon your help and asking you to take part in fighting against the enemy – your enemy and their enemy – the Americans and the Israelis. they are asking you to do whatever you can, with one own means and ability, to expel the enemy, humiliated and defeated, out of the sanctities of Islam. Exalted be to Allah said in His book: {and if they ask your support, because they are oppressed in their faith, then support them!} (Anfaal; 8:72)

O you horses (soldiers) of Allah ride and march on. This is the time of hardship so be tough. And know that your gathering and co-operation in order to liberate the sanctities of Islam is the right step toward unifying the word of the Ummah under the banner of "No God but Allah").

From our place we raise our palms humbly to Allah asking Him to bestow on us His guide in every aspects of this issue.

Our Lord, we ask you to secure the release of the truthful scholars, Ulama, of Islam and pious youths of the Ummah from their imprisonment. O Allah, strengthen them and help their families.

Our Lord, the people of the cross had come with their horses (soldiers) and occupied the land of the two Holy places. And the Zionist Jews fiddling as they wish with the Al-Aqsa Mosque, the route of the ascendance of the messenger of Allah (ALLAH'S BLESSING AND SALUTATIONS ON HIM). Our Lord, shatter their gathering, divide them among themselves, shaken the earth under their feet and give us control over them; Our Lord, we take refuge in you from their deeds and take you as a shield between us and them

Our Lord, show us a black day in them!

Our Lord, show us the wonderment of your ability in them!

Our Lord, You are the Revealer of the book, Director of the clouds, You defeated the allies (Ahzab); defeat them and make us victorious over them.

Our Lord, You are the one who help us and You are the one who assist us, with Your Power we move and by Your Power we fight. On You we rely and You are our cause.

Our Lord, those youths got together to make Your religion victorious and raise Your banner. Our Lord, send them Your help and strengthen their hearts.

Our Lord, make the youths of Islam steadfast and descend patience on them and guide their shots!

Our Lord, unify the Muslims and bestow love among their hearts!

O Lord pour down upon us patience, and make our steps firm and assist us against the unbelieving people!

Our Lord, do not lay on us a burden as Thou didst lay on those before us; Our Lord, do not impose upon us that which we have no strength to bear; and pardon us and grant us protection and have mercy on us, Thou art our patron, so help us against the unbelieving people.

Our Lord, guide this Ummah, and make the right conditions (by which) the people of your obedience will be in dignity and the people of disobedience in humiliation, and by which the good deeds are enjoined and the bad deeds are forebode.

Our Lord, bless Muhammad, Your slave and messenger, his family and descendants, and companions and salute him with a (becoming) salutation.

And our last supplication is: All praise is due to Allah.

Usamah bin Muhammad bin Laden
Friday, 9/4/1417 A.H (23/8/1996 AD)
Hindukush Mountains, Khurasan, Afghanistan.

OCTOBER 21, 2001

Interview with Tayseer Alouni

The following is a transcript of an hour-long interview with Osama bin Laden. It was conducted by Tayseer Alouni, the Kabul correspondent of al Jazeera, on October 21, 2001 and later translated by CNN.

TAYSEER ALOUNI: Dear viewers, welcome to this much-anticipated interview with the leader of the al Qaeda organization, Sheikh Osama Bin Laden.

Sheikh, the question that's on the mind of many people around the world: America claims that it has convincing evidence of your collusion in the events in New York and Washington. What's your answer?

OSAMA BIN LADEN: America has made many accusations against us and many other Muslims around the world. Its charge that we are carrying out acts of terrorism is an unwarranted description.

We never heard in our lives a court decision to convict someone based on a "secret" proof it has. The logical thing to do is to present a proof to a court of law. What many leaders have said so far is that America has an indication only, and not a tangible proof. They describe those brave guys who took the battle to the heart of America and destroyed its most famous economic and military landmarks.

They did this, as we understand it, and this is something we have agitated for before, as a matter of self-defense, in defense of our brothers and sons in Palestine, and to liberate our sacred religious sites/things. If inciting people to do that is terrorism, and if killing those who kill our sons is terrorism, then let history be witness that we are terrorists.

ALOUNI: Sheikh, those who follow your statements and speeches may link your threats to what happened in America. To quote one of your latest statements: "I swear that America won't enjoy security before we live it for real in Palestine." It is easy for anyone following developments to link the acts to your threats.

BIN LADEN: It is easy to link them.

We have agitated for this for years and we have issued statements and fatwas to that effect. This appeared in the investigations into the four young men who destroyed the American center in Ulayya in Riyadh, as disclosed and published by the Saudi government. The [Saudis] reported that they were influenced by some of the fatwas and statements that we issued. Also, apart from that, incitement continues in many meetings and has been published in the media. If they mean, or if you mean, that there is a link as a result of our incitement, then it is true. We incite because incitement is our [unintelligible] today. God assigned incitement to the best of all mankind, Mohammed, who said, "Fight for the sake of God. Assign this to no one but yourself, and incite the faithful."

[Bin Laden recites verses from the Quran.]

This is a true response. We have incited battle against Americans and Jews. This is true.

ALOUNI: Al Qaeda is facing now a country that leads the world militarily, politically, technologically. Surely, the al Qaeda organization does not have the economic means that the United States has. How can al Qaeda defeat America militarily?

BIN LADEN: This battle is not between al Qaeda and the U.S. This is a battle of Muslims against the global crusaders. In the past when al Qaeda fought with the mujahedeen, we were told, "Wow, can you defeat the Soviet Union?" The Soviet Union scared the whole world then. NATO used to tremble of fear of the Soviet Union. Where is that power now? We barely remember it. It broke down into many small states and Russia remained.

God, who provided us with his support and kept us steadfast until the Soviet Union was defeated, is able to provide us once more with his support to defeat America on the same land and with the same people. We believe that the defeat of America is possible, with the help of God, and is even easier for us, God permitting, than the defeat of the Soviet Union was before.

ALOUNI: How can you explain that?

BIN LADEN: We experienced the Americans through our brothers who went into combat against them in Somalia, for example. We found they had no power worthy of mention. There was a huge aura over America – the United States – that terrified people even before they entered combat. Our brothers who were here in Afghanistan tested them, and together with some of the mujahedeen in Somalia, God granted them victory. America exited dragging its tails in failure, defeat, and ruin, caring for nothing.

America left faster than anyone expected. It forgot all that tremendous media fanfare about the new world order, that it is the master of that order, and that it does whatever it wants. It forgot all of these propositions, gathered up its army, and withdrew in defeat, thanks be to God. We experienced combat against the Russians for 10 years, from 1979 to 1989, thanks be to God. Then we continued against the communists in Afghanistan. Today, we're at the end of our second week. There is no comparison between the two battles, between this group and that. We pray to God to give us his support and to make America ever more reluctant. God is capable of that.

ALOUNI: You said you want to defeat America on this land. Don't you think that the presence of al Qaeda on Afghanistan soil is costing the Afghan people a high price?

BIN LADEN: This is a partial point of view. When we came to Afghanistan to support the mujahedeen in 1979, against the Russians, the Saudi government asked me officially not to enter Afghanistan due to how close my family is to the Saudi leadership. They ordered me to stay in Peshawar, because in the event the Russians arrested me that will be a proof of our support of the mujahedeen against the Soviet Union. At that time, the whole world was scared of the Soviet Union. I didn't obey their order. They thought my entry into Afghanistan was damning to them. I didn't listen to them and I went into Afghanistan for the first time.

We sacrificed a lot in order to keep the Muslim faith alive and save the children. This is a duty for every Muslim, in general, not the Afghans especially. If I run to the rescue of my brothers in Palestine, it doesn't mean it's Osama's duty alone. This is a duty of all Muslims. The jihad is a duty for everyone, not just for the Afghans. The Afghans are suffering, that's true, but this is their Islamic duty. As far as the bombing of Afghanistan, this is not a personal vendetta. America didn't take my money or hurt me in any way. The bombing is a direct effect of our inciting against the Jews and the Americans.

America is against the establishment of any Islamic government. The prophet has said, "They will be target because of their religion." Not because Osama bin Laden is there. When I came here the first time it was because of a desire to revive the Muslim spirit and an attempt at rescuing the children and the powerless. The British attacked Afghanistan before Osama bin Laden was here, Russians came here before me and now the Americans. We pray that god will defeat them just like he did their allies before them. We ask God to give us the power to defeat them as we did others before.

ALOUNI: Let's get back to what happened in New York and Washington. What is your assessment of the attacks on America? What's their effect on America and the Muslim world?

BIN LADEN: The events of Tuesday, September the 11th, in New York and Washington are great on all levels. Their repercussions are not over.

Although the collapse of the twin towers is huge, but the events that followed, and I'm not just talking about the economic repercussions, those are continuing, the events that followed are dangerous and more enormous than the collapse of the towers.

The values of this Western civilization under the leadership of America have been destroyed. Those awesome symbolic towers that speak of liberty, human rights, and humanity have been destroyed. They have gone up in smoke.

The proof came when the U.S. government pressured the media not to run our statements that are not longer than very few minutes. They felt that the truth started to reach the American people, the truth that we are not terrorists as they understand it but because we are being attacked in Palestine, Iraq, Lebanon, Sudan, Somalia, Kashmir, the Philippines and everywhere else. They understood the truth that this is a reaction from the youth of the Muslim nation against the British government. They forgot all about fair and objective reporting and reporting the other side of the issue. I tell you freedom and human rights in America are doomed. The U.S. government will lead the American people and the West in general will enter an unbearable hell and a choking life because the Western leadership acts under the Zionist lobby's influence for the purpose of serving Israel, which kills our sons unlawfully in order for them to remain in their leadership positions.

ALOUNI: What is your assessment of the Arabic reaction and the effects on the Islamic world? Some were joyous. Others said, "We can't accept this. This is terrorism, not Islam."

BIN LADEN: The events proved the extent of terrorism that America exercises in the world. Bush stated that the world has to be divided in two: Bush and his supporters, and any country that doesn't get into the global crusade is with the terrorists. What terrorism is clearer than this? Many governments were forced to support this "new terrorism." They had to go along with this although they knew that we are defending our brothers and defending our sacred values. Many Western and Eastern leaders have said that the true roots of terrorism should be dealt with; they meant the Palestinian cause. Then we have a righteous cause, but they couldn't admit this out loud of fear of America. They say we are terrorists but solve the Palestinian cause. All of a sudden, Bush and Blair declared, "The time has come to establish an independent state for Palestine." Throughout the past years the time hasn't come, until after these attacks, for the establishment of the Palestinian state. They only understand the language of attacks and killings.

Just as they're killing us, we have to kill them so that there will be a balance of terror. This is the first time the balance of terror has been close between the two parties, between Muslims and Americans, in the modern age. American politicians used to do whatever they wanted with us. The victim was forbidden to scream or to moan. [unintelligible]

Clinton has said, "Israel has the right to defend itself," after the massacres of Qana. He didn't even reprimand Israel. When the new President Bush and Colin Powell declared in the first few months of their taking office that they will move the American embassy to Jerusalem. They said Jerusalem will be the eternal capital of Israel. They got a standing ovation in Congress and the Senate. This is the biggest bigotry, and this is tyranny loud and clear.

The battle has moved to inside America. We will work to continue this battle, God permitting, until victory or until we meet God before that occurs.

ALOUNI: Sheikh, I see that most of your answers are about Palestine and the Palestinian cause. In the beginning, your focus on killing the unfaithful and the Jews . . . and you specified then that the Americans should be sent out of the Arabian Peninsula. Now you're turning your attention to Palestine first and the Arabian Peninsula second. What's your comment?

BIN LADEN: Jihad is a duty to liberate Al-Aqsa, and to help the powerless in Palestine, Iraq and Lebanon and in every Muslim country. There is no doubt that the liberation of the Arabian Peninsula from infidels is a duty as well. But it is not right to say that Osama put the Palestinian issue first. I have given speeches in which I encourage Muslims to boycott America economically. I said Americans take our money and give it to Israel to kill our children in Palestine. I established a front a few years ago named The Islamic Front for Jihad against the Jews and the Crusaders. Sometimes we find the right elements to push for one cause more than the other. Last year's blessed intifada helped us to push more for the Palestinian issue. This push helps the other cause. Attacking America helps the cause of Palestine and vice versa. No conflict between the two; on the contrary, one serves the other.

ALOUNI: Sheikh, now let's talk about Christians and Jews. You issued a fatwa for jihad against the Christians and the Jews. As we can see, some other clerics also issued fatwas. There might be some who share your views, and some who oppose them and said this is against the teachings of Islam. They ask how can you kill a Jew or a Christian or a Catholic just because of his religion? They say that your statements contradict what Muslim clerics teach.

BIN LADEN: God bless Allah, many fatwas have been declared on these issues, especially in Pakistan. Sami Zai in Pakistan is a very well known authority on this. He has written many times on the subject. So did the famous Abdullah bin Ohkmah Al-Shehebi of Saudi Arabia. I read a book titled "The Truth About The New Crusades." They all wrote about and allowed the fighting of Americans and Israelis in Palestine and allowing their killings and destroying their economies and properties.

Q [interrupting]: How about the killing of innocent civilians?

BIN LADEN: The killing of innocent civilians, as America and some intellectuals claim, is really very strange talk. Who said that our children and civilians are not innocent and that shedding their blood is justified? That it is lesser in degree? When we kill their innocents, the entire world from east to west screams at us, and America rallies its allies, agents, and the sons of its agents. Who said that our blood is not blood, but theirs is? Who made this pronouncement? Who has been getting killed in our countries for decades? More than 1 million children, more than 1 million children died in Iraq and others are still dying. Why do we not hear someone screaming or condemning, or even someone's words of consolation or condolence?

How come millions of Muslims are being killed? Where are the experts, the writers, the scholars and the freedom fighters, where are the ones who have an ounce a faith in them? They react only if we kill American civilians, and every day we are being killed, children are being killed in Palestine. We should review the books. Human nature makes people stand with the powerful without noticing it. When they talk about us, they know we won't respond to them. In the past, an Arab king once killed an ordinary Arab man. The people started wondering how come kings have the right to kill people just like that. Then the victim's brother went and killed the king in revenge. People were disappointed with the young man and asked him, "How could you kill a king for your brother?" The man said, "My brother is my king." We consider all our children in Palestine to be kings.

We kill the kings of the infidels, kings of the crusaders, and civilian infidels in exchange for those of our children they kill. This is permissible in law and intellectually.

ALOUNI: So what you are saying is that this is a type of reciprocal treatment. They kill our innocents, so we kill their innocents.

BIN LADEN: So we kill their innocents, and I say it is permissible in law and intellectually, because those who spoke on this matter spoke from a juridical perspective.

ALOUNI: What is their position?

BIN LADEN: That it is not permissible. They spoke of evidence that the Messenger of God forbade the killing of women and children. This is true.

[Break in tape.]

ALOUNI: This is exactly what I'm asking about.

BIN LADEN: However, this prohibition of the killing of children and innocents is not absolute. It is not absolute. There are other texts that restrict it.

I agree that the Prophet Mohammed forbade the killing of babies and women. That is true, but this is not absolute. There is a saying, "If the infidels killed women and children on purpose, we shouldn't shy way from treating them in the same way to stop them from doing it again." The men that God helped [attack, on September 11] did not intend to kill babies; they intended to destroy the strongest military power in the world, to attack the Pentagon that houses more than 64,000 employees, a military center that houses the strength and the military intelligence.

ALOUNI: How about the twin towers?

BIN LADEN: The towers are an economic power and not a children's school. Those that were there are men that supported the biggest economic power in the world. They have to review their books. We will do as they do. If they kill our women and our innocent people, we will kill their women and their innocent people until they stop.

ALOUNI: Media organizations as well as intelligence information says that you run a big network in some 40 to 50 countries. There is information that al Qaeda is very infl uential and powerful and it is behind attacks and Islamic foundations and terrorist organizations. How much is al Qaeda dependent on Osama Bin Laden?

BIN LADEN: This has nothing to do with this poor servant of God, nor with the al Qaeda organization. We are the children of an Islamic nation whose leader is Mohammed.

We have one religion, one God, one book, one prophet, one nation. Our book teaches us to be brothers of a faith. All the Muslims are brothers. The name "al Qaeda" was established a long time ago by mere chance. The late Abu Ebeida El-Banashiri established the training camps for our mujahedeen against Russia's terrorism. We used to call the training camp al Qaeda [meaning "the base" in English]. And the name stayed. We speak about the conscience of the nation; we are the sons of the nation. We brothers in Islam from the Middle East, Philippines, Malaysia, India, Pakistan and as far as Mauritania.

Those men who sacrificed themselves in New York and Washington, they are the spokesmen of the nation's conscience. They are the nation's conscience that saw they have to avenge against the oppression.

Not all terrorism is cursed; some terrorism is blessed. A thief, a criminal, for example feels terrorized by the police. So, do we say to the policeman, "You are a terrorist"? No. Police terrorism against criminals is a blessed terrorism because it will prevent the criminal from repeating his deed. America and Israel exercise the condemned terrorism. We practice the good terrorism which stops them from killing our children in Palestine and elsewhere.

ALOUNI: What's al Qaeda's strategic plan in the Arab world. Some countries had commented about what's going on while others supported the Americans in their position toward you. The Saudi interior minister warned people against you, and against what you say, and against what you do and the path you follow. What's your reaction to his statement?

BIN LADEN: We are a part of that nation. We work hard to lift it out of oppression, and to stop those who want to manipulate its book and its God. I heard some of what the Saudi interior minister said when he said that we are turning Muslims to atheists, God forbid. Our goal is for our nation to unite in the face of the Christian crusade. This is the fiercest battle. Muslims have never faced anything bigger than this. Bush said it in his own words: "crusade." When Bush says that, they try to cover up for him, then he said he didn't mean it. He said "crusade." Bush divided the world into two: "either with us or with terrorism." Bush is the leader; he carries the big cross and walks. I swear that every one who follows Bush in his scheme has given up Islam and the word of the prophet. This is very clear. The prophet has said, "Believers don't follow Jews or Christians." Our wise people have said that those who follow the unfaithful have become unfaithful themselves. Those who follow Bush in his crusade against Muslims have denounced God.

[Bin Laden recites verses from the Quran on same subject.]

Those who support Bush, even with one word, have fallen.

ALOUNI: Even with one word: You are putting a big group of Muslims in the circle.

BIN LADEN: Know the truth and its roots. The book of God is our guide. Either Islam or atheism.

ALOUNI: Can small countries like Qatar, or Bahrain or Kuwait, which don't have much control, be excused? The Qatari foreign minister said, "I am surrounded by superpowers that will very easily wipe me off the map. That's why I have to ally myself with Americans and others."

BIN LADEN: In the subject of Islam and the killing of the faithful, what those people are doing cannot be excused. If the emir of Qatar orders someone to kill your child, and you ask this person why he did it, he'll say, "Look, brother Tayseer, I like you very much, but I was forced to do it." Nothing will excuse him for aiding the tyrant to kill your child. Your child's blood goes to waste like this. They claim that they don't have much control. Their claim that they were forced into it is not considered righteous in Islam. People's blood is being wasted in this case.

ALOUNI: What do you think of the so-called "war of civilizations"? You always keep repeating "crusaders" and words like that all the time. Does that mean you support the war of civilizations?

BIN LADEN: No doubt about that: The book mentions this clearly. The Jews and the Americans made up this call for peace in the world. The peace they're calling for is a big fairy tale. They're just drugging the Muslims as they lead them to slaughter. And the slaughter is still going on. If we defend ourselves, they call us terrorists. The prophet has said, "The end won't come before the Muslims and the Jews fight each other till the Jew hides between a tree and a stone. Then the tree and stone say, "Oh, you Muslim, this is a Jew hiding behind me. Come and kill him." He who claims there will be a lasting peace between us and the Jews is an infidel. He'll be denouncing the book and what's in it. Begin, the leader of the massacre of Kfar Yassin, and the traitor, Anwar Sadat, who sold the land and the blood of the mujahedeen both were given the Nobel Peace Prize. There will come some deceiving times where the liars will be believed and the truthful won't be believed. That's the situation in the Arabic world with its great leadership. They are lying to people. But god's relief and victory is coming soon.

ALOUNI: As you call it, this is a war between the crusaders and Muslims. How do you see the way out of this crisis?

BIN LADEN: We are in a decisive battle with the Jews and those who support them from the crusaders and the Zionists. We won't hesitate to kill the Israelis who occupied our land and kill our children and women day and night. And every person who will side with them should blame themselves only. Now how we will get out of the tunnel, that is the [unintelligible] of the other side. We were attacked, and our duty is to remove this attack. As far as the Jews are concerned, the prophet has announced that we will fight them under this name, on this land. America forced itself and its people in this [unintelligible] more than 53 years ago. It recognized Israel and supported its creation financially. In 1973, under Nixon, it supported Israel with men, weapons and ammunition from Washington all the way to Tel Aviv. This support helped change the course of history. It is the Muslim's duty to fight. . . .

[America] made hilarious claims. They said that Osama's messages have codes in them to the terrorists. It's as if we were living in the time of mail by carrier pigeon, when there are no phones, no travelers, no Internet, no regular mail, no express mail, and no electronic mail. I mean, these are very humorous things. They discount people's intellects.

We swore that America wouldn't live in security until we live it truly in Palestine. This showed the reality of America, which puts Israel's interest above its own people's interest. America won't get out of this crisis until it gets out of the Arabian Peninsula, and until it stops its support of Israel. This equation can be understood by any American child, but Bush, because he's an Israeli agent, cannot understand this equation unless the swords threatened him above him head.

ALOUNI: Do you have anything to do with anthrax that is spreading around the world?

BIN LADEN: These diseases are a punishment from God and a response to oppressed mothers' prayers in Lebanon, Iraq and Palestine. There is no wall between the prayer of the oppressed and God. This is God's response to these prayers.

ALOUNI: Do you have a message for the viewers of Al-Jazeera? You know Al-Jazeera is now translated into so many languages and transmitted around the world.

BIN LADEN: In this fighting between Islam and the crusaders, we will continue our jihad. We will incite the nation for Jihad until we meet God and get his blessing. Any country that supports the Jews can only blame itself. If Sheik Suleiman Abu Gheith spoke specifically about America and Britain, this is only an example to give other countries the chance to review their books.

What do Japan or Australia or Germany have to do with this war? They just support the infidels and the crusaders.

This is a recurring war. The original crusade brought Richard [the Lionhearted] from Britain, Louis from France, and Barbarus from Germany. Today the crusading countries rushed as soon as Bush raised the cross. They accepted the rule of the cross.

What do the Arab countries have to do with this crusade? Everyone that supports Bush, even with one word, is an act of great treason. You change your name and you help the enemy to kill our children, and you are telling me we are facilitating things between us and the Americans. What are they talking about? Those who talk about the loss of innocent people didn't yet taste how it feels when you lose a child, don't know how it feels when you look in your child's eyes and all you see is fear, don't know how it feels when, in Palestine, our brothers are being hunted by army helicopters in the middle of their own homes with their families and children. Everyday. They show you the injured and the dead, and they shed tears, but no tears are shed for our women and children killed in Palestine. Are they not afraid that one day they get the same treatment?

[Bin Laden recites verses from the Quran on same subject.]

The Europeans are free, but when they side with the Jews, that their [unintelligible]. I tell Muslims to believe in the victory of God and in Jihad against the infidels of the world. The killing of Jews and Americans is one of the greatest duties.

[More Quranic verses.]

Remember the saying, "If they want to exile you, they can't exile you unless it is written by God." Don't ask anyone's opinion when it comes to the killing of Americans, and remember your appointment with God and the best of the prophets.

[More Quranic verses.]

As far as Pakistan siding with the crusaders, our brothers in Pakistan and their actions will facilitate our attack on the coalition of crusaders. Everyone supporting America, even medically, is considered renouncing Islam. Our brother in Pakistan should react pretty quick and strong in order to praise God and his prophet. Today, Islam is calling on you to act quickly.

[Quoting the farewell speech of Mohammed] "Oh, Islam, oh, Islam, there is no other god than God, and Mohammed is the prophet of God."

DECEMBER 26, 2001

Speech Given Three Months after 9/11

The following is a transcript, originally in Arabic, of a 34-minute video of Osama bin Laden that was mailed to al Jazeera from unknown sources in Pakistan. It was aired in part on December 26, 2001, and later in full on December 27, 2001, on al Jazeera satellite stations within a program known as "First War of the Century." The text was translated by Justin Kitchens.

Thursday, 27 Dec. 2001, 18:12 GMT

Praise be to God; we praise him, seek help from him, ask his forgiveness, and seek refuge with God from our own evils and the sins of our making. Who is led by God shall not be misguided, and who is misguided cannot be led by any. I witness that there is no god but Allah, that he is one with no partner, and I witness that Muhammad is his servant and prophet.

And so, after the passing of three months since the blessed strikes against world infidelity and against the head of infidelity, America, and after the passing of almost two months since the fierce Crusade against Islam, it seems appropriate to us to comment on some of the details of these events.

These events revealed many matters of utmost importance to Muslims. It is now clear that the West in general and America at the forefront is carrying an indescribable Crusader's spite against Islam. Those who have lived these months under continuous bombardment from multiple kinds of American planes know that this is the truth.

Many villages were destroyed without a sin, and millions, were we to count, were displaced in this severe cold. These oppressed men, women and children are now harbored by tents in Pakistan though it was no sin of theirs, just a suspicion that caused America to launch this fierce campaign.

And if America had any evidence that reached any level of certainty that the ones who carried out this work were affiliating with Europe, such as the Irish Republican Army for example, then there would have been found many other means of treating this problem. But when nothing but suspicion points to the Islamic world, then the true ugly face was revealed as well as the Crusade against the Islamic world – with clarity!

And as these words are on my lips, I wish to confirm the truth of the conflict between us and America. This conflict is very important, and the seriousness of it impacts not only Muslims, but the entire world. What America accuses these mujahideen of is, for God's sake, not based on evidence, but rather depends on oppression, injustice, and aggression.

The history of the Arab mujahideen, thank God and glory be to him Almighty ["Subhanahu wa ta'ala", hereinafter: {swt}], has been pure as the driven snow since they left 20 years ago when the truly disgraceful terror appeared by the hand of the Soviet Union against these children and these innocents in Afghanistan. The Arab militants [mujahideen] left their work and their universities, their family and their people, to seek the pleasure of God, to support the religion of God, and to aid these oppressed Muslim sons.

Those who went to the support of the oppressed would not today turn to the killing of innocents, as some claim. At that time America was supporting all who struggled and fought against the Russians. But when God bestowed his grace upon the Arab [mujahideen] to support the oppressed in Palestine – those innocent children – America became enraged and turned its back to the killers in Afghanistan.

What is happening today in Palestine is abundantly clear, and all of humanity, since the time of Adam {pbuh}, agrees upon this. Nature may become corrupt and people may differ on many matters, but there is some of nature that Allah {swt} keeps from corruption – except for those whose souls deviated and reached the heights of injustice and aggression. It is from this preserved aspect of nature that people – even if some injustice and aggression have injured them – cannot let their souls kill innocent children.

And what is happening in Palestine – what is happening today – is the intentional murder of children. This is a matter, the great ugliness, the immense injustice, and the aggression of which threatens all humanity.

Has history known one who kills children? Only rarely, such as the ways of Pharaoh, and God {swt} bestowed his grace upon the Children of Israel because of him. "Since we saved you from the people of Pharaoh that afflicted you with the evil of torture, slaughtered your sons, and kept your women." [Koranic verse] Slaying children is infamous for being the height of injustice, disbelief, and Pharaonic aggression, but the Children of Israel have used the same style against our sons in Palestine. The whole looked on and witnessed the Israeli soldiers as they kill Mohammed al-Durra and many like him.

The whole world from the East to the West, despite difference of religions, but rather just as people themselves, denounced this action. But America continues to indulge in its delusion by supporting these oppressors and aggressors against our sons in Palestine. God {swt} has shown that the soul, if it unjustly attacks, comes to a limit where it kills another soul without reason. This is a very hideous matter, but uglier still is he who kills innocent children. God {swt} says: "For that reason, we have prescribed on the Children of Israel that he who kill a soul, unless it be for murder or a corruption on the earth, then it is as if he killed all people; and he who revive one revives all people." [Koranic verse]

It is as if these [of whom I speak], in truth, killed all of the children in the world – Israel with the support of America. What will prevent Israel from killing of our sons tomorrow in Tabuk and Jawaf and other regions around them? And what will the powers that be do if Israel widens its land, in accordance with their unfair, unjust books that claim their borders reach to Medina? What will our rulers do as they yield to this American-Zionist lobby?

The wise must wake up! What injured Mohammed al-Durra and his brothers will befall them tomorrow and their sons and their women. There is neither might nor strength except in God.

This matter is of utmost seriousness, and the disgraced terrorism America exercises is of its ugliest forms in Palestine and in Iraq. Bush the father, this ominous man, was the reason for the killing of more than a million children in Iraq, aside from men and women.

The events of September 11th were but a reaction to the continuing injustice that is being levied on our sons in Palestine, Iraq, Somalia, the south of Sudan, and elsewhere such as in Kashmir and Asia. This matter concerns the entire *ummah* and people must wake from their sleeping and hurry to find a solution to this disaster which is threatening human kind.

As for those that condemned these actions, they looked upon the event as if it were independent, not linking it with past events and the reasons that caused them. Their view is simple and comes neither from Shari'a nor reason, for they saw the people, America and the media criticize these actions and so criticized them themselves.

And such, they are like a wolf that saw a lamb and said to it, "You are the one who muddied my water in your first year." The lamb said, "No, not I." The wolf: "But you." The lamb said, "But I was just born in this year." "Then it was your mother who did it," the wolf said, and ate the lamb. When the poor mother saw her child torn between the jaws of the wolf, she was moved by her maternal instinct to butt against the wolf yet caused him no injury. The wolf cried out and said, "Look at this terrorist!" Then the parrots began to repeat what the wolf had said, "Yes, we condemn the sheep's butting of the wolf." But where were you when the wolf ate the lamb of that sheep?

The blessed, successful strikes, therefore, are reactions to what is occurring on our land in Palestine, Iraq and elsewhere. For America, in continuing this policy, and in the rising of the son George Bush who started his rule with violent air attacks on Iraq – these affirm the policies of injustice and aggression and show that the blood of Muslims has no value.

This was the blessed response, thanks be to God {swt}, and these blessed strikes have deep meaning, for they clarified that this arrogant and presumptuous power – the Hubal of our age – America stands is made of great economic might but yet is weak and fell quickly, thanks be to God {swt}.

Those who undertook this action were not nineteen Arab countries, and those that moved were not armies or ministries of the Arab countries that have become accustomed to the submission and injustice that afflicts us in Palestine and elsewhere. Rather, they were nineteen high school students – I urge God {swt} to accept them – that shook the throne of

America and struck at the American economy to the core. They struck the greatest military power deep in its heart, thanks be to God {swt}.

This is clear proof that the damnable, enslaving world economy that America uses with it military might to force unbelief and humiliation upon weak peoples, can easily collapse. Those blessed attacks, as America itself has admitted, have inflicted on the New York market and others, more than a trillion dollars in losses, thanks be to God {swt}. With small capacity, they used planes of the enemy and studied in the schools of the enemy. They did not need training camps, but rather God provided for them and they gave a tough lesson to those arrogant peoples who see the meaning of freedom, unless it is for the white race. These people think that others must be humiliated and enslaved. They do not move in response but rather praise their leaders when they strike us, as happened before in Iraq.

I say that American military might, and America's display of this might in Afghanistan in recent time, and the outpouring of its Anger on the weak – through these we learned, thanks be to God, {swt}, a great and important lesson in the way to confront this arrogant power.

For example, if the front line with the enemy reaches a 100 kilometers in length, that line must be wide, meaning, we are not satisfied with a line of defense of a depth or width of 100, 200, or 300 meters. Rather, this line must have a width up to a number of kilometers and it must be reinforced in length and width. The intensity of American bombing is reduced before it completes the destruction of these lines. There should be light and swift forces that move from one line to another and from one defense unit to another.

We benefitted from this knowledge after the intense bombing that the Americans practiced on the northern lines and the Kabul lines. In this way, years will pass and America will not, God willing {swt}, break the lines of the mujahideen.

On the other hand, it is well known that fighting is made up of two elements – the fighters themselves and money to buy weapons. This matter is confirmed in the Book of God {swt}, as said He {swt} in many verses confirming this meaning, in one of which saying, "For God bought from the believers their selves and their possessions so that they may have Paradise." [Qur'an, my translation]

So, yes, money and souls. The space between us and the American military base was very far, and our weapons did not reach their planes, it is possible to absorb these strikes by wide defense lines. Another way to strike at economic power, which is the basis of military power, is if their economy ended by people busying themselves with their own affairs rather than enslaving weak peoples.

I say it is very important to concentrate on striking the American economy through any means possible. Those who call for humanity and freedom – we saw their real crimes right here. A person is killed enough by a piece of shrapnel. A piece of shrapnel weighs seven gramms. So America, from its spite against those of the Taliban and Muslims, were throwing on our brothers on the front lines bombs, each of which weighing up to seven tons. Those who can add will tell you this is thousands of kilos, meaning seven million grams while a person needs but seven grams of shapnel upon him to die.

When the youths in Nairobi, we ask God to accept them as martyrs, detonated less than two tons, America said that was a terrorist strike and a weapon of mass destruction. However, it used two shells, each of which weighed seven million grams without restraint.

Then the secretary of defense responsed to us – after bombing entire villages without reason except to terrorize the people and cause them to fear giving hospitality to Arabs or coming close to them – the secretary of defense responded to us saying it was their right. That it was their right to annihilate people as long as they are Muslim or as long as it is not America. This is a crime in and of itself, clearly visible, and all that you hear them say about it being a mistake is a clearly visible lie.

A few days ago, they struck what they claimed to be al-Qa'ida positions in Khost and sent a guided missle into a masjid, saying it was a mistake. After an investigation, it was made clear that the 'ulema' were in Khost praying the Ramadan night prayer. They had a meeting after the prayer with a jihadi hero Sheikh Jalal id-Din Haqqani who was one of the most prominent former jihadi leaders against the Soviet Union, and who rejected the American occupation on the land of Afghanistan. They bombed the masjid while Muslims were at prayer, killing a hundred and fifty of them. There is no power but God and Sheikh Jalal was saved, we ask God to bless him with long life.

This is the spite of the Crusader. Those who repeat words without taking care as to their meaning should take care themselves when they say that they are against terrorism. We are terrorists against America, and that is terrorism commendable in the defense against the unjust working injustice, as America when it lends its support to Israel who kills our sons. The matter is clear, why cannot you be reasoned with?

America and the Western leaders often repeat that Hamas and the Jihad in Palestine and other fighting organizations are terrorist organizations. If self-defense is terrorism, what then is allowed? Our defense and our fighting do not differ from the fighting of our brothers in Palestine, like Hamas. We fight for the sake of Almighty God and to make the word of God the higher word and the word of the unbelievers the lower one, and to prevent the oppression inflicted on the weak in Palestine and elsewhere.

The matter is very clear. A wise Muslim should not stand in that trench under any kind of pretext. This is the most dangerous, fiece and savage Crusade advanced against Islam. God willing, the end of America is close. Its end does not depend on the life of the humble servant. Whether Osama is killed or remains, thanks be to God that the awakening has begun, and that was of the fruits of these actions. I urge God {swt} to accept these young men as martyrs and to join them with the prophets, the devout, the martyrs, the virtuous and the best of their companions.

These young men undertook a great deed, a glorious deed. God reward them with the greatest of rewards, and we urge God that they be the bounty of their fathers and mothers. They raised high the heads of Muslims and given America a lesson it will not forget, God willing {swt}.

In an interview with ABC, I warned America that by conflict with the sons of the two holy places, it would forget the horrors of Vietnam. This was exactly what happened, thanks be to God {swt}, and what shall happen will be even greater, God willing {swt}.

From the country of the two holy places came fifteen young men – we urge God to accept them as martyrs. They came from the land of faith, where the greatest treasure for Muslims is. The prophet {pbuh} said that faith clings to Medinah as the snake its hole. Also two came from the eastern part of the Arabian Peninsula, from the Emirates, and another from the Levant, Ziyad al-Jarrah – we urge God to accept him as a martyr. Another came from Egypt, Muhammad Ata. We ask God to accept all of them as martyrs.

These men, by their act, gave exceedingly great examples. They showed that the faith in their hearts demands many requirements and demands that souls must be exchanged for the sake of the one God. These men opened a great door to goodness and truth. Some say that these actions of the martyred fedayeen are unacceptable, but these are those whose voices we hear in the media, and they are only repeating the whims of tyrants and the whims of America and its agents.

A nation of 1,200 million Muslims is being butchered from its east to its west every day in Palestine, Iraq, Somalia, the south of Sudan, Kashmir, the Philippines, Bosnia, Chechnya, and Asam, but we do not hear their voices. But if the victim and oppressed rise up to offer himself for the sake of his religion, then we hear those voices. 1,200 million Muslims are being butchered, but if a man stands up to defend them, those otheres stand to repeat the whims of tyrants. They have no minds and no reason.

In the story of the boy, the king, the magician, and the hermit, there is clear evidence on the offering of oneself for the sake of the one God. There is another meaning here, and that is that victory is not considered only in evident gains, as people tend to believe. Rather, victory is adherence to principles.

God {swt} remembered the people of the rift and memorialized their memory in praising them for adhering to their faith. They were threatened with a choice between faith and being thrown to the fire, but they refused to give up belief in God {swt} and were put to the fire. In the end of the story of the boy, when the unjust king orders the filling of the rift with stones, there came a weak mother carrying her son. When she saw the fire, she became afraid for her son and was fill with despair. Then the son said to her, as had said he upon whom peace be, have patience, Mother, for you are right.

No Muslim would ever, in any situation, wonder how they profited or say that they wasted their lives. That would be the greatest of ignorance. They won the satisfaction of God {swt} and the paradise promised by God {swt}. For victory is not only material gains, but also adherence to principles.

There is a hadith of the prophet {pbuh} where a boy with little knowledge used to hesitate between magician and hermit. When an animal once blocked the road to people, the boy said he would now know who was better, the hermit or the magician. Due to his little knowledge, the boy was unable to decide who was better, which would guarantee him peace of mind. He asked God to show him who was better. If the hermit was dearer to God {swt}, then he would kill the animal. The boy then took a stone, threw it at the animal and killed it. The hermit came to the boy and said, "My son, you are today better than me." Despite the hermit's knowledge and the boy's ignorance, God {swt} filled the heart of this boy with the light of faith. The boy then started to sacrifice for the sake of the one God.

The youth of Islam are waiting for their scholars to say such words, to say to them, those who carried their heads on their shoulders for the sake of the one God, the words that the scholar told that boy. To say to them, "You are now better than us." This is the truth. There is also a hadith of the prophet {pbuh} that people differ from one another based on the extent of their faith in God. It is not only about the acquisition of knowledge, but also the use of it. As the prophet said {pbuh}, "He who struggled against them with his hand, upon him be peace; he who struggled against them with his tongue, he is a believer; and he who struggled against them with his heart, he is a believer." And whoever fails to do any of these has no grain of faith. They struggled against the biggest unbeliever with their hands and hearts. We urge God to accept them as martyrs.

Those are like, as said he upon whom be peace, the best of all martyrs Hamza bin Abd al-Muttalib, a man little known but whose heart God filled with the light of faith. This man stood up to an unjust imam, rebuked him, scolded him, and killed him.

This man won a great deal. He did not know the followers and did not know the esteemed companions of the prophet, God grant them rest, but yet God {swt} raised him up the his place in history as the best of all martyrs. Such was ruged by our prophet {pbuh}. How can a reasoning Muslim say, "How did this one benefit?" This is clear misguidance. May god spare us from it.

God enabled those young people to say to the head of world misbelief– America and its allies, "You are wrong and you are misguided. They sacrificed themselves for the sake of the one God.

There is much more that could be said about these great events. However, I will restrict my words and concentrate on the need to continue the jihadist action against America, both militarily and economically. America has declined, praise be to God {swt}, and the economic bleeding has continued until today, but it needs other strikes. The young people should make an effort to look for the pillars of the US economy and strike at them, at the will of the Almighty.

[Concludes with the reading of poetry in honor of heroes of faith.]

NOVEMBER 2002

Letter to the American People

The following letter was originally posted on a Saudi Arabian Web site previously used by al Qaeda to disseminate messages and was later published by the British newspaper The Observer. Its veracity has been doubted by some experts because the letter contains a series of issues never mentioned before in previous communications from bin Laden, such as AIDS and incest. The message cannot be fully authenticated as it does not have complementary audio or video. Whether or not it is from Osama bin Laden himself, it provides keen insight into the mind of the Islamist movement.

In the Name of Allah, the Most Gracious, the Most Merciful,

"Permission to fight (against disbelievers) is given to those (believers) who are fought against, because they have been wronged and surely, Allah is Able to give them (believers) victory" [Quran 22:39]

"Those who believe, fight in the Cause of Allah, and those who disbelieve, fight in the cause of Taghut (anything worshipped other than Allah e.g. Satan). So fight you against the friends of Satan; ever feeble is indeed the plot of Satan." [Quran 4:76]

Some American writers have published articles under the title 'On what basis are we fighting?' These articles have generated a number of responses, some of which adhered to the truth and were based on Islamic Law, and others which have not. Here we wanted to outline the truth – as an explanation and warning – hoping for Allah's reward, seeking success and support from Him.

While seeking Allah's help, we form our reply based on two questions directed at the Americans:

(Q1) Why are we fighting and opposing you?

(Q2) What are we calling you to, and what do we want from you?

As for the first question: Why are we fighting and opposing you? The answer is very simple:

(1) Because you attacked us and continue to attack us.

a) You attacked us in Palestine:

(i) Palestine, which has sunk under military occupation for more than 80 years. The British handed over Palestine, with your help and your support, to the Jews, who have occupied it for more than 50 years; years overflowing with oppression, tyranny, crimes, killing, expulsion, destruction and devastation. The creation and continuation of Israel is one of the greatest crimes, and you are the leaders of its criminals. And of course there is no need to explain and prove the degree of American support for Israel. The creation of Israel is a crime which must be erased. Each and every person whose hands have become polluted in the contribution towards this crime must pay its*price, and pay for it heavily.

(ii) It brings us both laughter and tears to see that you have not yet tired of repeating your fabricated lies that the Jews have a historical right to Palestine, as it was promised to them in the Torah. Anyone who disputes with them on this alleged fact is accused of anti-semitism. This is one of the most fallacious, widely-circulated fabrications in history. The people of Palestine are pure Arabs and original Semites. It is the Muslims who are the inheritors of Moses (peace be upon him) and the inheritors of the real Torah that has not been changed. Muslims believe in all of the Prophets, including Abraham, Moses, Jesus and Muhammad, peace and blessings of Allah be upon them all. If the followers of Moses have been promised a right to Palestine in the Torah, then the Muslims are the most worthy nation of this.

When the Muslims conquered Palestine and drove out the Romans, Palestine and Jerusalem returned to Islaam, the religion of all the Prophets peace be upon them. Therefore, the call to a historical right to Palestine cannot be raised against the Islamic Ummah that believes in all the Prophets of Allah (peace and blessings be upon them) – and we make no distinction between them.

(iii) The blood pouring out of Palestine must be equally revenged. You must know that the Palestinians do not cry alone; their women are not widowed alone; their sons are not orphaned alone.

b) You attacked us in Somalia; you supported the Russian atrocities against us in Chechnya, the Indian oppression against us in Kashmir, and the Jewish aggression against us in Lebanon.

c) Under your supervision, consent and orders, the governments of our countries which act as your agents, attack us on a daily basis;

(i) These governments prevent our people from establishing the Islamic Shariah, using violence and lies to do so.

(ii) These governments give us a taste of humiliation, and places us in a large prison of fear and subdual.

(iii) These governments steal our Ummah's wealth and sell them to you at a paltry price.

(iv) These governments have surrendered to the Jews, and handed them most of Palestine, acknowledging the existence of their state over the dismembered limbs of their own people.

(v) The removal of these governments is an obligation upon us, and a necessary step to free the Ummah, to make the Shariah the supreme law and to regain Palestine. And our fight against these governments is not separate from out fight against you.

(d) You steal our wealth and oil at paltry prices because of you international influence and military threats. This theft is indeed the biggest theft ever witnessed by mankind in the history of the world.

(e) Your forces occupy our countries; you spread your military bases throughout them; you corrupt our lands, and you besiege our sanctities, to protect the security of the Jews and to ensure the continuity of your pillage of our treasures.

(f) You have starved the Muslims of Iraq, where children die every day. It is a wonder that more than 1.5 million Iraqi children have died as a result of your sanctions, and you did not show concern. Yet when 3000 of your people died, the entire world rises and has not yet sat down.

(g) You have supported the Jews in their idea that Jerusalem is their eternal capital, and agreed to move your embassy there. With your help and under your protection, the Israelis are planning to destroy the Al-Aqsa mosque. Under the protection of your weapons, Sharon entered the Al-Aqsa mosque, to pollute it as a preparation to capture and destroy it.

(2) These tragedies and calamities are only a few examples of your oppression and aggression against us. It is commanded by our religion and intellect that the oppressed have a right to return the aggression. Do not await anything from us but Jihad, resistance and revenge. Is it in any way rational to expect that after America has attacked us for more than half a century, that we will then leave her to live in security and peace?!!

(3) You may then dispute that all the above does not justify aggression against civilians, for crimes they did not commit and offenses in which they did not partake:

(a) This argument contradicts your continuous repetition that America is the land of freedom, and its leaders in this world. Therefore, the American people are the ones who choose their government by way of their own free will; a choice which stems from their agreement to its policies. Thus the American people have chosen, consented to, and affirmed their support for the Israeli oppression of the Palestinians, the occupation and usurpation of their land, and its continuous killing, torture, punishment and expulsion of the Palestinians. The American people have the ability and choice to refuse the policies of their Government and even to change it if they want.

(b) The American people are the ones who pay the taxes which fund the planes that bomb us in Afghanistan, the tanks that strike and destroy our homes in Palestine, the armies which occupy our lands in the Arabian Gulf, and the fleets which ensure the blockade of Iraq. These tax dollars are given to Israel for it to continue to attack us and penetrate our lands. So the American people are the ones who fund the attacks against us, and they are the ones who oversee the expenditure of these monies in the way they wish, through their elected candidates.

(c) Also the American army is part of the American people. It is this very same people who are shamelessly helping the Jews fight against us.

(d) The American people are the ones who employ both their men and their women in the American Forces which attack us.

(e) This is why the American people cannot be not innocent of all the crimes committed by the Americans and Jews against us.

(f) Allah, the Almighty, legislated the permission and the option to take revenge. Thus, if we are attacked, then we have the right to attack back. Whoever has destroyed our villages and towns, then we have the right to destroy their villages and towns. Whoever has stolen our wealth, then we have the right to destroy their economy. And whoever has killed our civilians, then we have the right to kill theirs.

The American Government and press still refuses to answer the question:

Why did they attack us in New York and Washington?

If Sharon is a man of peace in the eyes of Bush, then we are also men of peace!!! America does not understand the language of manners and principles, so we are addressing it using the language it understands.

(Q2) As for the second question that we want to answer: What are we calling you to, and what do we want from you?

(1) The first thing that we are calling you to is Islam.

(a) The religion of the Unification of God; of freedom from associating partners with Him, and rejection of this; of complete love of Him, the Exalted; of complete submission to His Laws; and of the discarding of all the opinions, orders, theories and religions which contradict with the religion He sent down to His Prophet Muhammad (peace be upon him). Islam is the religion of all the prophets, and makes no distinction between them – peace be upon them all.

It is to this religion that we call you; the seal of all the previous religions. It is the religion of Unification of God, sincerity, the best of manners, righteousness, mercy, honour, purity, and piety. It is the religion of showing kindness to others, establishing justice between them, granting them their rights, and defending the oppressed and the persecuted. It is the religion of enjoining the good and forbidding the evil with the hand, tongue and heart. It is the religion of Jihad in the way of Allah so that Allah's Word and religion reign Supreme. And it is the religion of unity and agreement on the obedience to Allah, and total equality between all people, without regarding their colour, sex, or language.

(b) It is the religion whose book – the Quran – will remained preserved and unchanged, after the other Divine books and messages have been changed. The Quran is the miracle until the Day of Judgment. Allah has challenged anyone to bring a book like the Quran or even ten verses like it.

(2) The second thing we call you to, is to stop your oppression, lies, immorality and debauchery that has spread among you.

(a) We call you to be a people of manners, principles, honour, and purity; to reject the immoral acts of fornication, homosexuality, intoxicants, gambling's, and trading with interest.

We call you to all of this that you may be freed from that which you have become caught up in; that you may be freed from the deceptive lies that you are a great nation, that your leaders spread amongst you to conceal from you the despicable state to which you have reached.

(b) It is saddening to tell you that you are the worst civilization witnessed by the history of mankind:

(i) You are the nation who, rather than ruling by the Shariah of Allah in its Constitution and Laws, choose to invent your own laws as you will and desire. You separate religion from your policies, contradicting the pure nature which affirms Absolute Authority to the Lord and your Creator. You flee from the embarrassing question posed to you: How is it possible for Allah the Almighty to create His creation, grant them power over all the creatures and land, grant them all the amenities of life, and then deny them that which they are most in need of: knowledge of the laws which govern their lives?

(ii) You are the nation that permits Usury, which has been forbidden by all the religions. Yet you build your economy and investments on Usury. As a result of this, in all its different forms and guises, the Jews have taken control of your economy, through which they have then taken control of your media, and now control all aspects of your life making you their servants and achieving their aims at your expense; precisely what Benjamin Franklin warned you against.

(iii) You are a nation that permits the production, trading and usage of intoxicants. You also permit drugs, and only forbid the trade of them, even though your nation is the largest consumer of them.

(iv) You are a nation that permits acts of immorality, and you consider them to be pillars of personal freedom. You have continued to sink down this abyss from level to level until incest has spread amongst you, in the face of which neither your sense of honour nor your laws object.

Who can forget your President Clinton's immoral acts committed in the official Oval office? After that you did not even bring him to account, other than that he 'made a mistake', after which everything passed with no punishment. Is there a worse kind of event for which your name will go down in history and remembered by nations?

(v) You are a nation that permits gambling in its all forms. The companies practice this as well, resulting in the investments becoming active and the criminals becoming rich.

(vi) You are a nation that exploits women like consumer products or advertising tools calling upon customers to purchase them. You use women to serve passengers, visitors, and strangers to increase your profit margins. You then rant that you support the liberation of women.

(vii) You are a nation that practices the trade of sex in all its forms, directly and indirectly. Giant corporations and establishments are established on this, under the name of art, entertainment, tourism and freedom, and other deceptive names you attribute to it.

(viii) And because of all this, you have been described in history as a nation that spreads diseases that were unknown to man in the past. Go ahead and boast to the nations of man, that you brought them AIDS as a Satanic American Invention.

(xi) You have destroyed nature with your industrial waste and gases more than any other nation in history. Despite this, you refuse to sign the Kyoto agreement so that you can secure the profit of your greedy companies and*industries.

(x) Your law is the law of the rich and wealthy people, who hold sway in their political parties, and fund their election campaigns with their gifts. Behind them stand the Jews, who control your policies, media and economy.

(xi) That which you are singled out for in the history of mankind, is that you have used your force to destroy mankind more than any other nation in history; not to defend principles and values, but to hasten to secure your interests and profits. You who dropped a nuclear bomb on Japan, even though Japan was ready to negotiate an end to the war. How many acts of oppression, tyranny and injustice have you carried out, O callers to freedom?

(xii) Let us not forget one of your major characteristics: your duality in both manners and values; your hypocrisy in manners and principles. All*manners, principles and values have two scales: one for you and one for the others.

(a) The freedom and democracy that you call to is for yourselves and for white race only; as for the rest of the world, you impose upon them your monstrous, destructive policies and Governments, which you call the 'American friends'. Yet you prevent them from establishing democracies. When the Islamic party in Algeria wanted to practice democracy and they won the election, you unleashed your agents in the Algerian army onto them, and to attack them with tanks and guns, to imprison them and torture them – a new lesson from the 'American book of democracy'!!!

(b) Your policy on prohibiting and forcibly removing weapons of mass destruction to ensure world peace: it only applies to those countries which you do not permit to possess such weapons. As for the countries you consent to, such as Israel, then they are allowed to keep and use such weapons to defend their security. Anyone else who you suspect might be manufacturing or keeping these kinds of weapons, you call them criminals and you take military action against them.

(c) You are the last ones to respect the resolutions and policies of International Law, yet you claim to want to selectively punish anyone else who does the same. Israel has for more than 50 years been pushing UN resolutions and rules against the wall with the full support of America.

(d) As for the war criminals which you censure and form criminal courts for – you shamelessly ask that your own are granted immunity!! However, history will not forget the war crimes that you committed against the Muslims and the rest of the world; those you have killed in Japan, Afghanistan, Somalia, Lebanon and Iraq will remain a shame that you will never be able to escape. It will suffice to remind you of your latest war crimes in Afghanistan, in which densely populated innocent civilian villages were destroyed, bombs were dropped on mosques causing the roof of the mosque to come crashing down on the heads of the Muslims praying inside. You are the ones who broke the agreement with the Mujahideen when they left Qunduz, bombing them in Jangi fort, and killing more than 1,000 of your prisoners through suffocation and thirst. Allah alone knows how many people have died by torture at the hands of you and your agents. Your planes remain in the Afghan skies, looking for anyone remotely suspicious.

(e) You have claimed to be the vanguards of Human Rights, and your Ministry of Foreign affairs issues annual reports containing statistics of those countries that violate any Human Rights. However, all these things vanished when the Mujahideen hit you, and you then implemented the methods of the same documented governments that you used to curse. In America, you captured thousands the Muslims and Arabs, took them into custody with neither reason, court trial, nor even disclosing their names. You issued newer, harsher laws.

What happens in Guatanamo is a historical embarrassment to America and its values, and it screams into your faces – you hypocrites, "What is the value of your signature on any agreement or treaty?"

(3) What we call you to thirdly is to take an honest stance with yourselves and I doubt you will do so – to discover that you are a nation without principles or manners, and that the values and principles to you are something which you merely demand from others, not that which you yourself must adhere to.

(4) We also advise you to stop supporting Israel, and to end your support of the Indians in Kashmir, the Russians against the Chechens and to also cease supporting the Manila Government against the Muslims in Southern Philippines.

(5) We also advise you to pack your luggage and get out of our lands. We desire for your goodness, guidance, and righteousness, so do not force us to send you back as cargo in coffins.

(6) Sixthly, we call upon you to end your support of the corrupt leaders in our countries. Do not interfere in our politics and method of education. Leave us alone, or else expect us in New York and Washington.

(7) We also call you to deal with us and interact with us on the basis of mutual interests and benefits, rather than the policies of sub dual, theft

and occupation, and not to continue your policy of supporting the Jews because this will result in more disasters for you.

If you fail to respond to all these conditions, then prepare for fight with the Islamic Nation. The Nation of Monotheism, that puts complete trust on Allah and fears none other than Him. The Nation which is addressed by its Quran with the words: "Do you fear them? Allah has more right that you should fear Him if you are believers. Fight against them so that Allah will punish them by your hands and disgrace them and give you victory over them and heal the breasts of believing people. And remove the anger of their (believers') hearts. Allah accepts the repentance of whom He wills. Allah is All-Knowing, All-Wise." [Quran9:13-1]

The Nation of honour and respect:

"But honour, power and glory belong to Allah, and to His Messenger (Muhammad- peace be upon him) and to the believers." [Quran 63:8]

"So do not become weak (against your enemy), nor be sad, and you will be*superior (in victory) if you are indeed (true) believers" [Quran 3:139]

The Nation of Martyrdom; the Nation that desires death more than you desire life:

"Think not of those who are killed in the way of Allah as dead. Nay, they are alive with their Lord, and they are being provided for. They rejoice in what Allah has bestowed upon them from His bounty and rejoice for the sake of those who have not yet joined them, but are left behind (not yet martyred) that on them no fear shall come, nor shall they grieve. They rejoice in a grace and a bounty from Allah, and that Allah will not waste the reward of the believers." [Quran 3:169-171]

The Nation of victory and success that Allah has promised:

"It is He Who has sent His Messenger (Muhammad peace be upon him) with guidance and the religion of truth (Islam), to make it victorious over all other religions even though the Polytheists hate it." [Quran 61:9]

"Allah has decreed that 'Verily it is I and My Messengers who shall be victorious.' Verily Allah is All-Powerful, All-Mighty." [Quran 58:21]

The Islamic Nation that was able to dismiss and destroy the previous evil Empires like yourself; the Nation that rejects your attacks, wishes to remove your evils, and is prepared to fight you. You are well aware that the Islamic Nation, from the very core of its soul, despises your haughtiness and arrogance.

If the Americans refuse to listen to our advice and the goodness, guidance and righteousness that we call them to, then be aware that you will lose this Crusade Bush began, just like the other previous Crusades in which you were humiliated by the hands of the Mujahideen, fleeing to your home in great silence and disgrace. If the Americans do not respond, then their fate will be that of the Soviets who fled from Afghanistan to deal with their military defeat, political breakup, ideological downfall, and economic bankruptcy.

This is our message to the Americans, as an answer to theirs. Do they now know why we fight them and over which form of ignorance, by the permission of Allah, we shall be victorious?

JULY 18, 2003

Meaning of Jihad, Full Response to Saudi Cleric

The following are excerpts of a 90-minute speech delivered by Osama bin Laden. It was posted on a number of Islamist Internet bulletin boards and translated by the Middle East Media Research Institute.

'Without Hijra and Jihad, No Islamic State Will Arise'

"... Since the fall of the Islamic Caliphate state, regimes that do not rule according to the Koran have arisen. If truth be told, these regimes are fighting against the law of Allah. Despite the proliferation of universities, schools, books, preachers, imams, mosques, and [people who recite the] Koran, Islam is in retreat, unfortunately, because the people are not walking in the path of Muhammad..."

"In order to establish the Islamic state and spread the religion, there must be [five conditions], a group, hearing, obedience, a Hijra, and a *Jihad*. Those who wish to elevate Islam without Hijra and without *Jihad* sacrifices for the sake of Allah have not understood the path of Muhammad..."

'Islamic Countries Are Responsible For Fall of the Taliban'

"We are in a situation of no longer having a country to which to make *Hijra*. There was an opportunity [to create such a country] – a rare opportunity. Since the fall of the Caliphate, the Crusaders made sure not to enable the true Islam to establish a state. Allah decreed that there be events in Afghanistan, and the U.S.S.R. attacked [Afghanistan]. The Crusaders relinquished their resolve [to prevent the establishment of an Islamic state] because of their fear of the U.S.S.R. [They] had no choice but to repel the U.S.S.R. by any and all means, even by means of the *Mujahideen*, the fundamentalists, and the young Jihad warriors of Islam."

"Thus the gate opened. But unfortunately, a decade later, the [Islamic] nation – particularly the clerics, preachers, and sermonizers, and Islamic universities – did not meet the obligation. Those who came to the land of Jihad in order to support the Muslims and the Mujahideen were a small handful of the youth of the [Islamic] nation, in addition to the funds donated by some merchants; these were not sufficient to establish a strong country detached from geographical and tribal loyalties. Our Afghan brothers found themselves in a unique situation; an Islamic state could easily have been established according to Islamic, not national or geographic, standards. But unfortunately . . . this opportunity was lost, and the people did not take advantage of it. I mention this in order to tell you that it is not an easy thing, and that now conditions have become [even] harder."

"Then, Allah made it possible to establish the Taliban state. The Taliban established [the state] and removed the conflict among the Afghans. They remained [in power] for six years, more or less. But the people remained captive to their fixed ideas and captive to the world media, which launched a mad attack on the Taliban and harmed their reputation . . ."

"Afghanistan is [but] a few hours away from the Arabian Peninsula, or from any of the countries of the Islamic world . . . but the Taliban state disappeared, and they did not lift a finger. I say that I am convinced that thanks to Allah, this nation has sufficient forces to establish the Islamic state and the Islamic Caliphate, but we must tell these forces that this is their obligation. Similarly, we need to tell the other forces, those who [are] restricting these forces, that they are sinning by restricting these forces . . ."

'The Commandment of Jihad Versus Other Commandments'

"There are people who say, and it is no secret, that the *Jihad* does not require the [participation] of the entire nation; these words are true, but their intent is not. It is true that *Jihad* cannot include the entire nation today, and that repelling the aggressive enemy is done by means of a very small part of this nation; but *Jihad* continues to be a commandment incumbent personally upon every Muslim. But they [i.e. the clerics identified with the regimes] disagree with us [on] this ruling and say: 'If we sent you a few thousand, you would not manage to take them in. It is not logical that we abandon all the breaches [on other fronts] and go, all of us, to wage *Jihad*...'"

"If *Jihad* becomes a commandment incumbent personally upon every Muslim, it [*Jihad*] rises to the top of the priorities, and there is no doubt of this, as **Sheikh Al-Islam [Ibn Taymiya]** said: 'Nothing is a greater obligation than repelling the aggressive enemy who corrupts the religion and this world – except faith itself.'"

"There is no place to claim that if everyone went to Jihad it could not take them all in. This [claim] is the product of an abnormal flaw in Islamic religious law, and of the abnormal submission to the [concepts of] this world. When the number of [Mujahideen] will be sufficient to repel the aggressive enemy, Jihad will automatically be transformed from a commandment incumbent personally upon every Muslim to a commandment incumbent upon all Muslims as a collective... He who claims that Jihad is a tremendous ritual but that there are other [important] rituals does not understand the path of Muhammad..."

'Clerics Who Refrain From Inciting To Jihad'

"Most unfortunately, the young people who have the ability to sacrifice [themselves] for the religion are suffering by listening to and obeying Islamic clerics who refrain [from fulfilling the commandment of Jihad], even though such people must not be listened to or obeyed. Therefore, these forces [who obey these clerics] remain paralyzed; they [the clerics] incite them away from carrying out the commandment that is incumbent upon them personally and towards commandments incumbent upon the collective, such as study. [Even] if everyone became a cleric, there would be no religious revival that does not include [the five conditions of] a group, hearing, obedience, a *Hijra* and a *Jihad*..."

"Great evil is spreading throughout the Islamic world: the imams calling people to hell are those who appear more than others at the side of rulers in the region, the rulers of the Arab and Islamic world. Through the media and their own apparatuses, through their ruin of the country by their adoption of destructive ideas, and laws created by man... from morning to evening, they call the people to the gates of hell..."

"The heresy against Allah and His Prophet is being carried out before the eyes and ears of all in newspapers, television, radio, and symposiums, and none oppose it... In this situation, only one thing takes precedence over all other commandments, apart from faith itself... This immense obligation [i.e. *Jihad*]... has no place among the clerics today who do not speak of it. They all, except for those upon whom Allah had mercy, are busy handing out praise and words of glory to the despotic imams [i.e. Arab rulers] who disbelieved Allah and His Prophet. They send telegrams praising those rulers who disbelieve Allah and His Prophet. Their newspapers and media spread heresy against Allah and His Prophet. Other telegrams are sent from the rulers to these clerics, praising them for deceiving the nation."

"The nation has never been as damaged by a catastrophe like the one that damages them today. In the past, there was imperfection, but it was partial. Today, however, the imperfection touches the entire public because of the communications revolution and because the media enter every home. No home, in [the] city or in [the] desert, was spared this Fitna [internal strife]. None will be spared..."

'Clerics Are Civil Servants'

"The clerics are the prisoners and hostages of the tyrants. Some of them told me: 'We cannot speak the truth [because we are civil servants]...'

Young people must understand the nature of the connection today between civil servants and the ruler. A civil servant is a civil servant . . . It is amazing that some object to our linking them with this tyrannical ruler when that is what they are . . ."

"The true role of some civil servants is to bear false witness. The role of the information minister, for example, is to bear false witness. He and his apparatus deceive the public every day and portray the country as the best country and the ruler as an unparalleled genius. Likewise, the defense minister deceives the people and bears false witness, saying that our situation is good and our armed forces are good, while we have been under occupation for over a decade. The whole world knows we are under occupation and that the American planes take off whenever they want, with no prior notification, night or day, and then the defense minister comes to us and says: 'We are independent, and no one uses our land without our approval.' This is bearing false witness. God be praised, the people know that they are civil servants. Yet the danger does not come from the interior minister and his subordinates, because no matter what they do, they are unable to mislead anyone . . . because the people know they are lying to them and deceiving them."

"The true danger is when the falsehood comes from the imams of the religion who bear false witness every morning and evening and lead the nation astray. This is all the more so when the false witness comes from the house of Al-Haram [the mosque in Mecca] and from the *Ka'ba* [the holy black stone in Mecca] . . ."

"Bearing false witness is one of the biggest sins on any piece of soil, all the more so when you bear false witness in the house of Al-Haram every Friday and at every opportunity in order to lead an entire nation astray for a handful of coins . . . How great is the sin of he who does this. They are civil servants to whom no reasonable person can turn [to] on religious matters. The least you can say about them, as **Sheikh Muhammad bin Abd Al-Wahhab** said, the least you can say about the clerics who defend the tyrants, is that they are corrupt. The people must boycott and banish them . . ."

'Islam Ceases To Exist When the Ruler Is an Infidel'

"[They are mistaken], those who want to tell people that the religion exists even though the imam [i.e. ruler] disbelieved Allah and His Prophet a hundred years ago, ever since he rose through English strength, English support, English weapons, and English gold [i.e. the family of **Hussein bin Ali**, who in World War I conspired against the Ottoman Caliphate with the British]... It is inconceivable that there be faith, and that the religion will continue to rule, if the imam is an infidel. This must be clear: If the imam is an infidel... Islam ceases to exist and there must be an act that will elevate a [believing] imam..."

"The region's rulers deceive us and support infidels and then claim they still cling to Islam. What increases this deceit is the establishment of bodies to lead the people astray. People may wonder how it is that bodies engaging in [studying] Islamic law and jurisprudence play this role, whether wittingly or unwittingly. The aim of the regime in putting some [unfaithful] clerics on satellite television and radio stations to issue Fatwas for the people is not [to spread knowledge of Islamic law] – were this the case, the regime would put the faithful clerics on satellite television and radio; the goal of these authorities [in putting the unfaithful clerics on television and radio] is to [use them] when necessary."

"For example, when the regime decided to bring the American Crusader forces into the land of the two holy places [i.e. Saudi Arabia], and the youth raged, these bodies [the unfaithful clerics]... issued *Fatwas* and praised the behavior of the ruler, whom they called *Wali Amr* [men of authority, in accordance with the Koran requirement that believers obey those of authority amongst them], while in truth he was not really *Wali Amr* over the Muslims. We must pay attention to this."

"People may wonder and ask how it is possible that Sheikh 'So-and-So,' or 'Anonymous,' who is a respected elder sheikh with great knowledge of religion, could sell out his religion for a meager sum from this world. I say that no man is protected from error. If we examine the history of the Islamic world over the past centuries, we will find that these instances recur... Many clerics have misled [people] because of threats of beating, imprisonment, or perhaps even death [by the regimes]; only a few stood fast, and one of these, as you know, is **Imam Ahmad ibn Hanbal**..."

"The regime appropriates a huge budget for these bodies [i.e. the unfaithful clerics] whose role is to grant legitimacy to the regime... Imagine! The offices of the **Clerics Authority** [in Saudi Arabia] are adjacent to the royal palace, and the building of the **Fatwa Authority of Al-Azhar** is adjacent to **Hosni Mubarak's** Palace of the Republic... In such a situation [when even the offices are linked], is it reasonable to ask a civil servant, who receives his salary from the king? What is the ruling regarding the king, and should the king be regarded as supporting infidels?..."

"Civil servants don a robe and take for themselves grand titles, but they are in fact civil servants... We learned from their books, where it says that one of the 10 acts that contradict Islam is supporting infidels. In closed forums, they speak to us candidly, but [in public] they are afraid, and give [other interpretations]."

"The spirit of martyrdom is our strength and our weapon for the sake of the survival of our religion, and for resistance to any domestic or foreign attempt to distort our religion."

"*Jihad* is the way to attain truth and abolish falsehood. Therefore, the youth... who love the religion and sacrifice [themselves] for Allah must pay no attention to these civil servants and to those who refrain [from waging *Jihad*]... As a result of the communications revolution and the enormous advances in communication... the young people hear from a young age that Sheikh 'So-and-So' sent a telegram to the king, and the king sent him a telegram in return, and he appears at the king's right hand every Monday, and so on... The public is misled and says: 'If that king were no good, Sheikh 'So-and-So' would not visit him.' They disregard the fact that anyone who goes to see the king is a civil servant in the Royal Office or the Interior Ministry [and not an independent, faithful cleric]...."

"There is nothing of Muhammad's religious law in the religious law of the government clerics and sultans, and they do not understand the nature of the path of Allah. We must be aware that clinging to the religion requires us to show hostility to the people of falsehood..."

"The faithful clerics possess characteristics described in the book of Allah... The most prominent characteristics are faith and Jihad for the sake of Allah... Those who do *Hijra*, and those who support Allah and His Prophet and wage *Jihad* for the sake of Allah, are the faithful ones... In contrast, the other clerics [are those who] see [and remain silent when] the rulers support infidels and [do not] rule in accordance with what was sent down by Allah, who praise the tyrants and ignore the bank towers next to the Al-Haram Mosque, that charge interest [which is forbidden in Islam]... No faithful cleric can claim that interest is not a great sin..."

"A fundamental and realistic fact is that the land [of the holy places, i.e. Saudi Arabia] is occupied – and if it is occupied [by the U.S. military], the greatest commandment after faith itself is to repel the aggressive enemy. Their [the rulers of Saudi Arabia] statements attest to their situation. In an interview with some world press agencies, [Saudi] **Prince T alal bin Abd Al-Aziz** said: 'Were we to tell the American forces to leave, they wouldn't.' That is candor. Also, the Qatari foreign minister said: 'If we tell the American government and the American forces to leave Qatar, we'll be wiped off the map.'"

"The land is occupied in the full sense of the word. Yet despite this, people are busy with all sorts of [other] rituals. We must focus on making the starting point Jihad for the sake of Allah, guarding against those who refrain [from Jihad], and Hijra and Jihad for Allah. All these are obligatory in the present situation in order to establish the truth and abolish falsehood."

APRIL 2004

Speech Addressed to Europe

The following is a transcript of an audio tape broadcast by al Arabiya. The CIA claims to have determined that the voice on the tape is bin Laden. This translation was made available by the BBC.

Praise be to Almighty God; Peace and prayers be upon our Prophet Muhammad, his family, and companions. This is a message to our neighbours north of the Mediterranean, containing a reconciliation initiative as a response to their positive reactions. Praise be to God; praise be to God; praise be to God who created heaven and earth with justice and who allowed the oppressed to punish the oppressor in the same way. Peace upon those who followed the right path:

In my hands there is a message to remind you that justice is a duty towards those whom you love and those whom you do not. And people's rights will not be harmed if the opponent speaks out about them. The greatest rule of safety is justice, and stopping injustice and aggression. It was said: Oppression kills the oppressors and the hotbed of injustice is evil. The situation in occupied Palestine is an example. What happened on 11 September [2001] and 11 March [the Madrid train bombings] is your commodity that was returned to you. It is known that security is a pressing necessity for all mankind. We do not agree that you should monopolise it only for yourselves. Also, vigilant people do not allow their politicians to tamper with their security. Having said this, we would like to inform you that labelling us and our acts as terrorism is also a description of you and of your acts. Reaction comes at the same level as the original action. Our acts are reaction to your own acts, which are represented by the destruction and killing of our kinfolk in Afghanistan, Iraq and Palestine. The act that horrified the world; that is, the killing of the old, handicapped [Hamas spiritual leader] Sheikh Ahmed Yassin, may God have mercy on him, is sufficient evidence. We pledge to God that we will punish America for him, God willing. Which religion considers your killed ones innocent and our killed ones worthless? And which principle considers your blood real blood and our blood water? Reciprocal treatment is fair and the one who starts injustice bears greater blame.

As for your politicians and those who have followed their path, who insist on ignoring the real problem of occupying the entirety of Palestine and exaggerate lies and falsification regarding our right in defence and resistance, they do not respect themselves. They also disdain the blood and minds of peoples. This is because their falsification increases the shedding of your blood instead of sparing it. Moreover, the examining of the developments that have been taking place, in terms of killings in our countries and your countries, will make clear an important fact; namely, that injustice is inflicted on us and on you by your politicians, who send your sons – although you are opposed to this – to our countries to kill and be killed. Therefore, it is in both sides' interest to curb the plans of those who shed the blood of peoples for their narrow personal interest and subservience to the White House gang. We must take into consideration that this war brings billions of dollars in profit to the major companies, whether it be those that produce weapons or those that contribute to reconstruction, such as the Halliburton Company, its sisters and daughters. Based on this, it is very clear who is the one benefiting from igniting this war and from the shedding of blood. It is the warlords, the bloodsuckers, who are steering the world policy from behind a curtain. As for President Bush, the leaders who are revolving in his orbit, the leading media companies and the United Nations, which makes laws for relations between the masters of veto and the slaves of the General Assembly, these are only some of the tools used to deceive and exploit peoples. All these pose a fatal threat to the whole world. The Zionist lobby is one of the most dangerous and most difficult figures of this group. God willing, we are determined to fight them.

Based on the above, and in order to deny war merchants a chance and in response to the positive interaction shown by recent events and opinion polls, which indicate that most European peoples want peace, I ask honest people, especially ulema, preachers and merchants, to form a permanent committee to enlighten European peoples of the justice of our causes, above all Palestine. They can make use of the huge potential of the media. I also offer a reconciliation initiative to them, whose essence is our commitment to stopping operations against every country that commits itself to not attacking Muslims or interfering in their affairs – including the US conspiracy on the greater Muslim world. This reconciliation can be renewed once the period signed by the first government expires and a second government is formed with the consent of both parties. The reconciliation will start with the departure of its last soldier from our country. The door of reconciliation is open for three months of the date of announcing this statement. For those who reject reconciliation and want war, we are ready. As for those who want reconciliation, we have given them a chance. Stop shedding our blood so as to preserve your blood. It is in your hands to apply this easy, yet difficult, formula. You know that the situation will expand and increase if you delay things. If this happens, do not blame us – blame yourselves. A rational person does not relinquish his security, money and children to please the liar of the White House. Had he been truthful about his claim for peace, he would not describe the person who ripped open pregnant women in Sabra and Shatila [reference to Israeli Prime Minister Ariel Sharon] and the destroyer of the capitulation process [reference to the Palestinian-Israeli peace process] as a man of peace. He also would not have lied to people and said that we hate freedom and kill for the sake of killing. Reality proves our truthfulness and his lie. The killing of the Russians was after their invasion of Afghanistan and Chechnya; the killing of Europeans was after their invasion of Iraq and Afghanistan; and the killing of Americans on the day of New York [reference to 11 September] was after their support of the Jews in Palestine and their invasion of the

Arabian Peninsula. Also, killing them in Somalia was after their invasion of it in Operation Restore Hope. We made them leave without hope, praise be to God. It is said that prevention is better than cure. A happy person is he who learns a lesson from the experience of others. Heeding right is better than persisting in falsehood. Peace be upon those who follow guidance.

OCTOBER 29, 2004

Speech Addressed to the American People

The original videotape of this speech by bin Laden was delivered to al Jazeera and was a full 18 minutes long. The station created an edited-down five-minute version, which is the clip that they aired. The following transcript is from the shorter version of the speech, and was translated by the Middle East Media Research Institute.

"O American people, I address these words to you regarding the best way of avoiding another Manhattan, and regarding the war, its causes and its consequences. But before this, I say to you: Security is one of the important pillars of human life, and free men do not take their security lightly, contrary to Bush's claim that we hate freedom. Let him explain why we did not attack Sweden, for example. Clearly, those who hate freedom – unlike the 19, may Allah have mercy on them – have no self-esteem. We have been fighting you because we are free men who do not remain silent in the face of injustice. We want to restore our [Islamic] nation's freedom. Just as you violate our security, we violate yours. Whoever toys with the security of others, deluding himself that he will remain secure, is nothing but a foolish thief. One of the most important things rational people do when calamities occur is to look for their causes so as to avoid them.

"But I am amazed at you. Although we have entered the fourth year after the events of 9/11, Bush is still practicing distortion and deception against you and he is still concealing the true cause from you. Consequentially, the motives for its reoccurrence still exist. I will tell you about the causes underlying these events and I will tell you the truth about the moments this decision was taken, to allow you to reflect.

"I say to you, as Allah is my witness: We had not considered attacking the towers, but things reached the breaking point when we witnessed the iniquity and tyranny of the American-Israeli coalition against our people in Palestine and Lebanon – then I got this idea.

"The events that had a direct influence on me occurred in 1982, and the subsequent events, when the U.S. permitted the Israelis to invade Lebanon with the aid of the American sixth fleet. They started shelling, and many were killed and wounded, while others were terrorized into fleeing. I still remember those moving scenes – blood, torn limbs, and dead women and children; ruined homes everywhere, and high-rises being demolished on top of their residents; bombs raining down mercilessly on our homes. It was as though a crocodile swallowed a child, and he could do nothing but cry. But does a crocodile understand any language other than arms? The entire world saw and heard, but did not respond.

"In those critical moments, I was overwhelmed by ideas that are hard to describe, but they awakened a powerful impulse to reject injustice and gave birth to a firm resolve to punish the oppressors. As I was looking at those destroyed towers in Lebanon, I was struck by the idea of punishing the oppressor in the same manner and destroying towers in the U.S., to give it a taste of what we have tasted and to deter it from killing our children and women. That day I became convinced that iniquity and the premeditated murder of innocent children and women is an established American principle, and that terror is [the real meaning of] 'freedom' and 'democracy,' while they call the resistance 'terrorism' and 'reaction.' America stands for iniquity and for imposing sanctions on millions of people, resulting in the death of many, as Bush Sr. did, causing the mass slaughter of children in Iraq, [the worst] that humanity has ever known. It stands for dropping millions of pounds of bombs and explosives on millions of children in Iraq again, as Bush Jr. did, in order to depose an old agent and to appoint a new agent to help him steal Iraq's oil, and other sorts of horrible things.

"It was against the backdrop of these and similar images that 9/11 came in response to these terrible iniquities. Should a man be blamed for protecting his own? And is defending oneself and punishing the wicked an eye for an eye – is that reprehensible terrorism? Even if it is reprehensible terrorism, we have no other choice. This is the message that we have tried to convey to you, in words and in deeds, more than once in the years preceding 9/11. Observe it, if you will, in the interview with Scott in Time Magazine in 1996, and with Peter Arnett on CNN in 1997, then John Wiener [?] in 1998; observe it, if you will, in the deeds of Nairobi and Tanzania and Aden, and observe it in my interview with 'Abd Al-Bari' Atwan and in interviews with Robert Fisk. The latter is of your own and of your religious affiliation, and I consider him to be unbiased.

"Would those who claim to stand for freedom in the White House and in the TV stations that answer to them, would they conduct an interview with him [Fisk] so that he might convey to the American people what he has understood from us concerning the causes of our fight against you? For if you were to avoid these causes, you would take America in the right path to the security it knew before 9/11. So much for the war and its causes.

"As for its results, they are very positive, with Allah's grace. They surpassed all expectations by all criteria for many reasons, one of the most important of which is that we had no difficulty dealing with Bush and his administration, because it resembles the regimes in our [Arab] countries, half of which are ruled by the military, and the other half are ruled by the sons of kings and presidents with whom we have had a lot of experience. Among both types, there are many who are known for their conceit, arrogance, greed, and for taking money unrightfully.

"This resemblance began with the visit of Bush Sr. to the region. While some of our people were dazzled by the U.S. and hoped that these visits would influence our countries, it was he who was influenced by these monarchic and military regimes. He envied them for remaining in their positions for decades, while embezzling the nation's public funds with no supervision whatsoever. He bequeathed tyranny and the suppression of liberties to his son and they called it the Patriot Act, under the pretext of war on terrorism.

"Bush Sr. liked the idea of appointing his sons as state [*wilaya*] governors. Similarly, he did not neglect to import to Florida the expertise in falsifying [elections] from the leaders of this region in order to benefit from it in difficult moments.

"As previously mentioned, it was easy for us to provoke this administration and to drag it [after us]. It was enough for us to send two Jihad fighters to the farthest east to hoist a rag on which 'Al-Qa'ida' was written – that was enough to cause generals to rush off to this place, thereby causing America human and financial and political losses, without it accomplishing anything worthy of mention, apart from giving business to [the generals'] private corporations. Besides, we gained experience in guerilla warfare and in conducting a war of attrition in our fight with the iniquitous, great power, that is, when we conducted a war of attrition against Russia with Jihad fighters for 10 years until they went bankrupt, with Allah's grace; as a result, they were forced to withdraw in defeat, all praise and thanks to Allah. We are continuing in the same policy – to make America bleed profusely to the point of bankruptcy, Allah willing. And that is not too difficult for Allah.

"Whoever says that Al-Qa'ida triumphed over the White House administration, or that the White House administration lost this war – this is not entirely accurate, for if we look carefully at the results, it is impossible to say that Al-Qa'ida is the only cause for these amazing gains. The White House policy, which strove to open war fronts so as to give business to their various corporations – be they in the field of armament, of oil, or of construction – also helped in accomplishing these astonishing achievements for Al-Qa'ida. It appeared to some analysts and diplomats as though we and the White House play as one team to score a goal against the United States of America, even though our intentions differ.

Such ideas, and some others, were pointed out by a British diplomat in the course of a lecture at the Royal Institute for International Affairs; for example, that Al-Qa'ida spent $500,000 on the event [9/11] while America lost in the event and its subsequent effects more than 500 billion dollars; that is to say that each of Al-Qa'ida's dollars defeated one million American dollars, thanks to Allah's grace. This is in addition to the fact that America lost a large number of jobs, and as for the [federal] deficit, it lost a record number estimated at a trillion dollars.

"Even more serious for America is the fact that the *Jihad* fighters have recently forced Bush to resort to an emergency budget in order to continue the fighting in Afghanistan and in Iraq, which proves the success of the plan of bleeding [America] to the point of bankruptcy, Allah willing.

"Indeed, all of this makes it clear that Al-Qa'ida won gains; but on the other hand, it also makes it clear that the Bush administration won gains as well, since anyone who looks at the scope of the contracts won by large dubious corporations like Halliburton and other similar ones that have ties to Bush and to his administration will become convinced that the losing side is in fact you, the American people, and your economy.

"We agreed with the general commander Muhammad Atta, may Allah have mercy on him, that all operations should be carried out within 20 minutes, before Bush and his administration would become aware. We never imagined that the Commander in Chief of the American armed forces would abandon 50,000 of his citizens in the twin towers to face this great horror alone when they needed him most. It seemed to him that a girl's story about her goat and its butting was more important than dealing with planes and their 'butting' into skyscrapers. This allowed us three times the amount of time needed for the operations, Allah be praised.

"It should be no secret to you that American thinkers and intellectuals warned Bush before the war: all that you [Bush] need in order to assure America's security by ridding [Iraq] of weapons of mass destruction, assuming there were any, is at your disposal, and all the countries of the world are with you in the matter of carrying out inspections, and the U.S.'s interest does not require you to drive it into an unjustified war, whose end you cannot know.

"However, the blackness of black gold blinded his sight and his perception and he gave preference to private interests over America's public interest. And so there was war and many died. The American economy bled and Bush became embroiled in the quagmire of Iraq, which now threatens his future.

"His case is like that [described in the parable]:

"He is like the ill-tempered goat that dug out of the ground the sharp knife [with which it would be slaughtered].

"I say to you: more than 15,000 of our people were killed and tens of thousands were wounded, just as more than 1,000 of you were killed and more than 10,000 wounded, and Bush's hands are sullied with the blood of all of these casualties on both sides, for the sake of oil and to give business to his private companies. You should know that a nation that punishes a weak person if he is instrumental in killing one of that nation's sons for money, while letting go free a high-class man who was instrumental in killing more than 1,000 of its sons, also for money [sic]. Similarly your allies in Palestine intimidate women and children and murder and imprison men. [inaudible]

"Keep in mind that every action has a reaction, and finally you should consider the last wills and testaments of the thousands who left you on 9/11, waving their hands in despair. These are inspiring wills, which deserve to be published and studied thoroughly. One of the most important things I have read regarding their hand-waving signals before they fell is that they were saying 'We were wrong to let the White House carry out unchecked its aggressive foreign policy against oppressed people.' As though they were telling you, the American people, 'You should call to task those who caused our death.' Happy is he who learns a lesson from the experience of others. A verse that I have read is also relevant to their [last] signals:

"Evil kills those who perpetrate it,

"And the pastures of iniquity are harmful.

"There is a saying: a small amount spent on prevention is better than a great amount spent on treatment. You should know that it is better to return to that which is right than to persist in that which is wrong. A rational man would not neglect his security, property, or home for the sake of the liar in the White House.

"Your security is not in the hands of Kerry or Bush or Al-Qa'ida. Your security is in your own hands, and any [U.S.] state [*wilaya*] that does not toy with our security automatically guarantees its own security.

"Allah is our guardian but you have none.

"Peace be upon whoever follows the true guidance."

Index